A Crystal Goblet
& the Dragon

A Crystal Goblet
& the Dragon

Edna May Rawson

VANTAGE PRESS
New York

Cover artwork by Pamela Slavic & Earl Wilson, Holland Patent, NY

FIRST EDITION

Published by Vantage Press, Inc.
516 West 34th Street, New York, New York 10001

Manufactured in the United States of America
ISBN: 0-533-13622-9

Library of Congress Catalog Card No.: 00-91578

0 9 8 7 6 5 4 3 2

DEDICATED TO MY BELOVED SISTER, DOROTHY

Contents

Preface

Don Moser spoke of the China-Burma-India Theater as "the greatest untold story of WW II." We, who were there, called CBI "the forgotten theater." Over twenty years after the war Moser opened his trunk of war materials and began to write. The untold story slowly unfolded but it will never be complete. Beginning 1996 I read all published books pertaining to CBI. The bibliography is listed on the last page of this preface. The authors' writings covered government leaders and policies, military leaders and strategies, operations, battles, failures, successes. They told about the torturous experiences of fighting in Burma in the world's worst jungles—fighting the jungle-oriented Japanese. They told about flying the Hump, the world's most dangerous flight. They told about the clashing personalities of top leaders: Chiang Kai-shek, General "Vinegar Joe" Stilwell, President F. D. Roosevelt, and General "Leatherface" Chennault of the Flying Tigers. Important, informative, fascinating books that should be widely read.

However, an essential part of the story has not yet been told. What was done to try to maintain or to increase the morale of our fighting men, especially in that "forgotten" CBI Theater? Nothing had been mentioned in the above writings. So, like Don Moser, I too (only much later in 1997) dragged out a multitude of letters that my sister (Red Cross Field Director in the ETO Theater) and I (Red Cross Club Program Director in the CBI Theater) had sent home to our parents along with my monthly reports to ARC Headquarters; materials I had gathered on locations; 169 pictures given me by our men; and my never-fading memories. Before I could begin writing—for I decided I had to add another part to that story—I needed to satisfy my mind on questions that arose. Who were the Japanese back in that long-ago period? I had come home in 1945 and put away the war along with my feelings of hatred for and disgust with the enemy. Now I wondered what had made those Japanese so brutal, treacherous,

ix

almost inhuman. Back in December 1941, how did Japan dare to make an attack on our powerful country and what led her (her total islands smaller than our state of Montana) to the aim of world conquest? I became swamped with extensive reading of books and articles on Japan until I found sufficient and satisfactory answers. I wrote the following based on material I gathered from here and there.

The word "Japan" came from China, its meaning "sun origin." Nothing is known of Japan before the 3rd century A.D. when the name first appeared in Chinese records. But according to mythology, the Japanese islands were created by the gods apart from the rest of the world. It was the Sun goddess, the chief Japanese deity, who sent the first emperor to found her dynasty of chosen people. The emperor was the incarnation of the goddess who reigned over the universe, human but divine, the personification of Japanese destiny. The Japanese, a combination of Asiatic mainland and oceanic people, considered themselves also divine. So we have the beginnings of the Japanese superiority complex that rose to heights in the twentieth century. However, the individual was not important. It was the group that was superior.

Barbarism existed in Japan until the 6th century. Neither the Sun goddess nor the divine Emperor did anything about maturing the people. It was the Chinese who gradually brought to Japan the beginnings of civilization. Most important was a written language, an alphabet which is still used though the Japanese have added markings like punctuations, making it an extremely difficult language to read. In time the Chinese also brought religion, art, handicrafts, philosophy, and much more from their ancient culture. Even Japan's early government was modeled after the Chinese civil system with the court and nobles under the Emperor. For everything the Japanese borrowed (and in time they borrowed plenty from not only the Chinese but also the Koreans, Portuguese, Dutch, Spaniards, Americans...) they became jealous of all their benefactors, hated them, and in revenge warred upon them to prove their own superiority. Quite ungracious receivers, they!

Shinto, the Japanese religion (if one could call it that for ethically it's a vacuum) from the beginning up to and including the present (though it has been diminishing with the younger generation) does not appear in literature until the late 6th century of the western era. In its more remote stages as a system it was evidently nameless. There are no images of deities and adoration of deities is unknown. Coming to the Shinto shrine is not for worship but for reverence and veneration of their ancestors who have a common descent from the Sun goddess. When Buddhism was first brought to Japan it somewhat enriched the country but in the atmosphere of spiritualism and superstition it became a racket. The designation of "Shinto" came into existence after Buddhism was introduced and the word was used in order to distinguish the original Japanese cults from the way of the Buddha. Shinto is the Sino-Japanese reading of two ideograms that in pure Japanese terms mean "the way of the gods." Shinto also involves a great reverence of nature.

This early Japanese period lasted till about the year 1185 up to the beginning of the feudal period. A provincial warrior class had risen who challenged the court. There began a separation of civic and military functions or a dualism in government. Yoritomo, the new military leader, appointed himself Shogun. A Shogun was the highest officer in the Japanese government during the continuance of the feudal system and he gradually acquired all the real powers of government. The Emperor was pushed into the background and in time was almost forgotten. Through reading James Clavell's intriguing and shocking *Shogun*, published in 1979, and seeing the spectacular twelve-hour movie of the book on TV, most Americans were given a good picture, though fictional, of the feudal period. The Shoguns ruled (as had the Emperors) on an hereditary basis. Under the Shogun were various competing feudal lords known as the Daimyo. The Samurai were the feudal warriors who comprised about one-sixteenth of the population. They were held to strict rules that emphasized obedience, conformity, and loyalty to the Shogun. They were the only ones permitted to carry weapons, two swords each, and if any peasant or commoner failed to show proper respect off came his head. From this period there developed an ingrained quality of the Japanese that privileged people had the right to inflict punishment on any who offended them.

In 1542, there began a peaceful entrance of Portuguese and Spaniards in the interest of religious education. The Dutch language and western learning were introduced. Japanese scholars began to immerse themselves in Dutch studies—medicine, mathematics, and military science. Thus a foundation was laid for a later period. However, when the reigning Shogun discovered what was happening, he decided this was but a Trojan Horse for political conquest. He ordered all the "Pope's men" out of the country and in 1637 all foreigners were banned. There was no more intercourse with the western world for 216 years. No one could leave or enter Japan without facing death or imprisonment, nor could a ship be built.

In 1853, as the western nations were roaming the seas seeking commerce and colonies, President Fillmore sent naval Commodore Perry on a mission to open Japan to the world. Perry made two trips. On the second trip, after succeeding in coming ashore with his band of armed men and a group of brass players tooting their loudest (probably scaring the Japanese out of their wits) the militarily weak Shogun finally had little choice but to sign a treaty opening his country. In 1859, American missionaries arrived under the Harris Treaty and further opened the eyes of the thinking and scholarly Japanese not only to the past but promise of greater things to come. They encouraged education for the masses and urged Japan to send students abroad and to send an embassy abroad to explain to the world Japan's revolutions in thought and custom that could create a new nation. All of the preceding actions set in motion a series of events that snapped the long cord of past Japanese history. The Shogun era collapsed; feudalism was abolished.

Two great families, rivals of the Shoguns, established a new order. Needing a symbol, or figurehead, they chose the almost forgotten Emperor and made him the supreme embodiment of power. The new Emperor, a boy, acceded to the throne and in 1868 was reinstated to authority. He became known as Meiji and the event was called the Great Meiji Restoration. The Emperor Meiji was raised to an eminence unknown in previous periods. No official statement defined the Emperor's divinity, for political and human interpretations were suppressed. Since Japan had no great religion, emphasis on his mystical divinity was easy. This was accompanied by a growing military totalitarianism.

More and more the Japanese despised the Chinese because they owed them so much. They became determined to prove themselves the superior race with a "divine, imperial destiny and a holy task of achieving world peace." Japan moved forward quickly and effectively with an aim of surpassing that of the west. Her rapid move from closed doors to doors open to the world and from primitiveness to modern civilization surpassed that of any other nation with similar attempts in recorded history. "It was like a child leaping to maturity but skipping adolescence. This was a great cause of Japan's difficulties. Japan was never sweet sixteen." (This is a wonderful quote though I don't remember the source.)

The Japanese militants went through a long period of preparation for conquest of the world. As they approached the twentieth century their efforts were intensified to the nth degree. Following the Sino-Japanese War of 1894–95 and the Russo-Japanese War of 1904–05, Japan annexed Korea in 1910. This was an important base for launching their invasion of China.

In 1923 when the great earthquake leveled Tokyo, American ships came promptly with food and hospital supplies, plus 200 marines to distribute the rations. The Japanese probably hated us for that kindness along with our previous gifts to their people. They simply couldn't receive without resulting jealousy that made them feel inferior.

In 1927 came the Tanaka Memorial, a statement by General Tanaka (who was then the prime minister of Japan) regarding his country's aims: "For settling difficulties in Eastern Asia, Japan must adopt a policy of Blood and Iron...In order to conquer the world, Japan must conquer Europe and Asia; in order to conquer Europe and Asia, Japan must first conquer China; and in order to conquer China, Japan must conquer Manchuria and Mongolia. Japan expects to fulfill the above in ten years...In the future if we wish to control China, the primary move is to crush the United States."

In 1931 the Japanese occupied Manchuria, another important base for invasion of China, but also a country rich in raw materials which Japan badly needed.

The ruling race of Japanese needed to be increased since the world's population would be brought under their rule. So bonuses were offered to women to raise sons. The moral code was: "Whatever will advance Japan is right." In the schools, military activities and planned exercises to ingrain complete loyalty to the Emperor took priority over academics. Mere children were put through such powerfully emotional experiences to instill Emperor worship and loyalty that suicides occurred at an early age.

Japanese lacked respect for human life. Impersonality ran through Japan's history. From childhood they were taught at home and in their schools that the individual is of little importance. Their superior value is in groups. They learned to do things in teams. When it came to flying, their pilots worked well in formation, but a pilot alone was at a loss. He lacked initiative. Every soldier or worker in industry was merely an impersonal tool in the hands of the military, slaves of their own army. Japanese women had always been under the domination of the males. Overseas, Japanese soldiers showed contempt for foreign women and, though supposedly civilized, exhibited a streak of brutality.

Japan advanced fast due to low wages, excessively long hours, and slavery-like living for its citizens. The Japanese were indoctrinated to the thought that although the Emperor had unlimited wealth he lived very frugally, sacrificing in his love for his people. Thus the soldier was not ashamed of his coarse, uncouth uniform. Armies were not trained in tactics of retreat, for retreat was disgrace. To be captured was dishonorable. Suicide was common and expected if a Japanese felt he had failed the Emperor in even the slightest way.

Colonel Hashimoto, with the backing of the army, organized a group known as the Japanese Youth Party. Their international ideas were: "Britain, the United States, and France are the sinking sun at dusk. Nationalists and Fascists are the crescent moon against the evening sky. The Soviets are a bright star of early night, but adequate only to illuminate a corner of the sky. Things can revive only in the morning sunlight of great Japan. I am looking far and wide for pure-hearted youths to work for the cause of the imperial nation, whose policy is to write itself in letters of fire in the eight corners of the universe." (Hashimoto retired in 1936)

In 1936 the full possibilities of Emperor worship were brought into being by the army and surrounded with grave penalties. The Japanese had a perverse love of indirect government and so the country was ruled not by the Emperor but in the *name* of the Emperor. Hugh Blas in the *Japanese Advertiser* (Tokyo's American daily) said: "We see him as Priest-King entering into mystic communion with the spirit of the race. This mystic and religious element runs like a nerve through the ceremonies and explains their power to awaken the deepest national instincts in the Japanese people. They are a living link between past and present and not merely a picturesque survival." Japanese loyalty was not ordinary patriotism but "lofty self-denying enthusiastic sentiment for their august divine ruler." The Japanese sensed their unification of divine spirits through the Emperor. "He was the divine being who unifies." Japanese bureaucracy had inculcated among the people the thought that the Emperor is to be loved and revered above all things since he loves and protects the nation. The divine imperative is world conquest that the imperial way may be extended everywhere. The Emperor and the army became one. The army could ask anything in the name of the Emperor and the people obeyed. Reverence and loyalty were the cement that held the empire together. Without the prestige given the Emperor the army would have tumbled.

July 7, 1937: Japanese troops attacked Chinese soldiers at the Marco Polo Bridge near Peking in north China. In the same year, about 100 Japanese warships and a Japanese army bombed the capital of Nanking in a series of raids until much of the city was demolished. An estimated 250,000 civilians were slaughtered and several thousand women raped. The capital was moved to Chungking, a five-century old rural city in the province of Szechwan which dominates all western China. In this area lies China's most fertile land and some of her richest mineral resources. To maintain its strategic imports, Chiang Kai-shek had a 681-mile road to Burma built in 1937–38. Supplies to China had to come to Rangoon Port, Burma; then by rail to Mandalay and into the mountains to where the Burma Road curved its way to Kunming, China.

In 1939, Japanese bombers made an all-out air attempt on Chungking, killing over 5,000 citizens and injuring thousands. Over the next three years, 3,000 tons of bombs fell, destroying one-third of the houses and severely damaging another one-third of the rest. By the fall of 1941, Japan held all of China's important seaports and had cut off most of her supply of weapons and other needed equipment from other countries, especially America, though China still obtained a trickle of America lend-lease supplies over the Burma Road.

With their peculiar and intense sense of self-delusion, the Japanese waged war on China only because they were "friends of the Chinese and wanted them to have stability and peace." They claimed that "China was unable to govern herself properly." Yet in the twenties and thirties, Chiang Kai-shek had brought peace and unity to his country (which was an excellent beginning though he later failed miserably and his country deteriorated badly). In the *Japan Times* appeared the following: "What is termed guerrilla warfare by Chiang Kai-Shek, amounts to disturbing Japan's efforts to maintain peace in China..." It was clear that Japan wanted to prevent China from growing strong and becoming a world power. In September, 1940, Japan signed the Tripartite Pact with Germany and Italy.

From time to time, Japanese pamphlets were translated into English and published in the *Japan Advertiser*, Tokyo's American daily. Here are a few:

"Japan must have a powerful navy sufficient to defeat any state which will attempt to frustrate Japan's noble effort of making the Far East a paradise of peace and prosperity."
"The time has come when we must liquidate the modern civilization based on individualism."
"The establishment of world peace is Japan's aim. No

country in the world has so high a mission as Japan to save the world."

This was the enemy our men fought in the CBI Theater and the enemy who caused my first bombing experiences. The Japanese had made such amazing progress so far in their wars that they truly believed they were unconquerable. Pearl Harbor filled them with super pride in their strength over us. Another question as to why our military at Pearl Harbor were taken so completely by surprise had been clearly answered in the December, 1991, issue of *National Geographic*. Very succinctly it was a series of wrong decisions, false assumptions, and delayed messages. The officers at Pearl Harbor evidently didn't expect any threat from Japan. One arrogant officer said something like this: "When we have gotten rid of Hitler, we'll pat our Japanese brothers on the head and say: 'Now, now, little men, behave yourselves.'" The "little men" had big plans. It seemed to us in CBI that Washington never quite fully grasped this, for they directed almost full attention to getting rid of Hitler, while our CBI men lacked sufficient equipment and supplies in fighting the Japanese who were well on their way to gathering up all of Asia, three continents in one.

Bibliography

Inside Asia—John Gunther—(1939)
Thunder Out of China—White-Jacoby—(1946)
Burma Surgeon Returns—Dr. Gordan Seagrave—(1946)
Last and First in Burma—Maurice Collis—(1956)
(printed in Britain—mostly a biography of
Reginold Dorman-Smith, Governor of Burma in 1941)
A Secret War—Oliver Caldwell—(1972)
China, Burma, India—Don Moser—(1972)
Chancey War—Edward Fischer—(1991)

Acknowledgments

My deepest thanks go to the many men whose lives I shared for a brief moment or for a longer period and especially those on the two isolated air bases in China. I think of them with admiration. War was thrust on them with all its hideousness and they were assigned to the CBI "forgotten theater" and yet— with a few gripes and grunts, of course— they kept their courage, love of America, faithfulness, and sense of humor. I thank those who gave extra time, ideas, and energy in helping me make the barren, army-issue buildings into attractive clubs, retreats for all men in their few moments off duty. I thank those who taught me important techniques, and all who made me feel comfortable when a number of times I was the only woman on the base. I am ever grateful to those who gave me pictures, 169 total, which, of course, could not all be included in this book. I regret that I don't have recordings of mens' names. I have only a few.

I thank the American Red Cross for allowing me this privilege of war service, for sending supplies to China from America or India for our varied needs, and for supporting me up through my landing at New York Harbor, September, 1945.

I thank my niece and nephew (Patricia and Lewis Zuelow, California) for continuous encouragement in writing this book and for helpful suggestions especially during the final stages of preparing for printing; Carleen Taylor, friend-helper, for listening to my groans and moans during the whole period of writing pains and for doing the many little things that were important in getting the job finished; I thank Ruth Blynt, author, for reading my manuscript and for her helpful ideas and thanks to my many wonderful friends who believed in me and encouraged me to get the book written and published. Finally thanks to Beverly Seifried who called my attention to Vantage Press, Inc.

1

Beginnings

I leaped out of bed—not at all my usual style of rising but this was a special day of beginnings. My winter-smudged window showed the rising sun smiling. Light green baby leaves decorated the trees and "beneath the trees fluttering and dancing in the breeze" were golden daffodils. But I didn't have time for standing, admiring, quoting Wordsworth's poem, which I loved and knew from memory.

I showered quickly and breakfasted hastily. My father would not have approved. He said breakfast was the most important meal of the day. My most important meal for this day would be lunch at 1:00 with Jim. It was just a week ago at a party that I had met Jim and I liked him. This would be our first date.

Dressing had to be a slower, more careful job. The lovely black silk dress I had purchased recently at De Pinnas was my unquestionable choice. It had a scattered pattern of small rose flowers with green petals and I had rose crystal earrings to match. Black silk hose and high-heeled black pumps, an eye-catching wide-brimmed black straw sailor hat; three-quarter-length white gloves, and a small black purse completed my ensemble. A final critical look in my full-length mirror assured me: "Yes, you look quite stunning. Jim should be impressed."

In a short time I was whizzing along the highway to New York City feeling sorry for those I passed who were not so lucky as I. I was young and along with youth from every state in America, I was responding enthusiastically to the "Call to Service." I was headed now for an 11:30 A.M. interview at the American Red Cross building. The bombing of Pearl Harbor by the Japanese, December 7th, 1941, had thrust us into World War II. Overseas American Red Cross Clubs had come into being and were becoming one of the major operations worldwide. The War Department had designated the Red Cross as the one and only civilian organization to serve American troops abroad. With a home away from home retreat and planned recreational activities, the clubs were to be run as morale builders and relief periods for the soldiers when free from their military duties. A club program director's job sounded perfect for me and I felt perfect for the job.

The traffic became heavy and I drove carefully, but my mind was mainly occupied with the application letter I had sent to the Red Cross and possibly important things I had left out. I had my bachelor's from Keuka College, a master's from Columbia University, and at present I was teaching music at Dobbs Ferry High School, Westchester County. I was a PK (preacher's kid), brought up to like all people and treat them equally in a friendly, sensitive and sincerely responsive manner. At an early age I had learned to speak and sing publicly. In high school I had helped my father plan and enact programs for all ages. Often my father insisted I take a back seat in favor of someone whose ability, I felt, was inferior to mine. This was difficult and I thought it unfair but in time I realized its value. I had sewed since childhood and later made many of my own clothes. I had upholstered and re-covered a number of pieces of furniture. I loved books and read hungrily. At age four I had picked out melodies with one finger at the piano and (as my parents told me) then played the melodies in parallel sixths—with one finger of each hand. Years later I could play any familiar song by ear in any key with my own original harmonies and arrangements. Dad's salary was small. He taught us three kids to make or create what we desired and couldn't afford. There was no doubt about it, I told myself happily, I was really qualified for this job.

I found the Red Cross building and the right room and in a short time I was facing my interviewer. She was not especially friendly, probably tired, I thought, from interviewing so many women. The interview was short and I was told I would receive word by mail.

Confident that I would soon be overseas somewhere involved in club work, I looked forward all the more eagerly to a new romance before leaving our country. The restaurant atmosphere was perfect, the lunch delicious, the service excellent, and

2

Jim was a delightful luncheon companion. Our conversation flowed easily and at intervals humorous comments threw us into peals of laughter. Then Jim dropped a bomb. He'd be leaving the next day for officers' training camp. Why should I be so disappointed? I, too, would be leaving soon. Suddenly I knew our carefree, happy lives were changing—how, only time would tell.

For two days I waited impatiently for my Red Cross letter. Then it came.

Rejected. Rejected???

Impossible!

Rejected.

The only one I wanted to pour out my woes to was my beloved sister Dorothy who had already been accepted by the Red Cross, had completed her training at Washington, and was at Fort Devens, Mass., waiting for orders to leave our country for overseas. Over the phone she gasped: "How could they?" But when she found out how I was dressed she said: "Eddie: dressed like that, what did you expect? The interviewer assumed you were a romance-seeking dame out for a good time, exactly what they don't want!" She told me not to worry, she'd get me in by hook or by crook. But I did worry. I wept bitter tears at my foolish pride in my infallible self. How could I have been so stupid in wanting to make an impression on Jim and not giving a thought about the impression I might make on my ARC interviewer?

Dot, who would have moved heaven and earth for me, contacted a Red Cross woman of high position in Buffalo, explained what had happened and said (blessed Dot) "Red Cross can't afford to lose her." She asked for another interview for me and got it. Most assuredly I dressed conservatively and appropriately when I went to Buffalo for that interview. I was accepted on the spot and flew out of there in a delicious daze.

Two or three times while I was finishing my teaching year at Dobbs Ferry, I heard my brother Vinton lecturing on chemical warfare. He lectured throughout Westchester county. I was horrified at the thought of gases being used, though I realized there was a possibility and that we had to be prepared. The army was taking every precaution for our safety. Vint was later sent to Edgewood Arsenal where he became President of the Supervisory Board of Chemical Warfare. I'm proud of his contributions in this field both during and following the war.

I reread my sister's recent Fort Devens letter dated early June 1943. Her letter intrigued me, for I would undoubtedly be going through similar tactics before long. I quote from parts of it: "After my training in Washington I was designated American Field Director (AFD) in charge of the five Red Cross girls assigned to the 56th General Hospital. The whole hospital unit was sent here to Fort Devens, Mass., for further training." (My sister had a second masters from Chicago University in the field of Social Services. She was Children's Agent in Yates County, N.Y. when she applied to Red Cross December 20, 1942.) "I'm very lucky to be with a high quality of nurses—one hundred of them—who are the BEST (as their Head Nurse told me). We have over five hundred enlisted men in our unit, many will be orderlies in the hospital later and will do actual nursing.

"Every morning we have military training—Red Cross girls, nurses, enlisted men, officers—all wearing army fatigues, two-piece heavy cotton dark olive green fabric, slack suit type, fitting rather loosely. We also wear army issue field boots and helmets. It's a grotesque sight when everyone is dressed up with gas masks in place. Vint would get a big bang out of seeing me "properly clothed" for the gases awaiting us. This morning we had group calisthenics—rather trying on my bones and weak muscles (hadn't known they were weak); and then we went to the gas field and gas chamber which was quite an experience, for they gave us the works. As we entered the field they threw tear gas in our midst. I sniffed it, grabbed my gas mask out of its cover and got it on so fast that I surprised myself, but the tears streamed from my eyes and my nose ran. With our masks still on we went in the gas chamber where there was chlorine gas and then were taken back into the field where they played all sorts of tricks on us. We grabbed our masks as they demonstrated mustard gas and smoke screens and tear gas which we walked through. There were hand grenades, incendiary bombs, and magnesium, all to be very wary of.

"Later we returned to the gas chamber. Each person carries a special cover which is very compact but when opened com-

4

pletely covers the person squatting and is large enough to allow donning the gas mask while under it. This time we were told to take a deep breath of pure air, enter holding our breath, get our gas masks out of the covers and on our faces, clear the masks of any gas inside and don our helmets again. They kept us on our toes all morning. We returned in march formation to our barracks saturated with the various gas odors. I took a shower and washed my hair but it still held the odors like a new and repulsive brand of perfume. Everyone went through the experience with no casualties and the two ambulances returned to their station minus any victims. You have to test your mask, have faith in it, and not get panicky.

"This morning after calisthenics we marched over to a theater to see war movies following which I had to make a speech on Red Cross services. I had dreaded it and was uneasy having to deliver it after everyone would be tired from sitting so long, but it went off okay. It's the largest audience I had ever spoken to, and all in fatigues and helmets. We had to march all afternoon. Our drill captain says our platoon is sloppy and unless we improve we'll have to have special drills—and he means it! Tonight I am hostess for our barracks, which means I have to pull down all the shades after dark.

"Yesterday we finally got some furniture for our Red Cross office which is across the road from our barracks—two rooms, very rough and dirty. The Service Supply men came over with some things and helped us. Army posters, military courtesy, and Insignia illustrated in color brightened up the rough walls. We found some old drapes for the windows and I found a plant. The men laughed at me for wanting our crude office all fixed up for only a short time but I said it would be appreciated if only for one day. We have office hours from 6:30–7:30 P.M.

We all eat like pigs. Everything is cooked nicely and well seasoned, for we have excellent cooks in our unit—but the food is heavy; three heavy meals a day. With all our exercise we get starved even between meals.

I love the PJs with the very clever trimmings that you made for me, Eddie. I'll keep them for special wearing. The weather is so cold that I've been trying to buy an army comfortable padded

5

with cotton but they're sold out. The army blankets aren't too warm and the air gets through. I'm afraid I'm going to freeze this winter with only two blankets though I'm wearing my flannel PJs which I managed to buy. I've been wearing my wool army socks to bed to keep warm. Our barracks is cold and the heater is broken. Last night I wanted to phone you and hear your voice but the phone was kept so busy that I finally gave up . . . Love, Dot."

2

Washington, D.C. Training and Bay Ridge Merchant Marine Rest Center

It was painful leaving my parents. Mother was not well. She cried. Dad took me to the railroad station where we hugged and smiled and fought tears that fell in spite of our efforts. The train's whistle sounded faintly in the distance and as it grew louder our hugs tightened. The huge, roaring engine, with its passenger cars, chugged into the station. It was time to go. I climbed the steps, Dad following with my suitcase. One last hug and he was gone. No glimpse of him through the window. I understood.

Washington, D.C.

Dearest Mom and Dad:

I slept rottenly on the train. My eyes ached from crying and also holding back the tears that were deep inside me and the train rocked awfully. I did doze but then woke up to find only a half hour had passed. The trip seemed endless.

Luckily, when we arrived in Washington, I joined three others in taking a taxi to American University, for we rode on and on way to the other end of the city. So it cost me only sixty cents. I registered and found my room, which is literally a barn of a place with a cement floor, four bare walls, five army cots, and two old dressers covered with white paper. There were girls there full of pep which made up for the bare room.

At 2:00 we newcomers met and began general classes which will last all week, classes on everything imaginable: How To Fill Out Our Vouchers, History of ARC, Organization of ARC, Camp

Service, Hospital Service, Home Service, Club Service, Military Orientation, Insular and Foreign Operations, First Aid, Water Safety, and on and on and on . . . And now to bed. Love you very much, Eddie

End of First Week in Washington

My dear ones:

Today we had a four-page exam covering all those general subjects and I got a 94. Was relieved, for so much material had been thrown at us in a brief period and some of it was boring, making it difficult to listen. Yesterday I was embarrassed when our instructor, Commodore Longfellow, wanted a model for his Water Safety lecture and said: "that girl in the fourth row, third from the left." It was me! I had to stand on the platform while he demonstrated safety belts, saving people with blankets, etc. etc. Girls in the class spoke to me afterward complimenting me on my modeling (I guess they felt sorry for me) but I was very embarrassed to be singled out that way. It was, of course, a chancy thing. It could have happened to anyone, but I wish he had said "third row, second from the right" or some other combination.

We have a cafeteria here in this hall of the Printcraft Building where we can eat fairly reasonably but the vegetables are so overcooked that chewing is unnecessary and you know how I despise overcooked vegetables. So I often eat at the drugstore. Tell the kids that the other day I sat on a stool talking to Madeline Carroll, movie actress, not knowing for awhile who she was. She's pretty but so are all the girls. We have a Powers model in our group, very attractive.

I've had my uniforming and everything fits perfectly but the session from 5:15–8:00 P.M. took so long we were all wearied. I was issued a light gray seersucker suit and a dark gray winter weight suit (uniforms) with extra skirts, also two gray seersucker dresses. The overcoat issued me has a nice red flannel lining that can be removed. It's a complete coat in itself and can be used for an evening wrap. A jersey uniform dress in a lovely powder blue was optional, meaning we had to pay for it, but I bought it. It's worn at social occasions with pumps and is very becoming. It was too late to come back here so we ate in a Chinese restaurant.

Tomorrow, Saturday, we have special group classes. Mine will be Club-Job Function. Then we're free for the weekend to sew on name tags, insignia, buttons, etc. They're supposed to advance us $200 as a loan for emergency buying but I haven't seen mine yet. Next week I meet with club people for orientation courses of all sorts and that should be much more interesting than the general courses I've had.

As to business matters, tell the lawyer, Dad, that I wish to give you power of attorney so that you can sign any checks for me and take care of any of my business. As for my salary, for awhile I'll need it all to pay my debts. Later I'll save some for spending money, put part into bonds which will be sent to you and I'll send the rest to the bank for a savings account. I'll be given a $2000 life insurance made out to both of you in case I'm killed. Good heavens, I'm not worth much, am I?

11:00 P.M. is supposed to be the deadline for bed but here we are independent so at one o'clock radios are still blaring, people are taking showers and yelling all over the place and all those sounds are magnified in this building. Sleep is something I dream about in classes when I get bored which does happen occasionally. Someway I've managed to exist on a few hours of sleep but right now I'm going to fall into bed, hopefully blot out the noise and experience blissful unconsciousness.

I miss you so very much. You'll always be closer to me than the map says . . . Eddie

Monday After the Second Week in Washington

Dear Mom and Dad:

I've had all my shots—eleven of them—given to me in the Pentagon. I'm so full of shots I can't imagine how any sort of bug could possibly penetrate me or, if so, live very long to brag about it.

I'm sure you're probably interested to know how the face of

Washington D.C. has changed with all of us here. Buildings have sprung up like dandelions. Fifty-three acres of temporary wooden office buildings occupy an open stretch between the Capitol and the Lincoln Memorial. The Military occupy a mountain of buildings that overflow the District of Columbia into Maryland and Virginia. American Red Cross has taken over two additional office buildings plus the first floor of the Metropolitan Club and is also using part of American University. The massive Pentagon rises above the Potomac River about three miles from the White House.

I had intended taking no civilian clothes, thinking we weren't supposed to, but now we're told to take some. So will you send me an evening skirt and blouses, the black silk two-piece dress, earrings, necklaces, also some fine tacks, ration books to buy shoes, my birth certificate, 1942 income tax report. I hate to bother you but I'd be so very grateful.

I had my first interview which was very brief. They simply wanted to know what I wished to do if I weren't shipped out immediately. I said I'd rather go into one of our camps where I could do recreational work and they agreed that would be best for me. As for leaving I can give you no hints. We are warned definitely not to say anything. and it is the best policy. If you don't hear, you'll know I've gone. But even then, don't worry. The ships are quite safe. I'm not so concerned about being on the ship as getting on. I have to wear my suit, my overcoat with the flannel lining and my raincoat on top feeling like a stuffed pig. Then I'll be carrying my suitcase, musette bag, shoulder-strap handbag, gas mask, helmet, and ????—trying to look nonchalant as if it were my everyday attire with the usual paraphernalia. By the way there are "open" and "closed" stations. If I go to an "open station" you'll know where I am but if it's a "closed station" my whereabouts will be secret.

Saturday we had uniform inspection and then were given our extension assignment which will last until we receive our orders for leaving here. Finally we had graduation at 11:00 A.M. Saturday afternoon was filled with odds and ends. At 5:30 four of us were met at the Willard Hotel by a Navy photographer who took us to his home in Maryland. His wife served us tomato juice and lovely sandwiches while he posed us one at a time for our pictures. Received the proofs today, six different poses and all excellent. I was very pleased. He did a wonderful job. I had copies made from my final choice and am sending one to Vint, one to Dot, to a few friends, and the rest home to you, saving one for myself. I may want to look at it in the time ahead to see if I've changed.

Sunday and today; I've been terribly rushed with partial clearing, posing for newspaper pictures, packing my locker with stuff I won't need till a month after landing, painting my name on all sides of my locker, musette bag, duffel bag, etc. Some things, of course, will be put in the hole of the ship and entirely out of reach for a long time. Tomorrow Ann and I leave here for our temporary assignment. I'll write you from there . . . All my love, Eddie

Merchant Marine Rest Center

Dearest Mom and Dad:

We've been here a whole week though it seems much longer. Ann and I were met at Annapolis by a beach wagon driver and were taken out to this most beautiful spot on the ocean. It had previously been a summer resort with large dance hall, bath houses, baseball field and bleachers, and recreational facilities of all kinds. A most glorious spot for a Merchant Marine Rest Home.

We arrived about 11:00 A.M. and for the rest of the day were run ragged playing games with or talking with the men. They range in age from early twenties to older men who have been in the marines for many years—and all of them alcoholics. They're supposed to be drying out but after a week here I wonder whether that will ever happen. They're restricted to certain boundary lines and if caught slipping over they're dismissed. Most of them are recuperating from operations and many have been bombed or torpedoed. They're really a grand bunch of men, extremely courteous and thoughtful to Ann and me and seem to be entertaining us rather than our looking after their comforts.

The second day I complained that I wasn't doing enough for them and they assured me strongly that it meant everything to them just having us with them. My only real job has been taking inventory of all the clothes in nine closets, clothing that has been loaned the men while they're here. Ann and I prepare egg nogs, coffee, milk, and fruit at 10:00 A.M. and the same at 3:00 P.M. At 9:00 P.M. we prepare cocoa, coffee, and sandwiches. The men even help us with this process and insist on carrying the dishes and trays. They go to bed at 10:00 but so far we can't make it till 12:00 or 1:00.

Sunday I was thrilled that a number of men said they'd like to go with me to church in town. Ah, I thought, I'm having a good influence on them. I drove the beach wagon. It was Communion Sunday in the Protestant church. Now how did the men know that? They must have known, for part way through the service the man at my right leaned over and questioned in a loud whisper: "When do they serve the wine?" Oh, my sweet innocent self, you have so much to learn. So they had come just to get a small sip of wine—and it would be grape juice not wine! This was the strangest communion service I might ever go through surrounded by alcoholic marines with their tongues hanging out. The words from that old hymn: "My thirst was quenched, my soul revived" had no fulfillment for them. Poor thirsty souls. And that wasn't all. When we left the church to return home, they put on the pressure act for me to drive them to the business section to purchase a few things they needed. A few things they needed! Aha. You can fool me once but not twice. Thus ended the Church Episode. Amen and Ah, men.

I had wondered why the men looked forward to the Bingo parties town women put on regularly for them. They didn't seem the Bingo type. I soon found out. It was the special male prizes they wanted. Hair tonic has 85% alcohol. All prizes that contained alcohol were added to their egg nogs. No wonder they enjoyed that drink. I'm getting a real education not offered me in college.

We go for walks, shoot pool (I'm really not bad), play chess, ping pong, cards, dominoes, jigsaw puzzles, sing, talk . . . The younger men try to monopolize our time but we seek out the older men who look lonely. A group of young girls are brought by a chaperon every few nights to dance and play games with the men. Ann and I have had a hard time getting the men to cooperate more fully for they prefer our company and make it obvious. There are so many demands on us that it is an emotional strain.

The men have learned that I'm a minister's daughter and have been plying me with a thousand and one jokes to tell you, Dad—mostly the "Jew, Catholic, Protestant" conflict type. They've poured them out so fast midst loud guffaws that they all flow together in my mind and I couldn't possibly pass even one of them on to you. I heard Lowell Thomas on the radio last night and wondered if you were listening. It was announced that Ray Clapper, news commentator, was killed . . . My love to both of you always and ever, Eddie

Leaving Bay Ridge

Dear Mom and Dad:

A telephone message was delivered to us to report to R Street, Washington, that very night. It almost took our breath away. We hated to leave so abruptly. We had become well acquainted with the men and were a part of "The Family." The men seemed really upset. To see the old seamen with tears in their eyes was gratifying but also unnerving. I feel that I've learned more from them than they have gained from me although a familiar quote comes to mind: "Air and light pass through a window in both directions." I wonder, will I ever see them again? Our farewell around the waiting taxi left Ann and me speechless on our return trip.

Our present quarters back here in Washington are in a dirty old building taken over for housing girls on the alert. We arrived late, talked awhile, and went to bed. I suddenly was very, very tired, emotionally tired from the strain of the past weeks. At Bay Ridge we were on duty from 8:00 A.M. to 10:00 P.M. with no let-up. After the men retired we had conferences with the doctors and nurses till 1:00 and one night it was 2:00.

The next day I shopped, washed, and ironed. I did all of

Ann's washing for she had to clear the following day. Most of the girls here, except three of us, cleared with her—an all-day process. Today they left and I was busy helping them iron and pack. I clear tomorrow. I know the direction. Tomorrow I'll know all they can tell me. I'm happy. It's what I wanted.

I love you both so much. I remember what you said, Dad, that our love for each other is so strong we'll always be together in our hearts. Since my few days at Bay Ridge, I feel certain I can be of value if only I can keep a closeness to God. This war can't last too much longer and in the duration if Dot and I can be of use it will be worth it to you as well as to us. I have everything I need—enough soap to clean everyone in the universe. You won't hear from me for a long time but I'll be safe. I'll write en route and post a letter as soon as I can . . . Eddie

3

Malvern Wells, England—
Psychiatric Hospital

Dear Folks:

We had a good trip across the Atlantic and here I am in England. It is all very thrilling. I wish Eddie were here to share it with me. Yesterday I picked a bunch of holly and got such a kick out of it. I have it beside my cot. We're gradually getting settled though our living quarters are pretty bare. We live in Nissen huts with oval roofs and sides corrugated. They look like Eskimo igloos and are completely blacked out at night by curtains over the doors. Our floor is cement and always dusty and dirty. We sweep every morning before inspection. We tried to get some grass rugs but were unsuccessful. Our Sanitary is across the road. Everything is rationed. We buy mostly through the Army PX but things there are also rationed. We can't buy clothing or wool. Would you please send me my light blue wool sweater, my bright red wool scarf and mittens, my red cardigan and rainbow sweater and my red wool jacket which I can wear under my cotton uniforms. You can send a five-pound package the size of a shoebox each week. We can't get crackers or cookies. The flour is all one kind—dark. I'd love some good old graham crackers. I'm very grateful to you for all the thoughtful things you've done for me.

Today Terry, our secretary, had her radio changed over to the correct current by one of the boys so now we have music and speeches. We sat laughing at the German propaganda of which there is plenty. There are five hours difference between us—we're ahead of you. In the morning we get night club dance music from the States for our breakfast hour. Everyone goes wild with joy as we hear our various favorites played—good old American jazz.

15

I've been learning how to use English money but the pieces are so big they weigh me down. The billfold Eddie bought me in Italy comes in handy for the English notes. There hasn't been much social life but yesterday we rode a double-decker bus, like the New York City Avenue buses, to Worcester—lovely views across the valley. The houses all have many chimneys and are most picturesque and charming. And Dad, you would love the landscaping around the houses with beautiful flowers and hedges all unusually shaped. The soil is fertile and things grow profusely. High stone walls covered with ivy and other vines line the roads. Our writing is very restricted. I don't know how long we'll be here . . . Love, Dot

Still At Malvern Wells, England

Dear Mother and Dad:

We have been very busy. This is a psychiatric hospital and we have new patients coming in every day—some real difficult cases too. We of Red Cross have been accepted well by the doctors and I am asked in on the staff meetings when the patients' problems are discussed which is (so I've heard) unusual but also very helpful to me in my work with the patients. We've set up one of our buildings in one of the wards and have been functioning. The patients enjoy the privileges here.

They gave me an additional secretary to go with two of our girls to another section where some of our group are setting up another hospital. I have to supervise our girls in both places. It makes us a bit short-handed here but we'll manage. The British Red Cross is wonderful to work with and I'm thrilled more and more with their organization. They have marvelous personnel. The bombings around us are heavy and the patients keep coming in. It's most interesting trying to straighten out some of their tangled minds and often most encouraging and satisfying. Because Red Cross is nonmilitary, many patients feel freer to talk with us at times. It helps so much in the treatment process though, of course, I work closely with the military psychiatrist. We have all mental problems. I wish we could get Hitler here.

16

A few days ago I received your mimeographed letter, Dad, the one you sent to all the church young people overseas. I bet the kids got a big kick out of it with your wonderful sense of humor. You write so well. It was a nice thing to do. Repeat, please. My Evening in Paris perfume bottle is empty. Could you send me a new bottle? When I dress up, it brightens me if I smell sweet and the men seem to enjoy the smell too.

Last week I went to Birmingham and spent Saturday night in an English home with two fine typical English people. It was a grand experience. Seemed so good to get into a home again, sleep in a real bed with nice blankets, a puff over me, hot water bottle at my feet, and to wake up to a "Happy Good Morning" with a hot cup of tea. The day before they had made a fresh apple pie which they served at midnight with tea. We talked till 2:00 A.M. But I missed our American central heating. Their fireplaces keep you warm on one side while you're chilly on the other. They asked me back and promised to take me on a sightseeing trip to Stratford-on-Avon and Oxford University. We have many invitations to homes but haven't time to accept them.

I've had a cold ever since I came. It's hard to get acclimated to this weather which is damp and penetrating. Britain is a country with uniformly poor weather. I hope I'll be able to get a British Red Cross overcoat and winter suit. They're so much warmer than ours. Our huts are warm if we can keep the fires stoked but that's a job, for the stoves are so small and take only a little coke at one time. They're also dirty and our clothes get soiled and grimy. I can't send my overcoat or suit to the cleaners until I get replacements. I've been wearing my Palm Beach suit with snuggies and my gray sweater. I've worn out one pair of black shoes and had to send them to the repair shop.

Back to the weather, we've had little snow, only a few flakes a couple of times. It's surprising how the flowers bloom this time of year. Last week was quite warm and sunny. The grass has remained springy green all winter and the holly hedges are lovely full of red and yellow berries. We even have roses all winter... We're in a state of flux so no telling how long we'll be here... Love, Dot

4

On Board U.S.S. *Mount Vernon*

Dearest Mom and Dad:

I'm writing although I don't know when this letter will be posted. After my last call to you, I left Washington by train. A good trip to Los Angeles in spite of cramped quarters. I had to share a sleeper, rather crowded, and I marvel at how so many women could get into one small train washroom. I discovered that there were only two girls I knew in the group but they were a nice bunch of females. On arrival we were taken by Red Cross mobiles some distance to a staging area, Camp Anna. Our building was a roughly constructed affair but our quarters inside seemed luxurious in comparison to what we've had before.

There were meetings, issuings of necessary equipment, abandoning ship practices, gas mask drills, etc. Evenings we dated and danced in the officers' club. But the exciting episode of my stay there was a surprise reaction. As we stood in line with gas masks waiting our turn to go through the gas chamber, I suddenly felt nauseated. The next thing I remember was that I was stretched out on the ground looking up at mens' faces. They told me I went over backward like a flash and hit full on the back of my head just missing my helmet. I was taken in an ambulance to the hospital and stayed there for the major part of the day with a terrific chill. I couldn't believe that I had actually fainted for the first time in my life. I was told by a doctor that I couldn't ship out, I'd have to return home. Oh, No, No, No! Believe me, I did some fast and powerful talking. "I'm probably the healthiest person in this camp, have never been sick in my whole life. The only thing I ever had as a child was mumps. I don't get colds. Bugs ignore me." Then I mentioned Vint's lectures on chemical warfare and though I was not afraid of entering the gas chamber, perhaps some things in those lectures entered my mind and caused a physical reaction. So through words and determination I won, by golly. "Oh, thank you, God, I won."

We finally left Camp Anna in a pouring rain. I wished so badly that you could see me—wearing three coats (raincoat on top), helmet, gas mask in cover, pistol belt with canteen and first aid kit, musette bag loaded to overflowing, and a huge package tied on my back, bulging handbag hung from shoulder. Thank heavens our suitcases were sent on and, of course, our bedrolls and lockers had gone a few days before. We traveled to the Port of Embarkation and were thrilled at the sight of Red Cross women waiting to serve us coffee, sandwiches, and cookies. It was our dinner and we were grateful.

We sailed soon and the trip was marvelous, filled with all sorts of fantastic and hilarious events and most of the time, I'm ashamed to say, unaware of the headaches the captain and crew were having, zigzagging the ship over the submarine- and mine-infested Pacific to keep us from exploding into the waters. With the added zigzagging I have no idea of the total distance we covered but it took us a whole month. There were over 3,000 American men, 34 women, and the crew—quite a load. Of the women, four were assigned to clubmobiles, five to hospitals, and twenty-five, including me, listed as Staff Assistants.*

Red Cross Personnel on Board Ship, *Mt. Vernon*

Marion J. Bardot, Asst. Field Director
M. Otto Berg, Asst. Field Director
Daniel L. Brace, Asst. Field Director
William H. Colhoun, Jr., Asst.
  Field Director., Rec.
Ralph A. Rigden, Accountant
Herman H. Tonne, Asst. Field Director
Leo J. Will, Asst. Field Director
David K. Wood, Accountant
Elnora M. Anderson, Staff Asst.
Betty M. Atkinson, Staff Asst.
Betty B. Barr, Staff Asst.
Gogo Berenson, Staff Asst.

Ann C. Hemingway, Staff Asst.
Mary E. Huffman, Hosp. Secretary
Mary E. Johnson, Staff Asst
Blanche Jones, Asst. Program Dir.

Jane Kehrer, Staff Asst.
Elizabeth S. Luce, Hospital Rec Wkr.
Betty Mohlman, Staff Asst.
Theodora Morgan, Staff Asst.
Helena H. Neal, Asst. Club Dir.
Rachel A. Nommensen, Staff Asst.
Dorothy E. Palozie, Staff Asst.
Kate H. Pence, Staff Asst.

Barbara C. Bond, Staff Asst.
Jean M. Brott, Staff Asst.
Esther Campbell, Staff Asst.
Kathleen Crandall, Staff Asst.
Mildred E. DeVries, Staff Asst. (Clmob)
Margaret English, Staff Asst. (Clmob)
Carol Hagerman, Staff Asst.
Barbara Hamilton, Staff Asst.
Virginia H. Harris, Staff Asst.

Edna May Rawson, Staff Asst
Marjorie L. Riley, Staff Asst.(Clmob)
Mary E. Ringland, Staff Asst.(Clmob)
Georgia W. Schulte, Hosp. Secretary
Mary C. Shelby, Staff Asst.
Mary Sylvander, Psychiatric Soc. Wkr.
Virginia I. Trice, Staff Asst.
Sara H. Werden, Hosp. Secretary
Ruth H. Zang, Staff Asst.

The above named personnel will report to the senior American Red Cross official, Calcutta, India, for suitable assignment within its designated area.

This assignment is necessary in the military service.

Deputy Administrator, Services to the Armed Forces.

*I didn't become full Program Director until I reached China. I'm sure others' assignments also became changed in time.

There were daily afternoon programs where all the talent was pooled and what amazing talent there was. I worked hard arranging music for choruses, copied parts, rehearsed with dancers and soloists and choruses and loved it all. I sang a solo one night over an evening broadcast program and was elated that the captain asked for me on the next program—his only request! I sang a duet with a fellow who has a most glorious baritone voice, sang with him a number of times—"My Hero" from *The Chocolate Soldier*, Romberg's "Song Of Love," etc. and we were accompanied by a concert pianist, no less. The trained talent was overwhelming. I also sang the solo in a mixed chorus of Gershwin's "The Man I Love" (I made the arrangement). And all this to such a large, appreciative audience.

There were basketball games to watch, shuffleboard, sitting and talking or playing bridge, and dancing at night under the stars for one whole hour followed by one hour of listening to symphonic music. Dancing was sometimes hectic for we girls were cut in on so often by the men that we felt tossed from one to another. Following the dancing, I tried to mingle freely with the crowd but finally discovered it was safer to have one main escort to avoid getting tangled with the "wolves." My chosen companion was a jewel—and a superb dancer. I was in seventh heaven. When the dance music ceased and the symphonic music was broadcasted, we two continued dancing. Imagine dancing to Mozart's *Symphony in G Minor*! He was very sensitive to the music, very creative. I was privileged to dance with him. In the daytime he introduced me to the Chinese language. He was being sent as an interpreter for the Air Force. I have notes I took in my beginning lessons with him. I was to practice the four tone levels—high, rising, low, falling to the sounds of La, Ba, Ti, Ko. It is difficult enough to learn words and phrases let alone tones and yet a different tone gives the word a different meaning. Sometimes the difference in meaning can be humorous or even embarrassing.†

The most fantastic event was the initiation of everyone—and I mean everyone—when we crossed the equator. I was given five pictures which I'll show you someday. The outfits the men improvised were hilarious. There was, of course, Father Time, a central figure wearing a high headgear, a long white beard, and a flowing gown. The newborn babe was a fairly muscular man wearing only a diaper and a white bonnet. Everyone, so it seemed, was crazily garbed and eventually hosed with the proper ceremony. The girls were treated a little less rambunctiously than the men but all of us were sopping wet and foolishly happy. One would never know war was waging around us and that the poor captain was concentrating on keeping us from being blown to smithereens. We acted like idiots exploding with laughter. I have my card as proof of my initiation. It looks like this:

ANCIENT ORDER OF THE DEEP
This is to certify that
Edna May Rawson
was initiated into the solemn mysteries of

†Later in China, I bought a Phrase Dictionary put out by the military. That was a great help because it gave an English approximation in sound. Yet to master those different tones for each word was impossible for me. That ability takes years.

21

THE ANCIENT ORDER OF THE DEEP
on board the U.S.S. *Mount Vernon*
etc.
E.P. Eldredge, Captain U.S. Navy

I'll post this letter as soon as we land. I'm so happy I'm afraid I'll burst. I'll try to keep you posted on everything that happens but things happen so fast I can't keep up with all the events . . . Love, Eddie

5

Setting Up New Hospital Near Bristol

Dearest Folks:

We can give out our location now. We're about six miles from Bristol in the SW corner near the channel in easy reach of London and the train service is good. I wish Eddie and I could be close to each other. I haven't heard from her and am so anxious to know where she is.

We're in the process of setting up our hospital but, of course, have patients to take care of as well. Six of my Red Cross personnel are now together so we can get much more done. I've been going between the Ministry of Works and the London Red Cross trying to get furniture for our Red Cross building. Finally I went to Bristol in an army truck where there's a Red Cross depot and got action. The furniture arrived today. We're terribly crowded here and it's hard living with so many in one hut so I come down to the Red Cross building, which is one of the wards, to write a letter. Everyone is tired but now that we're all together, hopefully we can take off some time away from the hospital and get a change which will release the tension. Last week I had to go to London on business so I spent the weekend and had a wonderful time chasing around, also saw a play "Quiet Weekend"—very good.

We have a patient in the hospital from the musical show *This Is The Army, Mr. Jones*. Since he was feeling better Monday night, he sang some hymns for the chaplain's service—a beautiful voice and I was thrilled to accompany him. I play the harmonium (reed organ) twice a week for the chaplain's services in the wards. It means so much to the patients, especially those who are not ambulatory. Of course, we cover the wards regularly for recreation and crafts and especially for problems that arise with the patients. They look forward to having us talk with them.

Tonight I took two oranges to one patient who had not been enjoying his food. His eyes lighted up in gratitude. We have few oranges or fresh fruit.

I got coupons in London to buy some shoes and some mittens. My shoes wear out fast as we walk miles each day. Our hut is a good long block from the "John" which is a bad setup, and our hut is far from the Red Cross building. The wards are strung all over the place and up the hill. I got the blue wool suit and blue great coat, British material, which I'm enjoying. I'm really having the time of my life and wouldn't have missed this for anything. I know that I'm contributing something during this tragic period. There's so much to do that one could work twenty-four hours a day but I find myself getting terribly tired in the confusion of it all. There's never a chance of being alone. We're not a part of the Army but we're under the commanding officer and he is wonderful and very cooperative.

I'm so anxious to know where Eddie is. If she comes to England it will be a long dream come true. I would hop the next train and go find her. I'm so excited thinking about her possible arrival. With all of her abilities she'll make a real contribution. I'd love to see her in action. The clubs here are large, well equipped, and swarming with men...My love to both of you, Dot

Near Bristol, England

Dearest Eddie:

I'm sending this letter to Red Cross Headquarters and hope it reaches you. I'm so anxious to know where you are. If you land in London be sure to tell Headquarters that you're my sister. They know me and will contact me. I'm so happy that you're with ARC and will be a Club Program Director. The work should be fascinating. I've saved two eggs for you. They're scarce and precious but will be too old to eat if you don't come soon.

Received your picture you sent from Washington, Eddie, and it's marvelous—looks just like you except for the short bob but I like that too. You look so G.I., as we would say, with everything according to regulation. So many have seen it already on a little stand in my office and the comments are killing from "She's good looking," "Bring her around," "When is she coming?" to "She's as nice as you"—the latter coming from the diplomats. They suggested getting you into our outfit, but this is not a club. I pick your picture up several times a day and feel that you are talking to me. I still have hopes you are coming this way but where in heavens are you?

I received a box from home containing Kotex etc. and was so grateful. It's impossible to get American Kotex here. British Kotex is so cumbersome and expensive—they're like hammocks, the queerest things. Money doesn't mean much for there's nothing worthwhile to buy. I went all over London when I was last there on business trying to find a pair of shoes but there were none to fit my long narrow feet. My shoes are wearing out fast. The repair shops produce poor workmanship and their materials are poor. They really wreck the shoes.

I wonder and wonder where you are, Eddie. Have they sent you to the moon?

There's so much I can't write. Times are uncertain for all of us. The other day we received a radiogramophone, an electric radio and Victrola combination, with a marvelous tone. It's going from morning to night and thankfully we have a good selection of records. The walls all through the wards are a yellow buff top and a hideous green from the middle down. Pipes and electric fixtures all show and the coverings are all colors. The black pipes run up through the ceilings. But we're happy to have a ward rather than a tent for our building so we're really not complaining though it's far from beautiful. We have begun to wax our Red Cross floors that are covered with pitch-mastic, a tar base. The wax makes them shine and look much better.

The enlisted men can't understand why they can't date us. It's a touchy subject but we have officers' rating which forbids it. Yet we get along in a friendly relationship without dates, we doing much for them and they for us. Since the officers' club is in the process of renovation, the officers come into the Red Cross building after the patients have left. The place is full of music and noise.

Eddie, where are you? I look longingly at the moon and wonder.

The countryside is glorious this spring with the trees blossoming. Every place is landscaped, even in the country, with no rubbish anywhere. Hedges are everywhere and cut in all sorts of interesting shapes. England is very picturesque. Its main fault is the climate which not even the English are adjusted to. They go around coughing and blowing. Just now my cold is better but I don't get enough rest. There's so much noise in our hut till very late and then some girls get up very early and the noise begins again.

I found a patient whose birthday is the same as mine so Monday we'll celebrate together. I'll find some cake somewhere and take him some flowers. They all love birthday parties. We give a big one once a month . . . My love to you wherever you are, Dot

6

Arriving at Bombay, India

My dear Ones:

Bombay, that magical name, has become a reality. I stood at the crowded ship's rail watching land come closer and closer, a welcome sight after such a long trip on the Pacific. We were in the Arabian Sea approaching India on its western coast. I breathed a prayer to God thanking Him that I was here, for twice I almost didn't make it. It took quite a stretch of time, as you can imagine, to debark, to be reunited with all our luggage, and be taken to our quarters. Many of the girls left that day for their permanent assignments.

Five of us are housed in the Apollo Hotel (far from ritzy!) where I was introduced to cockroaches which were jumping happily about in our room. We evidently will be sharing the room with them but I'm not happily jumping over the idea. You know I can't handle bugs like Dot can and these bugs are huge. Each one is as big as my thumb. I'm told that India has more cockroaches than any country in the world. What a miserable outlook!

We five will be assisting in the Red Cross canteen until our orders come to leave. Orders seem to take an eternity to come through. Meanwhile I'll have time to see this city. I hadn't realized that Bombay is an island connected to the main land by a causeway. I'll write you about everything that happens, everything I see and hear and smell as best I can remember and get it down on paper . . . Love you much, Eddie

Bombay (2)

My dear Mom and Dad:

We arrived at a bad time of year weatherwise. It's getting hotter as we approach the monsoon season. Yet on a few hours of sleep per night and in this hot climate I'm all pepped up, feel grand, and bubbling with enthusiasm. I've been working each day and occasional nights at the Red Cross canteen. I'm just an assistant a-bidin my time an awaitin for the Big Moment when I'll be in 'my club' a-plannin an a-runnin the show for our men. I wonder where and when that day will be. I do what I'm told to do and much more but have no responsibilities in planning or having to write reports. Meanwhile so much happens each day that it's impossible to recall all that should be related to you.

To walk on the sidewalks is an extraordinary experience for me since they are crowded with such a variety of garbed Indians that I stare and stare. Dhoti clad Hindu men, the dhoti being a long piece of cloth wrapped around the waist, brought between the legs and tucked in at the waist, something like a glorified diaper (though I guess 'glorified' is not the right word)—Hindu holy men in their saffron-draped cloths with red and white markings on their foreheads—Jains (a cult or offshoot of the Hindus) wearing white muslin masks over their mouths and noses to keep them from breathing in and destroying the life of a microbe—Hindu women covered completely from head to toe with only their eyes exposed—Impressive looking Sikhs heavily bearded and wonderfully turbaned—Moslem women in gracefully draped saris—ambling unhealthy looking cows—and most of these (except the stupid cows) staring back at me, a strange woman in a short skirt with bobbed hair and face boldly exposed smiling at everyone. Probably I've shocked them as much as they have intrigued me.

I'm constantly stepping over sleeping bodies and seeing other outcasts cooking meager meals on the sidewalks or in the gutters and am shocked at the great poverty here in this city where there's evidence of great wealth and magnificent temples and mosques with domes and minarets rising all around. This is supposed to be the richest city in SE Asia and the best place for beggars and that last seems to be true for I constantly dodge them on the streets as they beg for annas. By the way, I've forgotten to mention money. Ten paisas equals one American cent. One anna is two cents and one-quarter of a rupee is sixteen cents. One-half a rupee and five and ten rupees are paper bills. I've been told that poverty is India's greatest problem but hopeless, I guess, due to the caste system which, as you know, is an ancient social structure. I'm told there are more than forty-nine million of these outcasts in India. They are said to be Hindus by religion but what can a religion do for them when they are debarred from spiritual and social rights by the two hundred million upper class Hindus. According to the Hindu belief, man is expected to remain in the station into which he was born. No hopes for these untouchables? I can't imagine living here and not doing something for them. It's all beyond my comprehension.

I've ridden in a taxi a few times but that's a scary experience. There are sacred cows roaming the streets as well as the sidewalks. Motor vehicles jam on their brakes with a screech to avoid hitting an apathetic cow but they only sound their horns at a pedestrian who might jump and still be almost run over. Seemingly, human life is cheap but a killed cow could cause a riot. I'm told there are over two hundred million cows in India. All the cows in the world should move here. It's a cow's heaven except I can't see as they are fed well or cared for—just kept alive. So perhaps on second thought, it's purgatory, not paradise. And, of course, along with the placid cows there are trucks and taxis and Jeeps all honking their horns, human rickshas weaving this way and that, rumbling bullock carts, and pedestrians running in between everything that moves and each one (except the cows) concerned with his own neck and to heck with anyone else's. The cows are safe wherever they are. I wouldn't drive a car here for a million.

I haven't yet used a human ricksha. I hate to see a man take the place of a beast. I'm reminded that these men need passengers for their livelihood but the men are so thin and gaunt and sickly looking, to use them and tip them well or not to use them in protest—it's a dilemma . . . My love to both of you, Eddie

*   *   *

My parents had received my letter that was mailed soon after we arrived in Bombay from our long ocean trip. The following is quotes from Dad's long reply with love and news mixed with spots of humor.

29

Parts of a Long Letter From Dad

It was a big thrill getting your letter from way out there somewhere. It's been a long stretch of time since we said goodbye over the phone at Washington. I've prayed constantly for you but could not but feel that all was well with you. If Uncle Charlie had only known you were in Los Angeles, he would have run over there from Hollywood and would have taken you out on a fishing expedition to get you used to being on the deep seas. However, you never mentioned "feeding the fish" so you must have been a good sailor. I could picture you boarding the ship with all that paraphernalia. How did you ever manage to walk? The image of you with all that luggage piled on you and hanging from you was far worse than the clown episode we saw once at Barnum's circus. Do you remember? The second clown said to the first: "Pull off your vest and I'll fight you." So the first clown took off his vest, then he took off a second vest, then he took off a third vest—another off and another off... There were a dozen in all. I should think you would have felt like singing and dancing when you got rid of that tremendous burden or collapsing on your bunk in exhaustion. You're young and healthy so it was probably the former.

What a crowd of musicians you must have had on your ship. I'm not surprised that the captain asked you for a repeat solo performance. He showed his good musical sense. If the Japs had ever heard that you were singing, they would have pulled down their rising sun flag and crawled in to listen. I didn't know you were so interested in Chinese. Are they sending you to China? Now you'll need a monkey wrench to turn your eyes slightly north-east by south-west...

Dot wrote that she traveled all night on a pokey train with poor connections and caught more cold. When she returned the doctor said she had conjunctivitis. She must have gotten it at the railroad conjunctions. But Mom and I were glad to hear the name for we had the same thing and didn't know what to call it. I've had two doctors on my trail but they couldn't finish me off. I guess I'm pretty tough. Dot says she's very tired and hopes to get a day or two to visit friends in Scotland. Maybe they'll give her some Scotch to build her up [this from my tee-totaler father!!]

Dot's been writing about rationing but we know all about that. The government has rationed our time so we have only three and a half days a week now. I come down from the pulpit on Sundays and before I have time to prepare another sermon it's Sunday again . . .

Bogram who owns the town drunk shop just had a stroke. Now the old gal who's been dishing up the hot stuff for the gang and has lived with Bogram for fourteen years has suddenly decided to marry him. A brilliant idea for if he croaks she'll get what he owns. Amazing she could think so clearly . . .

Mom says she's thinking of you all the time day and night. It must be you haunt her dreams. The old place weeps for you and so do I, but I'm proud of you. Love, Dad

*   *   *

Bombay (3)

Dear Mom and Dad:

This will be a short letter for we've received word that we're leaving here. I feel that I've been of value to the men in the canteen but I'm anxious to move on closer to my goal and closer to action.

Bombay is an ancient port and trading center and entrance to the British Empire's proudest crown jewel. It's rich in history, its settlement dating back to the Buddhist Maurya Empire about 300 B.C. The British have built an impressive arch in commemoration of the visit of King George V in 1911 and other commemorative buildings. The city has great beauty and extreme wealth but is surrounded by slums and extreme poverty. Possibly over half of the city's population lives below poverty level. I've been at the entrance to the slum area but not inside. Perhaps I'll be able to go into the slums at our next assigned place for the slums are everywhere and, it's said, they are the worst in the world. I'm told that on the streets of brothels, young teenage country girls are sold by their parents into prostitution for half

31

the price of a bullock. It is sickening. What a tragic situation.

There are about one hundred and twenty thousand Parsis in and near this city. Parsiism is a faith that swept Persia and the Mediterranean world several centuries before Christ. They worship Zoroaster and sacred fires of Zoroaster brought from heaven. You, Dad, are well informed on these religions but I write to impress it on my mind and to refresh yours. The Parsis operate the best hotels—(I forgot to ask if they own the Taj Mahal Hotel here). They're the best business men and the richest industrialists.

I would be happy to say I'm leaving cockroaches behind but I know they'll follow me wherever I go for they've become attached—dedicated to making my stay in India less than perfect. I haven't seen a great deal of them in daytime for they're mostly nocturnal. The fact that they're the most primitive of living winged insects doesn't produce awe in me nor unbounding fascination. I look at their brown flattened bodies with shining leathery covering, get a whiff of their disagreeable odor and I remove myself quickly in disgust. Each miserable jumper can live up to one year. That's one year too long. At night I pull the netting tight around me and pray none of them will eat through.

On three different nights I've attended an Indian movie, an Indian ballet, and a Dance Drama *Kovalan*. Classical Indian music is rooted in folk tunes and religious songs that are still sung in the villages. Though my understanding in the first two was about nil, I'm grateful I had these introductions to Indian culture. Dance is one of the most cultivated art forms in India and with the program notes for *Kovalan* that I'm enclosing I had a better grasp of what was happening. I enjoyed the dancing tremendously.

One night there was a big party at the plush Taj Mahal Hotel. Some officer (I don't know who) told the orchestra leader that I was a soloist. I was dragged up to sing with the orchestra. I was highly embarrassed and annoyed but at least I can say I sang in the plush Taj Mahal Hotel. So Goodbye to Bombay and love to you . . . Eddie

KOVALAN
A Dance Drama
Mrinalini Sarabhai – Nandita Kripalani – Medha Yadh
Music by Visalakshi

WE present here in dance the well known Tamil classic of South India, the 'Seelapadikaram' or the Epic of the Anklet.

In the second century, in the reign of Karikala, there lived in the Chola City of Puhar a merchant prince by the name of Kovalan. He is married to Kannaki. One day Kovalan sees the dancer Madhavi who has been rewarded for her superb dancing by the King and he is deeply fascinated by her. She, too, reciprocates his feeling until she finds that he is married. Knowing that their love will have no joy at the cost of another's happiness, she dedicates her beloved art to the Temple.

Kovalan and Kannaki go together to Madura to sell Kannaki's anklet, the only precious jewel that they have now. At Tanjore Kovalan falls a victim to the treachery of the Court Jeweller who alleges that Kovalan stole the Pandya Queen's anklet, which he has himself stolen. The king orders the execution of Kovalan.

Furious at the injustice done by the Pandya King, Kannaki proves Kovalan's innocence by breaking the anklet and showing the precious stones hidden inside. The king realising the terrible wrong done by him, dies at her feet. Kannaki heart-broken, does *tapas*, penance, and rejoins Kovalan.

The story has been slightly altered to suit dramatic requirements. The techniques employed here are the Bharata Natyam (the actual dance that was at its height those days all over Tamiland), the Kathakali (from Kerala) and the Manipuri (the lyrical dance of Manipur).

There has been much talk of mixing techniques. It is not in the mixing itself but in the way it is done that objection can be taken. Here, in this drama, we have mixed techniques, but not the steps of each separate style. Each individual dance is absolutely pure in itself, but dancers employ in their different dances two or more techniques which have been thoroughly studied.

The music also has been chosen to suit the different techniques and the only words used are Sanskrit, the beautiful language of an ancient culture.

ACT I

Scene 1

The Court of the Chola King. 2nd century. The king has heard of the famous dancer Madhavi and wishes to see her dance. She does so in the true classical style. He is very pleased and rewards her with a golden necklace.

Scene 2

Madhavi asks her friend Minakshi to sell the necklace and desires that whosoever buys it should be her husband. Kovalan, who is passing by just then, is fascinated by Madhavi and buys the necklace. He asks Minakshi to direct him to Madhavi, who has gone to the seashore where a great festival is taking place. They meet and are attracted to each other. As they sit by the shore watching the sea and talking, Kovalan's wife Kannaki comes there looking for her husband. Madhavi comes to know who she is and is extremely hurt that Kovalan has not told her of his wife. She leaves Kovalan and goes away. Kannaki asks Kovalan to come with her to Madura to sell her anklet, which is her last precious jewel. Kovalan realises his duty and goes with Kannaki.

CURTAIN

Scene 3

Madhavi goes to the temple and dedicates her art to God.

ACT II

MADURA

Scene 1

Kovalan sells the anklet to the goldsmith, who is surprised to find that it is exactly like the queen's anklet. He decides to steal the anklet of the queen and throw the blame on Kovalan. He persuades Kovalan to leave the anklet with him to be valued and goes to the king. The Pandya King who is annoyed at being disturbed, does not make any enquiry but tells the goldsmith to kill the thief who stole the anklet.

Scene 2 - The executioner is at first reluctant but his greed for reward overcomes him and he kills Kovalan.

Scene 3 - Kannaki is on the bank of the river bathing when a messenger runs in and tells her of the news.

Scene 4 - Kannaki accuses the Pandya King of the death of an innocent man. The anklet is brought as proof of Kovalan's guilt but she breaks it open so that the jewels hidden inside are scattered about on the floor. The king is astounded for he knows that his anklet did not conceal any precious stones in it and he dies repenting of his injustice.

Scene 5 - Kannaki by her tapas, her penance, rejoins Kovalan.

7

Near Bristol, England

Dearest Eddie:

I'm so disappointed that you weren't sent in this direction, for I had hoped so very much that we could be close enough to see each other. Take good care of yourself, for if anything happened to you I don't know what I would do. We have a new staff aide who reminds me of you—dark haired, wears her hair page-boy style, and has your build. She is sweet, refined, and cultured and has a major in music. She has a lovely voice but always takes the lead, never harmonizes as you and I do. The dampness has affected my throat terribly but now that the weather is clearing I should vocalize and start singing. Surely, Sally will be an incentive. Like you, she's eager to be at the piano or she's warbling. She's a little different from the other girls and a bright spot for me when I miss you so much. Your letter was written en route but heading where? I hope you'll be where it's interesting and with other girls. It would be hectic being one of a few women among so many men.

I'm ripping this letter off to you on a little portable we brought from the States. I can control it better than the British ones with all the extra doohickeys. I'm sitting at a lovely desk with mahogany finish all because I made friends with a man at the Ministry of Works. Right now the drawers contain everything from some Scotch that belongs to one of the officers to PX supplies, cosmetics, canned food, correspondence, my case files— a grand assortment. Some day soon I've got to get them cleared out. My private office is attractive and everyone remarks about it. I have flowers and extra touches here and there. I'm a special friend of the gardeners on the estate here. I cut across the fields to the hot houses and come back with my arms loaded.

There was a grand opening in the Officers' Club last night so three of us went to the gardeners and hiked all over the place looking for decorations. The estate covers 7,000 acres. There was a very interesting tree there, a Japanese cherry tree with branches shooting out from the top of the trunk and dropping low to the ground all covered with cherry blossoms. We brought back large branches of red rhododendrons along with other flowers. They made the club look beautiful. The club's been completely renovated with three fireplaces, a large bar, easy chairs, nice floor, etc. Our orchestra is outstanding, very smooth, and has wonderful rhythm. We're very proud of them. It was a grand dance but today I'm tired. There are always some men who enter and are ready to overstep the bounds. We in our unit are so close together that there is more respect among us than with those met just casually.

I have your lovely picture on a bookcase across from my desk, Eddie. I always keep a vase of flowers beside it and two white birthday candles fixed in a piece of wire at the base of the picture. It's a sanctuary for you. Everyone admires your picture. I covered it and the frame with a large piece of light blue X-ray film to protect it. The pieces protrude out from the sides of the picture and give an interesting effect. I do love the picture and am so happy to have it.

We are well organized now so we can get off duty regularly. I've impressed on the girls that we all need to get away from the grounds and see things whenever we have a chance. It gives us a new start on life. Sally and I are going to London sometime next week for the day to do some shopping. I need to buy some more perfume for mine is all gone. I'm still looking for shoes. Meanwhile I'm sending to Marshall Fields in Chicago for a pair of British Walkers, a brand that I've worn and have liked.

We have movies three times a week which is fortunate for some outfits don't get that many. Now I'm not working evenings except in rare cases. I'm so glad for I was getting so tired I was ready to blow up. My administrative job calls for plenty of strain but I like it and being the Head helps greatly. At first I was amazed that a bunch of girls could be so careless throwing things around, but I played Dad's old trick of handing them things they've thrown and insisting they be put in their places. At first the girls thought me fussy but now they say they're glad for things get done and our building is neat all the while. Miss Baker from Headquarters has praised us highly. The girls appreciate the compliments they're receiving from many different sources.

Our supply room is a beautiful sight to behold with everything out of the boxes and displayed. It's so convenient when we go there for something to find it easily. We've made a wonderful carpenter shop out of what was a kitchen with an old cabinet for tools that are taken care of and kept in order by an ambulatory patient assigned to the job. I've put Sally in charge of the cleaning job. She gets so ambitious at it that she gets more done than I ever did. I'm going to have one of the patients paint my office. The walls are the same as the wards with that hideous green. It will look very different all yellow and the pipes which run all over the walls yellow instead of black. I have green drapes which pull together for blackouts each night. The bombs still fall.

Mrs. Coates of the British Red Cross just came in with a basket of flowers for the wards. Take good care of yourself. Write as soon as you can. I'm anxious to hear from you . . . Love you, Dot

Bristol, England (2)

Dearest Folks:
Your letter came yesterday, Dad, and I enjoyed it so very much. I love your letters with your up spirit. Keep writing. The trees are in leaf and it really seems like summer. Flowers bloom everywhere and the fields are full of primroses. The people and children continually send flowers to our gate for the patients. Fruit trees have been planted against the brick walls in the gardens and have been pruned so that the trees are flat against the walls while other trees are planted in the open. The apple blossoms are going now but have been so very lovely as well as the peach blooms and others. England is colorful, full of bloom. Remember Browning's *Oh to be in England now that spring is there!?* He was right. I'm so glad to have been here in this season.

I am having the time of my life for life is far from dull over here and I'm adventuresome enough not to want to settle down too long and get in a rut. I am proud to be with the 56th hospital group. This is one grand bunch, all so interesting in their individual ways. We know each other quite well now, having been together so long and we have learned to laugh at each other's eccentricities. Mary is a howl, so full of life and enthusiasm and wise cracks. We all enjoy her as does our C.O. who thinks we Red Cross girls are very important to the total unit.

Our other social worker was taken away from us as there is a shortage of social workers just now so I have to do the social work all by myself. It's meant reorganizing our total program and assigning some of the minor inquiries to the secretaries so that I handle the case work problems as well as the administrative duties. It will work out for the staff is cooperative. Miss Baker gave us undue praise when she was here. It's good to have a supervisor who is inspirational and critical in a helpful way without making one feel defensive. We all felt like turning the world upside down when she left and the staff has been starting off with new zest again. Army life is something to get adjusted to when you live so closely with people all the while but it does a lot for us.

Now the patients have left the building for the night and it's time to close up for another day. I'm keeping Mary company for tonight as she's feeling rather blue. We'll stop down at the club for awhile along with the rest. I'll be having a different APO number but I can't tell you more at this time. I'll miss my nice office and wonderful mahogany desk. Someone else can enjoy it now. I expect to visit Liverpool soon. I was there once but really didn't have a chance to see it. We are very busy and I won't be able to get a letter to you for some time. I got a letter from Eddie the other day—so good to hear from her . . . Love to you, Dot

Bristol, England (3)

Dearest Eddie:

I was so happy to receive your letter from India. It practically traveled around the world—stamped with San Francisco

APO Directory Service, then written in pencil "received New York, N.Y." etc. etc. I wait and wait for your letters and long to know what you're doing and the kind of setup you're in. It doesn't seem right that we're so far apart. How I wish I could be with you. I've always wanted to go to India. As the war closes down we'll have to catch up with each other and meet in Berlin. These are exceedingly interesting days and I'm afraid we're going to find it hard to remember all the happenings when we get home.

Speaking of cows roaming the streets, they roam around us here in the country. They're fairly healthy looking but not sacred, of course. Yet we can only look at them for we're not allowed to drink their milk as the army says it's not safe. I've become so used to the army's powdered milk that I can't imagine what fresh milk tastes like. Once in awhile we get fresh eggs but they're very scarce. The food gets monotonous at times. We've had a great deal of pork lately. Do be careful of the germs and bugs and the food in that area.

I'm not permitted to write about what's going on at present so there's not much I can say except that I love you, think of you all the while, wonder what you're doing. Your picture is always and ever admired by the girls and me. It really is so like you though your hair is shorter but has probably grown longer by now. You mentioned a letter that I never received. You won't be hearing from me for awhile. I'll be having a new APO. I had a complete physical and I'm fine with plenty of exercise . . . All my love to you, Dot

8

Bombay to Calcutta by Troop Train

Dear Mom and Dad:

Dressed in our fatigues, the five of us rode in a truck to the railroad station sitting on top of our multitudinous luggage with cockroaches jumping all around. Those blasted cockroaches really like us and though the feeling is not reciprocated it doesn't faze them in the least. At the station we boarded a troop train that would take us on the long trip to Calcutta. The train looked sort of antique as though it might not endure the trip ahead and it differed from our U.S. trains. We five with all our luggage had a compartment with windows that had shutters, screens, and panes of glass which we could raise at will, also one door which was the outside entrance, and a latrine. After a long delay our door was banged shut and the train started—screeching, jerking and grunting along at moderate speed, rolling and shaking. There was no more moving from our compartment until the train stopped again. We were caged in. In spite of our overhead swishing fan, we had to open the panes of glass to get more air but the screens were no help. Fine dust and sand and even cinders blew in on us.

When we finally stopped for midday meal and our outside door was clanked open, we were immediately surrounded by villagers—children, beggars, vendors, barking dogs, monkeys, goats...but very soon they were pushed back by our men to clear a space. We were served in a mess line and ate out of our mess kits with the eyes of those gaunt creatures upon us—quite disconcerting. When the meal was finished, we stood in line again, scraped any refuse into a garbage can, washed our kits in a pail of hot water, rinsed them in a second pail, and dipped them for a final rinsing in a third pail. Very efficient but not deluxe. Every night we were sprayed to protect us from mosquitoes and bugs. Our beds were wooden planks pulled out from the walls and on them we put our bed rolls. There was no netting to cover us but the fan and the moving train seemed to compensate. Sleep was not peaceful with the rocking train and the hard surface but I dozed.

The days passed with the same routine but always with added new sights to fascinate and charm or to repel and draw pity. We passed village after village where the living conditions of the people were dreadful. Some lived in small crude huts that looked as though they would tumble if someone breathed heavily on them. For some, poles had been driven into holes in the ground and something had been stretched over the tops of the poles for a roof. For others, frameworks had been made out of scavengered odds and ends.

When we stopped for a meal, we picked up bits of interesting information. Three hundred million Indians live in over seven hundred thousand small, drab villages. Life there has not changed for one thousand years. There's a village well but no electricity and very scarce furniture or none at all. Each family has a rice plot that is very small. Cooking is done on a mud stove. Wood is scarce and coal is expensive so cow dung fuel is used. The dung is mixed with mud, formed into cakes, and plastered on walls or any other flat surface to dry in the sun. The main food is rice and vegetables which the people eat from leaf plates using their fingers. Very few peasants own their small bits of land and if the monsoon doesn't come or doesn't last long enough to nourish the land and there's no food, they have to turn to the moneylenders who milk them dry. Many are in debt all their lives trying to hang on and keep going. If they work for others they earn about eight cents a day but for large numbers of them there is no employment at all. Poor nourishment, tuberculosis, dysentery, and other diseases are prevalent. Progress seems to be hopeless with so much illiteracy, unemployment, and ridiculous strict religious traditions holding them down.

After we had eaten, we sometimes had a chance to move about in the villages. Beggars were always present pressing close for baksheesh. The children tried to capture our money by using English words they had heard. The results were hilarious but probably not so funny as my attempts at Hindu would have been. The most common request was "baksheesh, hubba, hubba, baksheesh." The childrens' bodies were scrawny and dirty, a sad sight. In the crowded bazaars with each small shop like an open shed, foods of various kinds were covered with flies. It upset me greatly to see flies on the faces of babies with mothers making no effort to brush them away. There were numerous things for sale but nothing I wanted. The vendors chased after us begging us to come back and buy something. We saw many women and children carrying loads on their heads that we knew must be very heavy. How could their heads bear those burdens without serious injury?

In the center of every village was a stone temple, usually Hindu, and we often heard the conch shell blown by the priests calling the people to worship. In more prosperous villages there were homes made of mud with grass roofs or even tile roofs but still no windows. Everywhere we saw the cowdung cakes. We were told that sheep dung is used if no cow dung is available but it's not considered clean by the Hindus. We saw no chickens. The Brahmans consider them also unclean. Everywhere were half starved dogs, thin sick-looking cows, old people who probably weren't nearly so old as they looked, and children, children, children. In spite of the high volume of deaths, India's population continues to rise due to the excessive number of births annually. The men have fun in the process while the women bear the pain and the responsibility. This birthing of children is awfully one-sided.

We finally arrived at Calcutta's large and noisy and crowded Howrah station. Along with the usual beggars and vendors calling out their wares and evidently selling everything imaginable, there were people sleeping on the floor and whole families established in areas with their cooking utensils set up but living there, as someone said, only until the police would arrive and oust them. This was the hottest time of the year, preceding the monsoon season with temperature at 105 degrees and at midday, rising to 115 with very high humidity.

After arrival we five were split up, each of us living temporarily with a family to whom we pay board and room. I'm in a house with an elephant porch but to my great disappointment so far no elephant has deposited visitors. The family is French-Portuguese and they're treating me royally. I'm getting established in the large Red Cross club and am being pushed right now but I'll write as often as I can and report everything I can possibly remember . . . Much love, Eddie

9

Calcutta, India (Continued)

My dear Mom and Dad:

This heat is debilitating. Taking a shower is only temporary relief for as soon as I dry off I'm wet again with perspiration. It takes the life out of me and instead of the usual G.I.s I've had constipation. I sleep under a mosquito netting and an electric fan that makes a struggling noise against the humid air and accomplishes nothing except it's given me a cold. We all take atabrin daily to counteract the loss of salt in our systems or we'd be flat on our faces.

I was sent from the DeCunha family to a rooming house. The DeCunhas were wonderful to me. When once I mentioned my love of ice cream, they made it for me in their freezer. Of course, it didn't taste like our super U.S. ice cream but it was okay and very kind of them to do it. The only son, a college graduate and very informed on cultural and political affairs, liked me and wanted to correspond but I didn't want to get involved with that. He gave me a beautiful jewelry box from Burma and a lovely pair of handmade shoes which fit and feel very comfortable.

I've worked at the large Red Cross club since I arrived and have enjoyed it. I'm there from 9:30 A.M. to 5:30, or from 2:00 P.M. to 11:00. I work at the information desk or at the censoring desk where men have packages inspected and wrapped or at the program desk. Sometimes I just float in the big lounge talking with or playing games with the men. Generally there's quite a turnover—some of the men leave shortly after arrival while others are here longer waiting for orders. They are sent to Burma, Assam, China. Friendships are made in five minutes and come to an end in sudden separation. These men—our American men—are wonderful, good spirited, full of humor and optimism, ready to fight and get rid of the Japs, anxious to get out of this often forgotten theater and return home to loved ones and good old U.S.A.

I've gleaned a little information about Calcutta from reading available material and also talking with old-timers here. This is India's largest city and one of the most prosperous cities in Asia with products from the mills, factories, and industries from all over the country coming in here to the bazaars and shops. It had a glorious past, was known as "the Paris of the East" but many of the glories were for the British and other white men, prohibited to the native Indians. The city is both beautiful and ugly, new and old, west and east. Calcutta is still India's intellectual and cultural center. A great deal of Britain's wealth, power, and prestige has come from the abundance of India's raw materials. But in turn, the British have united India politically, established law and order, introduced western medicine and sanitation (at least in some areas), built a railroad system and a few good roads, a postal service and telephone. I suppose it's hard to say who has benefited the most—Britain or India. But India doesn't have her freedom and what is more precious than freedom!

During this war the population has increased causing greater problems, for there's been an inpouring of peasants from the country—peasants whose crops have failed or who have lost their land, are without work and hope to find it here in the city. They leave disaster and come here into disaster. We see them on the sidewalks, which seem more crowded than Bombay, sleeping and sometimes wrapped in cloth looking like corpses. There are no public toilets so the people urinate and relieve themselves in the gutters and open sewers. This and their meager street cooking of anything they can obtain attracts more flies, rats, and cockroaches.

We had heard about people going to the Howrah Bridge evenings to get relief from the heat and humidity of the city center so a few of us, out of curiosity, went there last week. The bridge stretches over the Hooghly River, a tributary of the Ganges, and connects Calcutta with Howrah which is a small city of about two hundred thousand and an important manufacturing center. When we arrived in the evening the bridge was terribly congested with people including vendors on either side squatting behind their wares. You can be sure we didn't stay very long.

I've taken men on trucks for city tours a few times. Being their guide means having to read and prepare myself to answer some of their questions. It's been good for me since I'm learning more about the city. In the center is Marden Park, a huge expanse of acreage crowded with people including fortune tellers, holy men, and snake charmers. There are also some of the main public buildings, clubs, and stores. The most imposing building I've seen is the Victoria Memorial. It's a stone sister of the Taj Mahal at Agra (farther north), built of the same Jaipur marble and surmounted by a three-ton figure of Victory. It's a grand memorial to Queen Victoria of England and a vast treasure house of priceless collections relating to British-Indian history. It was in the reign of Queen Victoria in 1858 that India came under Britain's rule. Victoria was proclaimed Empress of India in 1877. The memorial was financed primarily by the wealthy Indian princes.

We visited the famous Parashnath Mandir Jain temple on Madridas St. It's built of snow-white marble, exquisitely and delicately beautiful and was very costly without a doubt. It was built in 1867 and dedicated to the Jain prophet Sithalnathji who founded the sect in 500 B.C. on the precept that no living creature should be denied its right to live. Jainism is a Hindu sect that arose in protest against Brahmanism. The Jains reject caste but they do believe in Karma and because of their ultra respect for the life of any living thing they wear masks of white gauze. I've heard that if they should kill a bug they would turn into that bug in the next incarnation which sounds rather farfetched to me. Maybe someone is pulling my leg and yet their beliefs here are so strange that I guess anything is possible. There are over one million Jain members in India. Most of them are very wealthy and many are traders in the city. There's no doubt but that flies have a heyday and so do the rats and those darned cockroaches. I can kill every fly that approaches me and am not afraid of Jain's hell, if there is one. I haven't been greatly bothered by rats but if only I could murder those darned cockroaches I'd rejoice. They're very fast moving at unbelievable speeds and they dart this way and that unpredictably. I'm just not clever enough for them. If I ever did catch one, the thought of crushing it makes me shudder.

A few days ago I took some men on a river tour in the general's boat and, believe it or not, I steered the boat and docked it. I had good instruction, of course, but it was exciting to be allowed to do it . . . Much love till the next time, Eddie

Calcutta (3)

Dear Ones:

Thank you for your wonderful letter. Your letters uplift me and bring you closer. Everything here is going okay. I'm managing to work and play in this awful heat and humidity though I'll never get adjusted to it and hope sometime before too long to get out of it. Don't worry about my walking on the streets. They're safe in that there's no crime I know of. No one is going to attack me. The streets are mostly unpleasant and mentally disturbing because of the poverty and the ghastly way of living these people are forced into. There are literally thousands living on the streets, more crowded than in Bombay which was bad enough. Every day some of these people die from lack of nourishment and resulting diseases. Others are killed on the streets by the congested traffic and also by clinging to the sides and rears of buses and trucks.

I have used a ricksha a few times though I had said I never would. I've overtipped to qualm my conscience. I had been told so much about these wallahs' dependence on passengers that I felt guilty not to use them. A perplexing situation to be in. Many of the wallahs rent their rickshas from owners who live in real comfort and even hire jobbers to collect fees etc. so they don't have to soil their hands. Those few wallahs lucky enough to own their own rickshas often sleep in them, especially if their families are not here with them. They send money home to their people in the country. One of the many street sounds is the ringing of their tinkly bells attached to the rickshas' shafts to attract customers. It's not an uncommon sight to see wallahs collapse in the streets from lack of nourishment. It must take enormous energy and endurance and determination to carry loads that are sometimes very heavy over the streets that have holes and ruts, dodging trucks, buses, and taxis whose drivers despise them, coping with cops who make life even more difficult for them, and ending up sometimes with passengers who try to cheat them. But a job is a job is a job.

I've been in the homes of two wealthy Indians for an evening's entertainment and had dinner in one home which was a gorgeous place. Though there are twenty languages spoken here (of the many more throughout India), English is one language that every educated Indian understands and these more educated and cultured are very alert on world affairs so that conversation flows somewhat (?) easily along interesting and informative lines. We were served on large individual silver platters with rice piled in the center and around the rim were small bowls of hot spicy foods and sweets. I couldn't find out what we were eating but my tongue told me some were dangerously hot. We ate as they did, our fingers making a small ball of the rice and then dipping it part way in a sauce. Sort of fun.

After dinner, still sitting crosslegged on gorgeously embroidered mats and piles of lovely pillows, we were entertained by two musicians and a dancer. The dancer had a gold loop in the pierced side of her nose and on her ankles were heavy silver anklets of intricate design with tiny bells that tinkled and jingled as she moved to the beat of the drum and the message of the melody played on the stringed instrument. I was sure she was relating a saga with the motions of her hands and body but I didn't understand what it was. It wasn't really explained and in an English colored with Hindu it was hard to grasp clearly everything our hosts said. No matter, for I was fascinated with the sounds and the expressive movements. In all I see and hear I wish you could see and hear with me . . . Love, Eddie

10

Uninvited Guests at a
Mohammedan Wedding

Dearest Mom and Dad:

I had a wonderful sightseeing day, not guiding the men around but being guided. Two officers hired a cab with an English speaking driver who could help in our understanding. Another girl and I were their guests.

We visited a few shops on some narrow side streets that were like alleys and I bought two matching brass vases with gold and silver inlay and also a brass bowl. At flower stalls children were threading flowers to make garlands for sale. They should be outdoors playing or in school learning but at least this was better than what I've heard about some industries employing children for ten to twelve hours a day for which they are paid from ten cents up to seventy-five cents a month, and where the working conditions are dark with foul air. The jobber working for the employer takes a fee for hiring the children. A funeral procession passed by, preceded by a band, and I was surprised that the music was spirited. At the fruit and vegetable markets the venders called out their wares in many different strange languages making an interesting cacophony of sound. Charles Ives would have liked all this and probably would have combined all the sounds into a new composition—orchestral or vocal.

We all wanted to get a glimpse of the slum area we had heard so much about though we knew we had better not penetrate too far or stay very long. It's another city by itself where people (the untouchables) were making things, repairing things, and selling things under the worst imaginable conditions. People had about three square feet each. There was no privacy with about ten to twelve people in one small room. There were no flowers or trees or bushes—only flies, mosquitoes, and rats. Hundreds die each year of TB, dysentery, leprosy, malaria, typhoid, cholera...The rooms were without windows and had earthen floors. At the end of the alley were open gutters for latrines and a pipe giving forth water, probably from the river. Filth, stink, mud, refuse, polluted air, noise, coughing. We took in as much as we could in quick glances and left. We sprayed ourselves with perfume from a vial I had in my purse. It was a haunting experience—one never to be forgotten.

Since the Hindus predominate in India, I've been anxious to see one of their temples. According to the most recent figures there are over two hundred and thirty-eight million followers in India. The temple we saw centered about a small dark shrine room that held the cult image. The construction was based on magical number systems and religious mysteries down to the finest detail. There was a porch for performances of dance and music to honor the gods, a large hall where the worshipers assembled, and a small vestibule that led to the heart of the temple. A tower rose from the shrine room and smaller towers rose from other sections. A rectangular courtyard surrounded the whole and was filled with lesser shrines which were also topped by towers. A rising spire holds heaven and earth in their proper places. We were not allowed to enter some parts.

I am bewildered by the Hindu religion which has such an array of gods. Besides the Trinity of Brahman (creator), and Vishnu (preserver), and Shiva (destroyer leading to recreation) there are all their incarnations and their consorts. There's Krishna, the romantic flute player; and Rama, the ideal man and his wife Sita; Hanuman, the monkey god; Ganesha, the goodluck elephant-headed god; Kama, god of love, and more and yet more. How can a poor peasant appease them all? I'm so grateful I was born in a Christian home where I know one God to whom I can talk and know He listens and cares. Yet it's no wonder these poor people cling to their gods. They are taught from early life that it's the only hope they have of attaining their promised Nirvana which is an escape from the unending round of monotonous striving and suffering.

At 6:00 our driver said "Look, a Mohammedan wedding." We got out just to peek in but when we arrived at the archway we were greeted cordially and passed along the line until finally we rested in the hands of a most gracious and hospitable Mohammedan who proceeded to escort us everywhere. We assumed that they thought we had been invited but it was too late to back out. The place was huge with imitation grass scattered all over the floor. Archways of flowers and streamers of flowers stretched overhead just below a pure white ceiling. There were two orchestras, one on each side of the hall, so that when one orchestra finished playing the other began. The saris of all the women were magnificent and I in my light gray seersucker uniform and black oxford shoes looked far, far, far from glamorous. We pinched ourselves to be sure we were not in a beautiful dream.

We were taken way back in the hall to a large room where all the wedding gifts were displayed in glass cases—many gifts of silver, saris of the most exquisite material beautifully embroidered with gold and silver threads and a multitude of lovely things. We met the bride's sisters and then rested a minute while we were served drinks—coconut milk (which had previously been boiled) with very finely chopped pistachio nuts, fruits, and essences, served cold. I had three glasses. It was super. We then were led to another room where we met the bride seated in a hammock-looking affair with a canopy of India's tiny sacred jasmine and roses. She smiled but I felt sorry for her missing all the fun while her future husband was the center of attention and having a ball.

Finally we met the bridegroom and saw him start off on his journey midst the guests. He was dressed in a gorgeous white embroidered suit, the coat long; reaching to the knees and buttoned tightly from the neck on down. A huge lei of roses was placed around his neck and in his hand he carried a scepter of flowers. After he had finished his round among the guests, he was taken into a small room—and us with him though we couldn't understand how we were getting all this attention—and wrapped from head to foot in a huge blanket of jasmine and roses. The next day, according to their tradition, this would be thrown into the sea. Around his head was also fastened a band from which hung long gold wires. There was a small opening

51

through which he drank coconut milk. The rest of the drink was taken to the bride to complete. He was placed on a pedestal while the bride's mother threw grain all over his body. The bride's father threw a coconut over his head which ended the ceremony. The groom was released from his wrappings. What an ordeal!

The real ceremony had been held the day before in a mosque, at which time the bride was not present but was represented by a priest. Meanwhile the two were not allowed to see each other until the ceremony of the second day was completed. It was later through inquiry I learned that a marriage in Islam must have the consent of the two to be married, and a dowry is given by the groom. Divorce seldom occurs. If it does, it becomes a very complicated matter. So a Mohammedan marriage is far different from a Hindu marriage where the girl has no choice and her parents have to produce the dowry with the groom often extorting as much as he can get. The saying goes among the Hindus: "Sons bring wealth, daughters take it away." I hope to see a Hindu wedding sometime.

For some puzzling reason our host and his wife had taken a liking to us and said they would take us to the races the next day. We got back to the hotel tired and happy, bathed and changed our clothes and went out to eat and dance. I've danced just about every night since I left Camp Anna. I didn't intend to serve my country dancing but the men want to dance, dance, dance . . .

The horse races the next day were spectacular and exciting. The sight of women all in beautiful graceful saris at a sports event seemed incongruous to us Americans.

It's late and I'm tired and the bed is waiting. My love to you both, Eddie

Calcutta (5)

Dear Mom and Dad:

The five of us have been moved again. It seems as though we're constantly moving and it's a pain in the neck with all our luggage. I'm enclosing the bill from Mrs. Hurley. At the rate of 1 rupee = 64 cents and 1 anna = 2 cents, my room per night cost

$3.20, one dinner cost $1.28, one luncheon cost 96 cents and a phone call 4 cents. My total bill was $81.92—a lot of money.

But we five are together now in what was a former Rajah's home, a marble structure with balconies and big halls. My corner room has windows with iron bars, colored panes of glass above and French windows below that open outward. My four-poster bed holds up the mosquito netting which tucks under the mattress. It sounds like a royal place to live but without the rajah's furnishings or any furnishings it's bare and far from homelike.

Dating has been a problem. We're not supposed to date enlisted men. We have no rank as do the military, for we're Red Cross civilians, but if we were ever captured, the army has authorized our having the rank of captain. A heck of a lot of good that would do if we were ever captured by the Japs who have no respect for women. Yet every enlisted man wants a date and easily gets the idea, when refused, that we're interested only in the officers. We are here primarily in the interest of the G.I.s. So I've broken the ruling and have gone to movies with them, had luncheon dates and dinner dates in my off moments but I've discovered that I have only so much strength and it's impossible to go continuously. The officers too offer complications, for they want dates. The men get attached so easily in this uncertain tension-filled war period that I have to be on my guard without hurting anyone's feelings, if possible.

It seems as though there's one religious celebration after another in this city but when I realize that the main religions have many important sects and even subsects I guess it's not surprising but it surely is confusing. The more I learn about them the more grateful I am that I'm a Christian. There are more Mohammedans here in India than in any other country and three times as many Hindus as Mohammedans and there's obvious great tension between the two.

Due to Hinduism, the cows disrupt traffic and spread disease. Because their milk is poor, there is very little milk consumption which deprives the children of proper nourishment. Yet I've been told that a certain mixture of cow products cleanses the body: milk, butter, curd, urine, and dung. Can you imagine? Ugh! Death was once the penalty for killing a cow even accidentally but now it's years in jail. Though the cows are a blamed nuisance, I do feel sorry for them, sacred so they can't be killed but neglected in any sort of care.

I've seen pictures of Gandhi in public places and have heard his name mentioned but haven't seen him. I don't know where he is. It's been said of him that he would do anything to lift the untouchables out of their miserable condition—those of the lowest class who do the most menial tasks. He calls them "the chosen ones of God," but unless they're relieved from Hinduism, how can that happen? Gandhi's about 64 years old and still pressing for independence of his country.

There's a possibility I might be going to Benares. I'm excited over the thought . . . Love, Eddie

11

Benares on the Holy Ganges

Dear Mom and Dad:

Through influence and rank, two officers managed a one-day visit to Benares up NW for another girl and myself. Benares is the Hindu's holiest city on the sacred Ganges. Before we went I read the story of how the Ganges became sacred and picked up what other info I could that would clarify what we might see.

In the Hindu *Ramayana,* it tells how the sons of King Saga went out searching for something that had been stolen from their father and that the King desired. When it was found the thief cursed them, burned them to ashes, and condemned their souls to wander the earth. King Saga asked Kapilo, the sage, how the souls of his sons could be redeemed. He was told to pray to Brahma that the goddess Gandhi be allowed to come to earth and wash their souls in his holy waters. His prayer was granted but the gods were afraid that the earth might be destroyed by Gandhi's descent. Thus Shiva, of the Trinity, helped to break Gandhi's fall by straining her waters through his long hair and abating the force. The ashes of the princes were washed in Gandhi's waters and the princes' souls were transported immediately to join Lord Shiva in his Himalayan paradise. So the goddess Gandhi is personified in the river and the Ganges flow from the hair of Shiva. Shiva is also Lord of the Dance. He dances the world into destruction and recreation. Shiva chose Kashi, City of Light (now known as Benares) for his permanent home and made it a place of spiritual life. The Ganges plain and river are sacred, the very heart of India's history and Hinduism.

Benares is at the foot of the Himalayas and may be the oldest inhabited city in the world. Nomads from western Asia settled here 3,000 years ago. Their beliefs and practices united and blended with those of the more ancient people of the area thus forming the religion known as Hinduism. To die in Benares is to attain freedom from the cycle of reincarnations and to achieve bliss through the extinction of individuality in Nirvana. Every devoted Hindu plans to come here at least once. It's said that about five million come every year to worship and bathe in the Ganges' waters. Some who can afford it live out their final years in houses and palaces that rise one on top of the other along the banks of the Ganges.

From our plane the four of us drove in a Jeep. As we came closer to Benares the road became terribly congested. The scenes were so amazing that as I started to write you about them I got a sudden crazy idea of picturing it in verse for you write in verse so much, Dad, and so excellently. I really struggled, for it wasn't easy, but here's the result.

> Heavy loaded bullock carts
> Their wooden wheels a clattering;
> Donkeys, goats, and scraggly dogs.
> Their noisy sounds a shattering;
> Hindu pilgrims devout but poor,
> Their hymns and prayers declaring;
> Anxious and impatient us,
> Our own Jeep horn a blaring.
>
> People piled in old rickshas,
> Their wallahs a transporting;
> Dead bodies wrapped and placed on biers,
> Sad mourners them escorting;
> Clothing, food, and trinkets cheap,
> The vendors all a hawking;
> Anxious and impatient us,
> Our own Jeep horn a honking.
>
> Holy men in saffron robes,
> Their begging bowls a carrying;
> Both high and low and in between
> And not a soul a tarrying;
> Monopolizing carefree cows
> Their raw-boned selves a plodding;
> Anxious and impatient us,

Our own Jeep horn a throbbing.

Hypnotic, raucous, raspy sounds
Into my ears discording;
Brilliant, drab, and nondescript,
All sights my eyes recording;
Dirty, foully, dusty smells
Into my nose a rising;
Anxious and impatient us
Will soon be there arriving.

There are many ghats but we headed for the busiest ghat in the heart of the city. Heavy smoke was rising from the burning pyre. We watched a cremation and had helpful information as to what was taking place. A shrouded body that had been brought on a litter previously and immersed in the river had dried out sufficiently to be placed on the pyre along with sacred offerings. Ghee, which is melted butter that has been purified five times, was poured on the corpse's forehead for anointment while ritual mantras were recited. The body was then covered with chips of wood and more ghee poured on the chips. A man, probably a family member, walked around the pyre five times, struck the skull to break it and free the soul, and then lighted the pyre with a torch. When the body would be completely burned to ashes, the ashes would be collected in a container and scattered in the river. We were told that because wood is expensive and the cremation attendants have to be paid, many bodies are thrown into the Ganges without cremation.

We descended a ghat's wide flight of steps that led to the river. There are many ghats. I would estimate the steps of this one were between 25´ and 30´ wide and about that many in number, though it's only a guess. Around us was the singing of sad sounding melodies, undoubtedly religious, accompanied by cymbals and drums. There was continual chanting of the name of Rama. I had heard before that constant repetition of his name would lead to freedom from the cycle of rebirths. And there was the ringing of bells in the nearby temples.

In the air was the heavy scent of jasmine flowers but mixed with foul smells making breathing unpleasant. On the river were floating corpses of animals and humans and in the water that looked far from clean men and women were bathing themselves and chanting mantras to wash away their sins. In spite of the city's filth being carried down into the river by open channels from the streets above, and in spite of the corpses of humans and animals thrown into the river, and in spite of the people bathing and washing their clothes, the Hindus believe the waters can't be polluted for they are holy and sacred so they drink from it and believe they gain virtue and physical strength. They take containers of the water home for it will keep for years. A few drops of the water on a man's tongue when he is dying cleanses him from sin and ensures salvation. They pray to the river and cast sweetmeats, flower petals, and rice on its waters which is the nice positive side of the picture but not enough to blot out the appalling negative side. Mark Twain said a self-respecting germ wouldn't live in the Ganges but Twain wasn't a Hindu.

We saw a Sadhu, a wandering holy pilgrim who has no possessions and is easily identified by his tattooed mantras which are just a few words or prayers from the sacred Hindu writings. Repetitions of the mantras have magical powers. I should imagine that the tattooed Sadhu would be ultra rewarded. He certainly should be.

We visited the Temple of Vishnanath but were not permitted to enter for we would have defiled the place. Lingams, small icons, were brought by pilgrims and anointed by a Brahman priest with ghee. They were then washed with milk and water. The lingams are shaped from stone and represent Lord Shiva's regenerative powers. Very large ones, we were told, were inside the temple and we assumed these small ones would be taken in after their purification.

Benares is certainly a religious city with countless temples and brimming over with Hindus who exert themselves in an amazing way to follow the strict traditions of their faith. Though their faithfulness is admirable, it's sad that they don't know the one and only God.

I have heard that in the fall a whole month is devoted to enactments of various parts of the *Ramayana*, the great Hindu epic. Rama, a Vishnu incarnation, is the "ideal man" and Sita, his wife. The monkey army is led by the monkey god, Hanuman. The victory of good over evil is celebrated with great rejoicing. The final night they have torch processions and finally the burning of huge effigies of the demon Ravana. I'd love to see some of it but certainly hope I'll be out of India by that time.*

This letter has taken days to write but I wanted it all recorded while I had it fresh in mind . . . My love to you, Eddie

*   *   *

*Though I never saw enactments of the *Ramayana* in India, Dot and I saw two different marvelous performances in Bali in the 1970s with the fantastic 200 member male chorus (the monkey army preparing for battle). In physical movements and in the vocal monkey sounds the 200 gave a performance that was perfectly synchronized and stunning in effect. Once seen and heard one can never forget. So that others could at least hear, I obtained a recording through a New York City company.

The *Ramayana* according to tradition, was written by a sage and dictated by the gods. Two and a-half thousand years ago Prince Rama was the only one able to bend the bow of Shiva and thus was given the Princess Sita for his wife. The King, his father, influenced by one of his ladies, exiled the two to India's central wild forests. There they were attacked by Ravana, and his demon followers, who carried Sita away to his distant quarters. Rama turned to Hanuman and his army of monkeys for help. In a furious battle raged with the demons the terrible Ravana was defeated and Sita was freed. But Rama could not accept her back as his wife for she had lived in Ravana's home. Sita declared her innocence. To prove it she cast herself into the flames of a funeral pyre but her virtues kept her from perishing. Thus Sita was spared and Rama took her back as his wife. They returned to his kingdom where he was crowned. It's said that even the illiterate Indians know verses of the epic by heart. The last words on Gandhi's lips when he was dying were "Rama, Rama."

12

The Sikhs, and The Monsoon Arrives

My dear Mom and Dad:

We wish to heavens it would rain but we're told that when the monsoon starts we'll wish to heavens it would stop. So we continue to wilt and perspire.

And I continue to gather information through reading and asking questions. This vast subcontinent of India, so-called because of its physical isolation as well as its historic seclusion, is larger in size than continental Europe (excluding Scandinavia and Russia). It has a five-thousand-year-old history and is one of the world's oldest cultures but it's so complex that "we foreigners" wonder how these greatly varied peoples continue to exist together without killing each other off. India is not a melting pot like our U.S.A. for I'm told that people in the provinces and in the native states know little about each other. Our melting pot of America is far from perfect but compared to India our country is heaven. In many respects, though, from all I've read and heard, I would say that India is the mostest of any country in the world. She has the most cockroaches, flies, mosquitoes and cows—the most people, for one out of every five people in the world is an Indian—the most languages and dialects though only eight or ten are used in politics, Hindustani being the most used, (by the way, on a one-rupee bill the word "rupee" is written in five languages)—the most illiteracy—the most religions and cults and sects, though Hinduism has by far the most followers—the most customs and traditions connected with the religions that affect every phase of the peoples' daily lives—the most mosques and temples and shrines—the most holy rivers and pools—the most torrential rains—the most torrid heat—the highest mountains and the broadest plains. If this isn't the mostest, what is? India is a fascinating country in its sounds, colors, and smells but I've seen enough and smelled enough. I'm ready to leave.

I haven't mentioned the Sikhs to you and they are interesting. They are very prominent here, being the fourth largest religious group. Some of them are tailors. I had slacks with matching jacket made and was surprised at the excellent fit. Some of them are taxi drivers. We had been warned never to ride in a taxi alone with one of them. Evidently some sexual disasters had happened. One night I called a taxi to meet a friend and save time as he came off duty. When I got in the taxi I suddenly realized the driver was a Sikh but we were already moving. I spent a few panicky moments but I arrived safely. So much for warnings.

The Sikhs are a dissenting and reformed group of Brahman Hindus and are disciples of the Gurus who were and are their religious leaders. They respect many Hindu and Moslem beliefs but they denounce idolatry and the caste system. They believe in one God who is the supreme truth and is represented on earth by ten Sikh prophets. There are no images in their temples but simply their Holy Book which contains writings of the first gurus and some of the Hindu and Moslem scholars. It was in the 15th century that Guru Gobind Singh organized his followers into a military group of men who would be strong and brave enough to fight their foes. They adopted the custom of uncut hair as a sign of virility and strength. Did they get this idea from Samson in the Old Testament? Wearing turbans became a definite part of their attire. With their military bearing, their Greek-like noses, and beautifully draped turbans they make an impressive appearance. They are famous as soldiers and make excellent police. Some are quite handsome and many of the women, who also let their hair grow, are striking looking. The men don't smoke but are heavy drinkers.

The Sikhs' turbans completely fascinate me for they're so cleverly and artistically draped in comparison with other turbans I've seen. I inquired and got information which I'll pass on. Really, Dad, you'd look stunning in a turban and with your cut hair you wouldn't have to follow each of the set steps. You could grow a small beard that would be quite becoming. Well, this is their procedure: They rinse their hair in milk curd and rub it with oils, usually scented. The turban is anywhere from six to twelve yards long and forty-five inches wide. A cheap inner turban is worn to protect the outer one from oily scalp. The long hair is combed with a wooden comb and then twisted into a strand and tied into a knot on the top of the head. The Sikh then holds his beard out, combs it, and tucks it around the string with a stick shaping it into a roll. A cloth is tied around the beard holding it tightly in place. The inner turban, which later will be pushed out of sight, is wound around his head. Then the outer turban is wound around his head in folds giving a pleated look. While winding, he grips the bottom of the turban with his teeth to keep it in place. The finished job is perfect. The outer turban shows neat pleats on the left side and is plain on the other side. The cloth that covered the rolled beard is slipped out from under both turbans. Those who can afford it buy silk and fine imported muslin. The poorer Sikhs wear rough cotton cloth. It takes long practice to complete the whole procedure and even when the technique is conquered the complete winding of a turban from scratch takes fifteen minutes.

This was a long involved description, Dad, but I thought the kids in our church might enjoy experimenting under your "highly qualified instruction." It's a wonderful opportunity for the kids to learn more about religions and customs in other countries through the letters of us serving overseas in various areas . . . Goodnight and sweet dreams, Eddie

*   *   *

Additional Information in 1998

In more recent reading I have found that the history of the Sikhs is quite long and fascinating. The following is a very brief summary. Jaidev, in the 12th century, taught that yoga was worthless in comparison to worship of God in thought, word, and deed. At the close of the 14th century Ramanana freed his followers from caste restrictions. Later on, Kabir denounced idolatry and ritualism. A whole century later in 1469 Nanak was born, he who was to become the first founder of Sikhism. It's an interesting coincidence that he was a contemporary with Martin Luther who led the Reformation and thus was excommunicated from the Catholic Church.

The tenth and last Guru was Gobind Rai Singh who remodeled the Sikh organization and named it Khalsa. He made the Sikh initiation into a rite of admittance. Following this rite a Sikh had to wear the five Ks: Kes—unshorn hair signifying virility and strength, Kachh—drawers reaching only to the knees signifying self-restraint, Kara—an iron or steel bracelet indicating obedience, Kirpan—a sword which later was usually a tiny facsimile set in the comb, Khanga—a small wooden comb. Tobacco was forbidden. Each Sikh thereafter has taken the surname of Singh. Before his death, Gobind declared the line of Gurus extinct. Those preceding him were God's representatives on earth.

Calcutta (8)

Dear Ones:

I'm glad you don't have to experience this heat as much as I wish you were here to see all that I'm seeing. Though it's too hot to shop, I've shopped for I knew I'd regret it very much if I left here without buying a few things.

The market place is huge with endless stalls and most of them open in the front so sometimes it's hard to tell who is the owner and who is the customer. They have wonderful offerings of everything one could desire—ivory work, fine embroidery, metal work, pottery, beautiful fabrics etc. and all made in various parts of India. I've purchased a long red embroidered hanging with mirrors and yards of black satin and flowered silk to make dresses when I get home. I bought two identical silver ornate anklets made into necklaces for Dot and me and a beautiful pin for you, Mom, a large stone in a gold filigreed setting and a stone on a cord that can be worn with a sport shirt, Dad. I couldn't resist buying a sari—pongee with a band of colorful design. I've learned how to drape the material and become a real Indian woman. I'll demonstrate when I get home.

The saris are usually six yards long and forty-five inches wide. Underneath I have to wear a blouse preferably with short sleeves and of a color that contrasts but blends with the pongee, also a petticoat with a tight drawstring. With a good section of the sari I make a row of pleats across the front to give it fullness, then tuck that tightly in at the waist under the petticoat. The other half is drawn across the back and to the right, then gathered up and pulled diagonally across the front to the left shoulder. The sari should hug the hips tightly and yet ripple at the front in loose graceful folds. It's wound around the waist counterclockwise. The rest can be draped over the head or over the shoulders. I also bought a sari band with gold and silver threads for which I paid thirty-five dollars—costly, but it's quite special. I thought I might use it on the bottom of a full skirted black evening gown with also a piece of it around the waist. Since Benares on the Ganges is famous for its silk fabrics woven with gold and silver threads, I wonder if this was made there. Could be.

I had a number of dates with a major who showered me with attention and gifts. He left for Mussurie and was planning to stay for awhile with a missionary who is the son of a famous missionary in India. I'm sure you would recognize the name if only I could remember it. Watch your diet, Mom, and take good care of yourself...Love to you both, Eddie

Calcutta (9)

Dearest Mom and Dad:

I've received orders to leave Calcutta so this will be my last letter from here. Though I'm relieved to get out of this heat and to be moving forward to my goal and closer to the action, I'm grateful for all my experiences here and for the men I've met who have in many ways contributed to my life. I hope with all my heart I've done as much for our men as they've done for me for my purpose for being here was to serve, not to be served.

Three officers invited three of us girls to Pandeveswar for a dance. We left here Saturday at noon. It was a five-hour long

64

train trip with all expenses paid by the men. When we arrived we were amazed at the tremendous job they had done with obvious much time and thought given to the preparations. They had used a tennis court for the dance floor with lanterns strung all around and had made a platform out of odds and ends for the orchestra. Grand refreshments had been planned. We danced quite a long time and had just started on the refreshments when a wild wind arose blowing sand and dirt and in no time everything was ripped to pieces. We ran for shelter. What a destroyer of dreams! We felt so badly for the men but they were good sportsmen and we did have great fun in spite of the sudden coming of the monsoon. The rain fell like mad. We returned Sunday (the next day) on the ten A.M. train. I went on duty at the club as soon as we returned and worked till eleven P.M., beginning again the next morning at eight o'clock. What price pleasure!

So the much talked about monsoon season has begun and I now know a little of the reality of the word "Monsoon" It's been called "the gift of the gods to the people," necessary for enrichment of the land and production of rice, celebrated with joy by the farmers for it means survival. But the monsoon is also unpredictable. If it doesn't come, famine takes the lives of the people. I've heard this season pictured many times—temperatures rising, a violent wind blowing dust and sand and anything not firmly grounded, the sky darkening, thunder roaring, and then raindrops that are large, heavy, noisy, pounding the ground, the rain pouring as if the heavens were emptying endless rivers of water in a continuous sustained storm. Though it brings relief and nourishment, it also brings floods and areas can become uninhabitable.

I'm leaving Calcutta and don't know what awaits me. I'll write as soon as I'm settled someplace and can find a spare moment...Much love always, Eddie

13

Arriving in France Midst the Fighting

Dear Folks:

I can tell you now that we're in France and I'm excited to be here near the real action. Before leaving England, we were sent to an area where we were given an extensive physical training period and classes each day. We couldn't write about it at the time. We Red Cross girls were billeted in British homes. I had a room to myself with a very nice family, white bed sheets, lovely light colored blankets, and a downy puff like we have at home. We were spoiled at this time but we took advantage of it while we could knowing that soon we'd be living army style again in a mass without comforts. We went from there to a place near our former hospital for a week. When we finally left for the marshaling area, to my great surprise, Mrs. Coates, British Red Cross Liaison Officer, was there to bid us goodbye. How she learned that we were there and were leaving I'll never know but it was grand seeing her again and having her wish us well. She was a minister's daughter and the best friend I had in England.

We had an excellent crossing on the Channel in a large ship with no difficulty and were brought to shore on the Utah Beachhead in small landing crafts. The Utah Beachhead looked much as it was pictured in the movie. We were grateful there was no loss of personnel or equipment. We had quite a walk heavily laden with our personal belongings and blanket rolls. Our bed rolls, duffel bags, lockers were taken care of for us by our enlisted personnel who had to take them off the ship and handle them on and off the trucks until they were delivered to us later. Not having had access to all these for some time, we realized how much simpler it would be to cut down to the barest necessities with less to keep track of and to carry when we move. Many material possessions mean very little after all. One can get along with the clothing one is wearing and a toothbrush. How the army ever got all the equipment and conveniences over here is more than I can understand—an enormous undertaking.

We arrived in France ahead of schedule. The fields where we were to set up our hospital hadn't yet been retaken from the Germans and the grounds around us had not been demined. We girls sat on the ground in a place made safe for us while de-mining was finished in a large field and pup tents set up by the enlisted men. Every day has brought new developments and our own little village is growing. We watch with fascination and admiration as the men put things together. We're in a really beautiful spot that reminds me more of the States than did England. Now we are in tents as we were previously for a time.

I'll write you as soon as I get a spare moment and have a typewriter which is so much easier than writing by hand . . . Love, Dot

France (2)

My dear Folks:

When we arrived, as I said in my last letter, we were ahead of schedule and the place where we were to set up our hospital hadn't as yet been taken from the Germans. That first night it seemed that we were in the midst of things with firing going on around us. In the first few days we didn't dare venture away from our field for fear we would be blown up. We stayed pretty close to our own area taking no chances. When we first arrived, one of our boys picked up a hand grenade and it went off doing a terrible job on him. They thought he wouldn't live but he did and will be returned to the States shortly. It was his fault for we had all been given lectures before we came and plenty of warnings.

Now as I write you, the front has advanced quite a distance and our men are doing wonders in the new demined fields across from us setting up our hospital which will be ready soon for occupancy. Meanwhile many of our group have been out to other evacuation hospitals on detached service relieving the nurses and doctors. I took a trip to Cherbourg the other day to our Red Cross Headquarters there and am visiting some of the Evacuation Hospitals to get ideas for our Red Cross tents. Our 56th will be a tent hospital but more permanent than some for they're laying all the foundations in cement. We will have at least two Red Cross tents.

I had an attack of pyelitis (infection of the kidney) which seemed to be going around our group but it's cleared and now I'm fine. The water situation is not very good. A truck comes in daily with water. We have lister bags in the fields where drinking water is placed and chlorine added and then one large tank for wash water. Our helmets are our best friends over here, used for every purpose imaginable. We wear them everywhere we go and also carry water in them to our tents where we use them to wash our clothes, our hair, and our bodies (all in cold water). We rinse our hair with the lemon powder from our K rations. The water is soft. Every few days we manage to get to an Evacuation Hospital for showers which feel wonderful.

At night it is so cold that we sleep in heavy woolen underwear and flannel pajamas and have a dark bathrobe handy to put on in case we have to run out to our foxholes. During the day we wear fatigues or our Red Cross combat suits with brown field shoes, leggings, and helmet given us by the Army. Our helmets have a red cross painted on the front for identification whereas the other helmets have painted insignia on the front according to rank.

Since we have been in our present location we have picked up German bomb crates which we use as bedside tables. Also other German equipment comes in handy. One of the girls and I bought some rope mats which we use as rugs on the ground in front of our cots. We have only two army blankets each so we use a shelter half (tent half which is part of our equipment) over the top of our cots for warmth and to keep the dampness out. But the air is wonderful. This is a healthy spot.

Day by day our little village grows and is improved to fit our needs. We couldn't ask for a better spot for a rest center, which it is at present. We've managed to get a lot of salvage from the area around us. I keep my perishable supplies in an ammunition box under my cot. We have one corner fixed up as a washroom with a large piece of glass fastened to the tent, a bomb crate as a stand and a box as a seat.

Of course, the whole layout of our unit is somewhat camouflaged with the tents being on the edges of the fields. We have foxholes in back which we have used. We are careful not to venture into the unknown hedges around us which have not been de-mined. We're collecting all sorts of things to furnish our tents, parachutes for decoration and material for ditty bags, cans for ash trays which we will cut down and decorated cartons for waste which we will paint, bomb crates for tables, German beds for making pieces of furniture. We will be given salt, sugar, and flour bags from the mess tent for ditty bags and also blue burlap which we will make into covers for G.I. cots as studio couches.

Take care of yourselves and I'll be writing again as soon as possible . . . Love, Dot

France (3)

Dearest Eddie:

Dad sent copies of two of your letters. I have read and reread them but I still want to know more. Please write. I wish you were here with me. This must have been a very, very lovely place in peace time. The trees and shrubs are beautiful. The sun shines all the while. The days are hot and the nights are cool. There are wide open spaces with fields surrounded by trees and shrubs and hedges reminding me more of the States. The air is clear and fresh. I feel fine now and in the peak of health.

I am straddled across a cot trying to type. It isn't very comfortable but still easier than trying to write by hand. I must get carbon paper and make duplicates in order to keep up with correspondence. Mail coming in is slow. Letters from home and friends are tremendously uplifting.

We are in the midst of preparations. I will be most happy when we begin to operate as a hospital. A General Hospital is a big undertaking. Ours was one of the very first to arrive here. In this interim period, many of our personnel are out on detached service to other smaller hospitals where they are needed. I have been going out with the Chaplain and his assistant playing the reed organ for services with various groups. I've enjoyed it as much as the fellows seem to appreciate it. They also appreciate seeing a woman. Females here are scarce. As we drive along, the fellows holler, wave, and whistle at us. Our arms get worn out with waving. Here in our tent village there are many officers around all the while. They come streaming in from every place. We have good looking nurses who are a big attraction. Plenty of dates for all.

Living quarters for Red Cross, nurses, and officers are in large tents around the edge of two large fields. Across from us scattered in another field are the enlisted men's pup tents. There's a separate Chapel tent. Our "john" is a tent with a large ditch with drainage dug in the middle and with seats—good old country style. Our enlisted men work hard to make all sanitation excellent. Even our mess hall in a tent is run very sanitarily. We eat out of mess gear which each of us owns and takes care of. Outside the tent are three large containers where we wash and rinse and store our utensils. We lived on K and C rations for quite a while but now we're able to get more variety. We're thankful for we get tired of those rations.

We Red Cross girls live with a number of the nurses in a large tent and get along beautifully. I can't imagine what it would be like to live alone again. There's something about group life that is appealing and it certainly gets one out of selfish ways. We sleep on canvas cots and use our bedrolls for mattresses filled with our excess clothing. In fact, at present, we have all of our extra clothing in our bed rolls to keep them off the ground.

As you well know, there were always plenty of chances for dates for us in the States but here we are almost bombarded with requests. Officers come from everywhere to visit and want to take us places. I was taken over to a large cemetery one night where General McNair is buried. It was one of the most impressive sights I've seen. Grave after grave with the men placed regardless of rank and for each one his identification tag was nailed to the back of his cross.

I have been dating a pilot commander. A bunch of us have had some wonderful times together. When I was at the air base the other night I asked him to let me see the inside of his plane. Much to my amazement as we drove up to the plane, I saw "Dotty" painted on the side in bold red letters. I was thrilled over the idea more than I dared express. I got in the plane and sat in the pilot's seat while he stood on the wing and explained all the contraptions to me. He told me what he could about his flights. All during the day I wonder how things are going with the group. Rare experiences happen with them. One night when I was over there for a party, a pilot returned who had been shot down last June. We were intrigued listening to all that had happened and amazed and grateful that he had come through to safety.

The French people are anxious to talk to us Americans. They have learned to speak a few words in English and even the children can say "candy, chewing gum, thank you" etc. Some of our girls can really converse with the children but my French is very bad. I'll have to get out my little Army *French Phrase Book*.

Last week some of us were taken in our army transport to a lovely little French church near here where we attended a high mass for the Allied dead. The church had been untouched by the war. They had black bunting with white stripes on the edge draped around the church. In front of the altar was a casket, representing all who had died in this war, covered with flowers and lined on the sides with tall candles. The service was most impressive. Afterwards the French people were friendly to us and talked with some in our group who could communicate in their language. Again I wished I could use my French better. Outside the church is a cemetery and we were interested in the way the graves were decorated. Some were very old. There were large wreaths with patterns of flowers all done in colored beads and on top of the graves there were flowers of all kinds made of china.

I must quit. Please write as often as you can. I miss you so very much . . . Love, Dot

France (4)

Dear Mother and Dad:

I keep thinking I wish you could see this or that or that I could talk to you as things happen. It will be all old stuff when I get home. The magazines carry many pictures. Save all those copies because some day I will appreciate looking back. *Life Magazine* was supposed to send a photographer over today to take pictures of various sections of the hospital including our Red Cross Recreation Tent, so we worked like mad getting it in super condition—but the photographer didn't come. Anyway we had over three hundred new patients today and many of them viewed it and commented that it was the nicest they have seen. Some of them have seen many over here.

There are some of the most unusual trees here, tall and very crooked with short branches and leaves growing all the way up to a certain point and then on the top they branch out into quite a foliage, very interesting against the skyline. I haven't found out what type they are. The country must have been very lovely here before the war. I can see, though, how hard it must have been for our men to fight their way through with so many places for the Germans to hide out.

It's quite something to set up a general hospital and it's been most fascinating seeing it built and organized, all in tents. We Red Cross are in quite an isolated spot from the rest. Our Red Cross tents are behind the Patients' Mess tent on the side of the first field but the Mess Boys are always around and nothing ever bothers me. Right now I am here alone in our Peremidal Tent which is an office for now. We have fixed up a large ward tent as a recreation room. We also have a squad tent for a carpenter shop.

I'm very lonely tonight. I'm very tired and, along with the nurses, I have the G.I.s. No one seems to know what's causing it—the water? The blackberries we picked in the fields? Some particular food? At last our tent hospital is set up covering several fields. We know it's plenty large in area when we start walking. We already have many patients, including some German prisoners. The ambulatory ones, under guard, have done quite a bit of the constructing. We are far behind the lines now, whereas when we first came we were on the front lines.

We have been busy making things out of nothing as it is almost impossible to get equipment. I wish you could see our efforts. We have the cutest snack bar painted dull red and decorated with a bright blue. Paint and brushes are hard to get around the area. We hired a French carpenter to make writing tables and also a beautiful slant-top desk for painting as well as for other activities. In the middle is our music section with our piano, Victrola, and radio we brought with us from the States. I picked up a few pieces of furniture I obtained from the outside including desks and German cabinets for our supplies. On the other end of the tent is the library. We made bookcases but have few books and little reading material. We made benches and also use wire spools for chairs. On the walls of our tent one of our very clever boys drew pictures representing the various departments. There are music notes on the wall over the music section, clever little drawings over the writing tables, also over the library and snack bar. In one section he drew pictures of each one of our staff and painted the first name and address under each.

Some Time Later

Our Red Cross office has been completed. We have two desks for Terry, my secretary, and for me, three cabinets in the center where we store and lock away our comfort supplies for the men (combs, toothpaste, toothbrushes, soap, shaving equipment, sewing kits, towels, matches, cigarettes, chewing gum, candy, etc.); also office supplies including stationery and envelopes for the patients. I found a French washstand with a basin in the top and also a place for soap. It has drainage into a pail in a compartment in the bottom. and towel racks on the sides. I have a bookcase, a record case, and a small stand. We have three French straight chairs. I carted along my desk equipment which I've set up. I feel quite at home with all my little gadgets, inkwell that a patient made way back in Malvern days, bookends with hand-wrought vases on either side, desk pad and blotter, a black pitcher for flowers. I found a nice large German map that covers the lower part of England, all of France, and other countries around Germany. I am quite the scavenger, so everyone tells me.

For a while the weather was heavenly, a relief from England's weather, but for the past few weeks it has been raining and clearing and raining until the area is deep in clay mud. I wear my overshoes all the while and continually feel damp and cold and wish I could get some place where I could get warmed. We have no heat in our tents and the ground is wet where the rain comes in. I have to walk through clay mud. Thank heavens I have a good G.I. flashlight for night-time.

One day I went back to the little French church where they had held mass for the Allied dead. Remember I wrote you about it? The black drapery around the church had been removed and the casket also, of course. The church was simple and lovely with gorgeous stained glass windows, light walls. and a beautiful altar with two large forty-five-inch figures of angels in front.

I have toured around a bit seeing the villages which have been demolished, and I've been to Cherbourg to our Red Cross Headquarters. They serve doughnuts which melt in your mouth. They make ten thousand a day all by hand since their equipment hasn't arrived yet. It's a lovely club set up in what was a department store. I saw workers I had met in London, so grand seeing them again. We go everywhere around us now. At night the vehicles have on bright lights whereas before they traveled with tiny dimmers. How we arrived safely from place to place I don't know for on many nights the roads were black.

I about live in my combat suit and feel very comfortable in it. The paratrooper boots are beautiful and many of the girls have them. I didn't get a pair for myself as they are so heavy and warm for this weather. Very soon we'll be wearing seersucker dresses in the hospital. Hope to see Paris soon. Take good care . . . My love, Dot

14

From Calcutta to Chabua
and Cherapunji

Dear Mom and Dad:

Here I am in a new spot, Chabua, Assam. Assam is a small Indian province bordered on the north by the Himalayas and east by Burma. I'm supposed to take off from here for China. At least I'm closer to my final goal. When I received orders to leave Calcutta, I was warned that the plane ride north would be rough due to the monsoon. It was more than rough. It was *very rough* and I did feel nauseated but luckily I held on to my insides. However, for the two days following I had a beautiful hangover of headache and chills.

When we arrived in Chabua, I was sent to the infirmary as there was no scheduled place for me elsewhere. The way I felt the infirmary was a good place to be. The next day I was moved to the quarters where I am now. It's an absolute mess here. There seems to be no one in charge and the natives working here have no conception of cleanliness. Last night I slept on someone's dirty sheets but I was so tired and achy that it really didn't matter. Everyone is in tents that are scattered about.

As usual there's a delay in orders so I'll help in the club while I wait. The club director and the girls are lovely and the club is set up nicely. There was dancing in the club last night. First time I've danced in one month. We dressed formal in our blue dress uniforms even though it was pouring rain outside. It's not real dancing for there were just a few of us girls and each of us was cut in on twenty times during one dance. It was like old home week for I saw men I had met in the States before leaving California. I kept refusing dates but finally agreed to go to the officers' club (after the G.I.s' club closed) to eat and listen to classical music recordings with a medical man interested in both music and theology. A good combination, eh?

My flashlight was stolen. Could you get me another? I can't get one here. There are so many poisonous snakes around us and also the path from the club to our quarters is so muddy and ditchy that at night a light is a must. The mosquitoes are terrible. They've greatly increased since the beginning of the monsoon. My arms and hands are covered with bites. Except for being exposed to the mosquitoes, I wish you were beside me.

As I'm writing you, I'm facing a gorgeous sunset. We're at the foot of the mighty Himalayas with its hundreds of great mountains and thousands of the world's highest ice-clad peaks rising above 20,000 feet. The ancient faiths consider the Himalayas as dwellings of the gods and Mt. Everest at 29,028 feet at the top of the world is Goddess Mother of the Earth. Soon, I hope, I'll be flying somewhere over some of those peaks. The valleys around us are beautiful, green, fertile and produce huge crops of tea. The tea plantings cling to those steep slopes. I know little of what's going on in the outside world for I very seldom see a newspaper, which would be an old issue, or hear a radio. We're stranded in this CBI Theater apart from the world. Some of our men have been here for a long time. I feel sorry for them but I also admire them for their good humor and optimistic spirits. Our American men are bricks—wonderful—amazing!

I'm seeing the officer I mentioned quite regularly. He reminds me of you, Dad. Until my next move, my love to you both, Eddie

From Chabua To Cherapunji, Assam, India

Dearest Ones:

I received word that the next day I'd be traveling further north on a temporary assignment until transportation over the Hump was available for me. This is my tenth move. With all my luggage, it's a darned nuisance to whoever has to move me, far more nuisance than to myself. Though I'll try hard, I'll fail, I'm sure, in picturing where I am now and how I got here. I was told that this would be a sixty-mile Jeep ride but that didn't take in to account what the monsoon had done to the road. With all our ups and downs the mileage must have been doubled.

I've ridden in Jeeps ever since I've been in India and over some very rough roads but the road to this place tops them all as a "hopeless passage." It's been raining steadily and it rained all the while we were struggling forward in deep, deep mud. To me the road seemed utterly impassable but my stupendous driver fought the road like a mythical hero forcing the Jeep to its utmost strength and endurance. A large truck followed us. We went down into a three foot mudhole. It seemed the Jeep was standing almost perpendicularly and I held on with all my might. The truck moved up and pushed us out only to see us dive forward into another three-foot hole. Suddenly we leaned so far to the right I was sure I'd be dumped out into that mud disappearing from sight, never to be seen again. I was completely fascinated by what might happen next and marveled at our miraculous American machinery and our unbelievable super American drivers. It was a unique trip never to be forgotten.

We actually reached our destination, Cherapunji in the Assam Hills, the most primitive place I've ever seen. The Hill tribes, I'm told, are very backward and undeveloped. My living quarters is a basha with thatched roof lined with burlap and the "john" is another basha way down the line midst the bushes where one sits on a plank of wood over a hole in the ground. It rains continually. I've been loaned high boots which I remove when I go to bed. Otherwise, I sleep in my clothes. I am the only woman here.

My second day I opened my locker to get my Hoyle Game book and discovered the rain and dampness had played havoc with my things. The lovely black satin material I had purchased in Calcutta had run into the flowered silk. I wanted to weep but then it struck me funny. This is no place for silks and satins, for ribbons and bows, for partying and dancing. My precious feminine apparel along with make-up and perfume were so out of place here that the thought was ludicrous. In this area where the mountains catch the masses of vapor as it rises off the sea, the rainfall is enormous averaging 500 inches a year—that's 41 and 1/3 feet and the monsoon rainfall can last three or four months. Can you imagine? Mildew appears overnight. Every day I have to wipe it off my possessions. A special kind of mosquito increases and after a while the most unhealthy season arrives when malaria is most prevalent. This is not a place to spend a vacation or go on a honeymoon!

The club (far from what we'd call a club) is a very crude, narrow, rectangular building of just one room with bare walls— nothing, nothing to add a bit of cheer. Tables are placed as close as possible on either side where the men can write letters or play table games and just enough space between them in the center for two men to squeeze through sideways . . . The men jam in like an overflow in an elevator. It's the only social life they have. When the club closes at night, everyone returns to his basha cot and listens to the rain pound down in torrents. Occasionally I hear strains of Negro spirituals and popular love songs—beautiful and moving. The men here are American black engineers working on a very important project. They have been most courteous and gentlemanly to me and interesting to be with. But I wonder why Red Cross sent me here. There's nothing I can do for the men except talk with them, listen to them, play cards with them. When I leave I'll never know whether I was of any value or not.

Though this is a horrible place to be, I'm very grateful to be here to catch a glimpse of "history in the making" and to see and feel (in a very small degree) what our men are experiencing and the sacrifice they're making to rid this part of the world of the Japs and end this tragic war. This is one place where I'm glad you're not with me though I miss you . . . All my love, Eddie

*   *   *

1998 Notes

I couldn't mention in my letter home what the above "important project" was. In July 1937, Japanese troops had attacked

78

Chinese soldiers at the Marco Polo Bridge in North China. This was the beginning of Japan's plan of conquest of Greater East Asia. As Japan's bombing of China continued, Chiang Kai-shek ordered a 680-mile road built during the years 1937–38 to safeguard the import of strategic Lend-Lease supplies from America. This was known as the Burma Road. Originally this was the old Tribute Route over which elephants bore gifts from the Kings of Burma to the Emperor of China and coolies carried silk from China to middle and lower Burma. In the thirteenth century Marco Polo, famous Italian adventurer, traveled this route to Cathay, a name he gave to North China, and the route became known as the Marco Polo Trail.

In the fall of 1941, after years of bombing, Japan held all of China's important eastern seaports. The Burma Road was the only land route left whereby China could receive supplies from America. The supplies arrived at the Port of Rangoon, Burma, were unloaded and sent by rail to Lashio, a little NE of Mandalay, and twenty miles from the border, then by trucks over the Burma Road that twisted its way to Kunming, China. The road was far from smooth. A *London Times* correspondent said: "A truck passing over the Burma Road is like an ant crawling latterly across a sheet of corrugated iron." In other words, like crawling up an old fashioned metal washboard (for those who have ever seen this antique piece).

In 1942 Japan captured Rangoon and pressed northward closing China's last land supply route on the Burma Road and raising a threat to invasion of India. The only route left was the shipping of supplies to Calcutta where they were sent by railroad 800 miles north to Assam and then flown over the Himalayas—a very dangerous flight that resulted in a great loss of lives as well as planes and supplies.

General Stilwell said the only effective action against the Japanese was to construct a new road to China beginning seven miles east of Ledo, Assam, where the railroad from Calcutta ended, then join the Burma Road and on into Kunming.

The first black American engineers who came to upper Assam had to convert tea plantations and virgin jungle areas into encampments. With only a few light bulldozers and British lorries they began work on the new project directing 200,000 Chinese, Indians, Burmese, and British workers in what was practically a handbuilt Ledo Road. Powered drills were used for planting dynamite charges, but coolies squatting by the roadside had to break rocks with hammers and carry the pieces in baskets on their heads to the men who fitted the pieces into the roadbed by hand. Finally the road was further leveled by large handmade stone rollers drawn by a great number of coolies. The whole amazing project was accomplished by the most primitive methods. Thousands of workers died during the period from numerous causes, but especially malaria. The new 500-mile road from Ledo to Mong Lu where the two roads were joined made the longest supply route in the world with a six inch pipeline laid beside the road to carry gasoline for the bombers. Work was done while dodging bullets from the Japs. It was an amazing engineering feat, cutting through dense jungles and crossing mountains in snake-like curves with drops thousands of feet below. About 500 bridges had to be built, crossing rivers and streams, bridges that would withstand the monsoons. The tight switchbacks of sharp curves had four curves to one mile. There was no hard rock to surface the road, only red porous clay and soft river rock.

The road opened January 1945, six months before Japan surrendered to the Allies. Hundreds of trucks carried war supplies over the Ledo-Burma Road linking North India with Yunnanyi Province, China. It was gratifying but humorous that Chiang Kai-shek of all people (for he opposed Stilwell at every possible moment) suggest that this road become known as the Stilwell Road from now on. "Vinegar Joe" Stilwell certainly deserved this tribute! Without his determination and inspiring leadership Burma would never have been retaken from the Japs. Before the war ended, more than 5,000 vehicles made the trip, carrying 34,000 tons of war supplies.

I'm thankful I was there for a period of time with those black engineers who were working under such terrible conditions, living in most unhealthy surroundings, making noble sacrifices to bring the war to an end. I dreaded the return trip over that impossible "mile deep mud road" but still was anxious to get transportation over the Hump to China.

From Cherapunji Back to Chabua, Assam

Dear Mom and Dad:

I received a call: "Leave tomorrow for Chabua and be prepared to leave the following day for your permanent assignment." Again I was jeeped over that impossible, impassable road paved with mud a mile deep while the monsoon rains pressed down on us. Miraculously we made it to Chabua (I should say the driver made it—all I had to do is hang on and pray I wouldn't become a mud corpse). In Chabua I was told there was no transportation available. I was beginning to wonder if there really was a China.

I've seen the *Hey Rookie Show* which has traveled through various war theaters. I also saw Noel Coward right up close. That was thrilling. By the way, I'm pleased to hear of Vint's promotion. Chemical warfare preparation is necessary, I'm sure, but I hope no one starts using gases over here. I'm enclosing a picture, given to me by an officer, showing half-starved Indian children, typical of what I've seen everywhere in this country. They have been and still are suffering enough without the hellish addition of gases.

So far I've escaped malaria and I'm okay. We're compelled to use mosquito repellent and to wear slacks and long sleeves in the evening. I do wish I had high boots to wade through puddles and protect me from snakes when coming from the club at night. The men often carry me when the water is too deep for my short boots. There was a tiger near the club the other night so we're all cautious until he's caught. Don't worry. I won't walk unaccompanied until he *is* caught. I'm not anxious to wrestle with a tiger.

Most of our dinners are quite starchy and greasy. The club closes at 10:00. We eat dinner at 10:15 and by then we're so hungry we overeat and the food lies heavy on our tummies. We miss fruit and vegetables. I'm still seeing the officer I mentioned. Miss you and love you both, Eddie

81

Chabua (3)

Dear Ones:

Well, it's happened! I've fallen in love with Dick.* Dad, he is the nearest to you in make-up of anyone I've ever met. He has a searching mind delving into every subject that's worth looking into, loves the out-of-doors and is stirred by nature, enjoys classical music, is affectionate, fun-loving, and a wonderful dancer (though I've never seen you dance). Like you, he worked his way through college and medical school. His father, a doctor, died last March. He's made quite a study of theology, is full of pep and even drives a Jeep like you drive the DeSoto—top speed. He loves his mother deeply, is courteous, thoughtful, 6´ tall, blond, curly hair, brown eyes, good looking.

I've had more male attention since I left home than I ever had in my life (which is natural with so few females around) but I never felt the lack of attention in the States, nor lack of proposals. Of course, there have been proposals here—some impetuous and some seemingly sincere, but Dick's proposal was most beautiful for I felt he was the right man for me. It was in a tent. I said "No" but I wanted to say "Yes." I'm older than he though he says that makes no difference. The people on your side of the family, Dad, seem to look and act younger than they are. I guess it's the good healthy stock the Rawsons have been blessed with. But also Dick and I are of a different Christian religious group.

I'm grateful to have had you, Dad, as my father and pastor. I have freedom to think my own religious thoughts. I have freedom to interpret the scriptures according to my intelligence and knowledge which I know will increase as I grow older. I have freedom to talk to God in an intimate way any time, any place, for through you and your personal prayers at meal times and many other times, I have known God to be a truly personal caring God. With these freedoms I could never change to a religion that is more restricting and I believe that Dick would not change from his religion.

Why—when I have much love to give and when I've wanted

*Almost all the names used in this book are authentic but this one is an alias, for the experience was very personal and meaningful.

to have children and always expected to bear children for as far back as when I was in my teens—why have I not fallen in love till now? And why have I fallen for someone with whom marriage is impossible? We've exchanged rings and we've exchanged pictures. He has the ring I bought in Africa. We'll correspond when I leave here and we'll have to wait and see what develops. I wish I could be with you for an hour and we could talk . . . Much love, Eddie

15

Over the Hump to Kunming, China

Dear Mom and Dad:

This will be a short letter just to assure you I'm safe in China—here where very few American women have been allowed to come—here in this country that has enchanted me for so long a time. I thought I'd never make it with so many delays. General Stilwell didn't want American women in China. I don't know why. My orders came for passage from Dinjan Air Freight Depot to Kunming through Services of Supply.

I was strapped into a C47 wet with perspiration and wondering if we would ever take off. It seemed an eternity while thoughts of the trip ahead suddenly hit me seriously for I had heard so very much about flying over the Hump, the toughest air route in the world. The C46s and C47s are the workhorses in this CBI war area carrying freight, war equipment and supplies from India to China. I was alone with a pilot and co-pilot/radio operator who were both Chinese. I had a strange feeling of being quite alone gliding over those glorious tremendously high peaks I had seen at a distance when I first wrote you from Chabua. The peaks were covered with snow and the scenery was spectacular. As the air became rarefied the men made me lie down with an oxygen mask where I couldn't see anything. The altitude didn't bother me and soon I was up again drinking in my surroundings. The flight was sensational.

I even took the landing standing up behind the pilots. I thrilled over the instruments because only a short time before a pilot had given me an hour's lecture on flying and then put me in a link trainer for another hour. How much I had hoped I could continue those lessons but they were cut short by my orders.

The picture of landing at Kunming will never leave me—the rosy red soil with purplish tint, and blue, blue skies, large black

84

pigs (or hogs?) lying on their backs on wheelbarrow rickshas being taken to market by farmers all dressed alike in faded blue cotton jackets and trousers. On the hills were terraced rice paddies with their charming variety of shapes and variety of shades of greens. The pilot told me that the importance of Kunming as the unofficial military capital of "Free China" was greatly due to its fine weather. When pilots leave Assam, India, for the treacherous 525-mile sky route over the Hump, they are practically assured of blue cloudless skies at Kunming and that the field will not be "closed in." And, by the way, he said that it takes three tons of gasoline for a Liberator Bomber to make the round trip. Imagine that!

The radio operator had sent a message on the plane that I was arriving so I was met by a man with a Jeep and driven to temporary quarters. The air was lovely, clear and cool—what a tremendous contrast to hot humid India with its rain and mud! I'm rooming with a Chinese girl. I'll write as soon as I can but right now I'm rushed and want to get this letter on its way . . . Am happy, Love to you, Eddie

*   *   *

1998 Notes

I had tried not to say much to my parents about the Hump in previous letters so as not to worry them. Being among pilots I naturally heard all the gory details of the hazardous flights over those massive ranges, the highest in the world. In the 500 plus mile route over the rugged Himalayas, planes were subjected to many great dangers. Freak winds could rise up to 248 miles per hour tossing the planes like toothpicks. Turbulences caused planes to flip over or plummet 3,000 feet a minute landing in the jungles below where death could await them. Bitter cold formed dangerous ice formations on the wings and the monsoons brought visibility down to zero. In addition there was harrassment by Jap fighter planes based in North Burma. It's no wonder I perspired, and not just from the Indian heat, while strapped in the C47 waiting for the take-off at Chabua. But, though I had a lucky flight, I gained a keener awareness and concern for the men I was later with on our Yunnanyi Air Base who faced that flight time after time and I wept for those who didn't make it back. The pilots named this flight THE HUMP.

Fatigue caused accidents for those pilots working sixteen-hour shifts. They needed 650 hours to qualify for a return to the States and thus some of them pushed their luck. Air pilots had to take off and land on quickly and crudely constructed air strips. Mechanics also worked round the clock and often under enemy fire. More than 1,000 men and 600 planes were lost over the Hump during the war, lost in trying to get supplies to China to keep China fighting the Japs. Many times, however, Chiang Kai-shek was more concerned about fighting the Communists than fighting the Japs and saved supplies sent from America for that purpose. From Kunming, where the planes landed, supplies were transported to airbases over horrible roads by trucks and donkey carts taking weeks or more. I was to find out in time why supplies I needed for the club arrived so slowly and, of course, club supplies were second in priority to war supplies.

16

France in a Tent Hospital

Dearest Eddie:

I wish you could see our beautiful tent hospital, a complete setup all under tents. Our enlisted men are geniuses and have improvised equipment out of next to nothing to complete the supplies they brought. We Red Cross have scouted around the countryside gathering up all sorts of things to furnish our tents. Others are envious of some of our collections of desks, chairs, cabinets etc. We have a squad tent for carpentry and noisy crafts. The desks which I obtained from the outside were dirty and worn so we're still in the process of sanding and staining as well as painting some pieces bright colors. We now have a stove in our office which we've already used and three double cabinets where we keep all the comfort articles. Much of our time is spent in doling out supplies for the fellows who come in with next to nothing. Many a time I've sewed on buttons for them. These kids have been through so very much. They're a grand bunch of boys and so appreciative. We have various groups here as patients including Germans. Many of the German prisoners, housed in a stockade which is well guarded, work on the hospital area and are excellent workers.

I'm so glad to be here in France nearer the action rather than in England. Our hospital covers a vast space of fields. Living quarters for the Red Cross, the nurses, and officers are in large tents pitched around the edge of the field. Across from us and in the other field are the enlisted mens' pup tents. There are also tents with built-in "johns" country style, also the Chapel and Officers mess tent. For a long time we have been eating K and C rations out of our mess gear. Today we were surprised to enter the mess tent and find tables and chairs and dishes and cutlery and our cooks baking, making pies and cakes. Our cooks are not only the best in the Army but are also wonderful men too. At 9 P.M. they place bread, butter, jam, and peanut butter and hot water in the mess tent for the whole group so we can have a snack. We all have cans of Nescafé or lemon powder for mixing drinks.

Our hospital covers a vast space of fields. It has the most beautiful entry of any of the hospitals I've seen over here. The entrance to the two fields is a wide road and at the gate is a very large sign: 56TH GENERAL HOSPITAL, U.S. ARMY. The wide road leads through the grounds and we now have roads all over the place. At all the other hospitals I've seen, the tents are placed right next to the road. The nurses, officers, and enlisted men live several fields back of the hospital and it calls for much walking during the day as the wards are also scattered among the various fields. Every day brings new improvements. Red Cross has four tents, two have been put together for a large recreation room. When scouting after furniture I found some Army furniture that had been stored, all needing sanding and staining.

I made friends with the Navy and they brought me down a beautiful handmade ping pong table and writing boards to be used in the wards. They're now making me a file, bulletin boards, etc. for our office. I was fed wonderfully well and the surprise was a large bowl of chocolate ice cream just like in the States. I thought of you. Remember how I always enjoyed a small amount and you could eat on and on and never gain weight? Well! I ate it all up on top of a big dinner and thoroughly enjoyed it. Only a few times has our hospital made ice cream and then only for the patients.

I have been bothered with kidney trouble since I came over here. Doctors want to put me in the hospital but I persuaded them to let me stay out. However, I've been having tests made. This week they're going to take X-rays to see if they can locate the trouble. I have been taking medication. I worry about you in that particular area for you know I always did mother you and yet I know you're perfectly capable of making your own decisions.

Our Red Cross Headquarters are now in Paris so I suppose

I'll be traveling there soon. I wonder how long war is going to last in this part of the world. Maybe I'll be coming your way next. Wouldn't that be something! I think about it often. I'm still in Normandy in the area where there was so much fighting and there are signs of it all around us.

I have to quit for now but please write. I long to hear from you and also be assured that all is well . . . Love to you, Dot

France (6)

Dearest Folks:

I'm okay but I was in the hospital as a patient for over a week. I guess I was tired out when they sent me in. I had a chest cough, sore throat, and achy muscles and also another slight infection of the bladder. They're giving me a complete checkup and overhauling. My back has been tormenting me. They did an X-ray of it including an intravenous pylogram which means that they injected a dye in my veins and took X-rays of the kidney and bladder and urinary tract to see if they were functioning okay. The report was fine on that. The X-rays didn't show anything out of order in my lower back or my neck but the doctor is going to consult with a specialist here and I hope to talk with him also. They seem to think at present that nothing can be done about my back except to give me therapy treatments—heat and massage. I've begun the treatments, go every morn and lie under electric lamps for half an hour. That seems to help. My chest has cleared up a lot. I should be out again and back at work soon. I hope so for there's so much to be done. One nice thing about being with a hospital unit is that one has the advantage of the best advice and help one could get anywhere in the States and all free, and even the services of a psychiatrist if you have worries though I haven't had to use that service.

We have a full hospital. I don't know where any more patients could be put. We have many Germans and French as well as our own American boys, most of them transferred here from other hospitals nearer the front. We have mixed feelings about the Germans, of course, but they're human beings and it's impossible for me to treat them any differently than I treat the others. We also have some German nurses as patients. They are ambulatory and we've had to inform them that they can't trot around the area as one started to do. She wanted to get on the German wards. There's a stockade in back where the German prisoners live under guard. They work in squads on construction of the hospital area.

We have a beautiful hospital in a lovely site, well equipped and all under tents—the operating rooms, laboratory, X-ray, dental, dispensary etc. Our enlisted men have improvised much to supplement the equipment given us. It's more thrilling to me than civilian hospitals in the States for so much has to be done by hand to make the departments convenient. Equipment (machines) are the very best from the States. The hospital covers a vast area of fields. Our Red Cross section is improving all the time. A German PW has sanded some of the furniture ready to be stained. Some has already been done but when I'm not there pushing, things slacken up.

You might be interested to know that the PWs (prisoners of war) wear fatigue suits (olive drab 2-piece twill material) and on the back of the blouse is painted PW in big letters. The German patients don't wear our American dark red corduroy robes but rain coats issued by the army. I am wearing the Army men's flannel pajamas (light blue) and the dark red corduroy robe embroidered MD USA in white (medical department).

Later:

My treatment today made my back feel wonderful. I had the lamps on both my spine and neck. There are 2 nurses especially trained in massaging and the way they massage is something out of this world—beautiful.

Our Red Cross Headquarters has moved to Paris so one of these days I'll have to plan to go in for an official visit and look the place over. I have a map of Paris. There are scheduled trips to places of interest round about us. On time off I want to get some of these in while the getting is good. I'm sorry I didn't get more in while I was in England. I've decided I'm too conscientious for my own good. Others seem to get around . . . My love to you, Dot

France (7)

Dear Folks:

I love you both so much and miss you terribly. Dad, thank you for your wonderful letters. Don't use Captain in addressing them to me. We have that rank only if we are taken prisoners and I feel confident that can't happen.

We now have wonderful showers with hot water which we can regulate—all set up in a tent. Today the doctor let me go over to shower and to wash my hair. Now that we have the hospital so beautifully set up, they will be moving us again. How do you like the news of the war on the Siegfried Line around Aachen? I wonder what the weather is like over there. Maybe soon I'll have first-hand information. It looks like things will move fast in that section now that they have broken through. I love to talk to the patients who come to us. It all seems so real. We do much in our Red Cross unit in supplying the boys with comfort articles when they come here with no personal supplies—no razor and they've grown a beard they don't want, no toothbrush and their teeth haven't been cleaned for weeks, etc. Many of them are happy to get a package of cigarettes no matter what the brand and are grateful for all our supplies. They have plenty of tales to tell. My French and German (taken in college but seldom ever used) get mixed up at times but the universal language seems to work. The boys here from the front are so anxious to talk that I stay a long time going through the wards. I just saw one of our own hospital unit boys who was burned badly when he poured gas in a stove instead of kerosene to light the fire.

When I write I wonder what you would like to know. What questions are on your mind? If there's really something you wish to know which I can answer without divulging forbidden information, please ask.

Later

Whenever I start a letter in the office, I have interruptions

91

and then have a hard time getting back to the writing again. Today we rushed around getting ready for inspection. Just as we finished, one of our enlisted men came in with a refrigerator tray of chocolate ice cream made in the patients' mess tent refrigerator. We three sat eating it out of the tray when the inspectors popped in very suddenly. I didn't have a spoon in my hand at the time so I directed their attention to the other side of the office while Terry got the tray behind her and disappeared out of the tent just in time. I'm sure the inspectors didn't suspect. At least there was no comment.

Our setup is lovely and everyone remarks about it. Mary, one of our staff, is very clever with excellent ideas. She is from Seattle, Washington, and is Head Recreation Worker. Terry, my secretary, is from Ohio. Katherine from Ohio and Etta from Oklahoma are recreation workers. Each one is different but we seem to fit in well together. Where one leaves off, the other fills in. Of course, we have our ups and downs but we manage to get along as well as any group could. Each one of our group is a natural leader and that always makes a bit of a problem. Ours is an excellent group as I compare it with other groups.

It's so hard to settle down to writing for I'm always busy. Yesterday I went to Cherbourg and brought back 3,500 doughnuts made in the Red Cross kitchen there. By the time they bumped over the miles of ROUGH roads coming back they had settled down a lot and the bottom ones were no good. We're serving doughnuts and coffee tonight to the total troop.

We are training a group of Red Cross girls who just came from the States with another General Hospital. They are bivouacking across the road from our hospital in the fields that we previously occupied. When we leave they'll take over our hospital. The same old story. We set up and move on. It's always a mess trying to pack up the necessary things and train the new workers mid all the confusion. But we will be glad to go from here as we are now so far back and away from anything of interest. We may get near Paris and possibly in a permanent building setup for the winter. I hope so for we're fed up with living in tents in the rain and dampness with mud all around us. We have had our time roughing it and look forward to a better layout. But we're grateful for the conveniences we've had when we think of our men living in foxholes full of water and also maneuvering around in the thick clay mud.

It's interesting working here as the patients come from the front and most of them here will return to duty so we get first hand information. They're a grand group. I feel much more of service to those going back to the front. As much as I'd like to return home, I wouldn't want to leave here till the war is over. These boys are giving their all, anything I can do to help is important to me.

I've also talked to some who have just come over from the States, getting a bit of the situation there. The German prisoners in the States are being treated very differently than they are here. The men from the front have no use for the German prisoners. Over here prisoners are treated decently but not served ice cream. From what I've heard the German prisoners are given everything they want in the States and more too . . . Love, Dot

France (8)

Dearest Eddie:

I long to hear from you but I know how difficult it is to find time to write. I think of you so often. Since our portable typewriter got on the blink I have to write by hand and it doesn't go so fast. The food is excellent but too heavy and I'm losing my appetite. I haven't had too much pep since I went to the hospital as a patient. I sort of drag around and tire easily. I guess I take things too seriously and work on my nerves. Our hospital is observed constantly by others for ideas. I marvel at the things that have been done here for convenience and efficiency. So now what happens? As soon as we get a good setup we move on.

Later

I had to leave this letter and go to choir rehearsal. I've been playing the little reed organ for Sunday morning services. We rehearse Friday nights. I'm getting quite attached to the little organ. I can't seem to find anyone in our unit who plays hymns.

Strange! But I don't mind the job too much. The tent chapel is always overcrowded.

I haven't been to Paris yet. They say everything is booming there. Styles still persist and one of our girls came back saying she felt very unfeminine in her uniform with everyone so dressed up on the streets. They have things there you can't buy in the States. Clothing is very expensive and not worth the price. Even souvenirs are expensive. Mary bought a silk nightie costing $20.00 which was not worth $5.00 at the most. Cotton hankies were $1.60 apiece etc. Everyone on the streets tries to get American cigarettes and offers almost any price or commodity for them.

We still have to be careful of our clothes because of dampness. We're in the rainy season and how it penetrates the tents. We have only wood fires for our quarters. The mud is terrific. Never did I think I'd wear 4 buckle arctics but we all do.

It's a strange thing about love, isn't it, Eddie? I guess I'll have to wait until it happens and hope that when it does happen I'll make the right decisions. I've dated so very much and have had serious proposals, insistent proposals, but I can't reciprocate though they are fine men. I hope I'll fall in love before too long. Both of us, Eddie, should be married and have children for we love children so much.

We have officers' dance every Saturday night. It's a unique experience dancing in tents on cement floors. We still have our marvelous band. At present the only piano in our unit is the Red Cross piano which we brought from the States. When we move we manage to convince our C.O. to take it along with us.

Please write. I'm always so grateful to receive your letters for I know what an effort it is to write. We're always being lectured on security so it's impossible to write what I'd like to tell you. I miss you so very much... Love, Dot

17

My Stolen Possessions
in Kunming, China

My dear Parents:

I'll be leaving here tomorrow but will bring you up to date while happenings are fresh in my mind. Tomorrow I'll be involved in a new life.

My first evening here I was taken to a Chinese restaurant for dinner—three high ranking officers, two girls and myself. It was my first experience with chopsticks and although the men gave me good instructions my efforts were hopeless. They asked for a fork or I would have starved. That's a technique I have to acquire. A fork might not always be available and anyway while in China I want to eat as the Chinese do. I'm enclosing the bill (I asked for it as a souvenir) to impress you with what I'll have to get used to in money exchange. As you can see, the bill is on thin rice paper and all the items are in Chinese characters except the total bill for the six of us of $2440–Chinese yuan (CN) which wowed me even though I was warned not to faint when I would see it.

After dinner, though it was getting dark, I was taken on a brief sightseeing tour of Kunming, capital of Yunnan Province and known as the Eternal City of Spring. The city is surrounded by a thick red mud brick wall with four ornate gates surmounted by stone dragons. The most important gate has a magnificent dragon. The narrow cobbled streets are lined with little shops. While other Chinese cities are being devastated by the Japanese, Kunming is growing in size and wealth as refugees pour in from the east during this war.

It was quite late when I returned to my room. The first thing that hit my eyes was the stand in front of the screened window. It was completely empty. Impossible! Impossible but true. Chinese thieves had cut through the screen and taken all my cosmetics and all my family pictures as well as Dick's picture. I was angry through and through. Why hadn't someone warned me of prevalent thievery? I land in China to be of service and the Chinese rob me. So I go to my first real assignment with no makeup and no pictures of my loved ones. Of course, I cried. The next day I learned that stealing has become a major problem for the temptation is great but if the thief is caught the punishment is ruthless. My thieves got away scot free and there was no way I could obtain a police dog and track them down.

The next day, with helpful guidance, I had my money exchanged in the black market. I'm enclosing four different yuan bills. Aren't they delightful? One with the picture of a large ornate double curved temple roof and the other with the sedan chairs and Chinese figures—much more attractive than our bills. The rate of exchange before the war, so I'm told, was two Chinese yuan to one American dollar. The present rate is 100 to 1. Though the rate is terrifically in our favor the prices of things in the market and at the restaurants are enough to knock one unconscious. The rate keeps increasing. Money changers walk the streets daily chanting "Change money? Change money?" American troops brought wealth to Kunming and gold has become the standard in the black market. Yet only a small percentage of Chinese benefit from this. Illiterate ricksha coolies' income has soared while the white collar class are having to sell their personal belongings and precious family heritage possessions to buy food. How very sad.*

Next I reported to the Red Cross Headquarters which are in the Town Club, the most elaborate Red Cross installation in the CBI theater. Though it looks like an extravagance in a "five-story skyscraper" (known as the Alliance Building), the military has said it's the greatest single morale-building factor in China with good fellowship and good food, books, magazines, entertainment, dancing, coffee and doughnuts and all together an American atmosphere for G.I.s who are homesick. From Mrs. Kerr,

*Before I left China 1 American dollar bought 2800 yuan. In other words 28 yuan (CN) would equal 1 American penny. I was carrying CN from the Snack Bar to my quarters in a suitcase—packed solid with bills that were worth so little.

Regional Supervisor, I received my long awaited assignment. I will be flown west from here to a post where Naomi Thompson will be the club director and I (the only other woman) will be the Program Director. They say Naomi, known as Tommy, is older than myself, intelligent, capable, experienced, well-groomed, and likable. Now that my big moment has come, I'm a little scared and yet I know I can do it—I hope, I hope.

I've been entertained royally here. I enjoyed another sight-seeing trip, only this time in daylight. The people fascinate me and I'm so anxious to know them better. The coolies are colorful in their cartwheel hats and faded blue cotton trousers and tunics and the blue trousered old women shamble along on bound feet. Yes, though a law has been passed against binding the feet, they are still much in evidence. The deformity making walking difficult saddens me. Old men with leathery faces sit and smoke their water pipes while lovely young girls in sheath dresses with mandarin necks stroll by. Some young women still wear tunics and trousers. There are always plenty of children holding up their thumbs to us in a "Ding hao" greeting.

But midst the people, the romantic pagodas, the medieval moongates, the ornate curved roofs of many buildings, all the beauty and fascination there are the odors. Whew! There is no sewage system and no plumbing. Human excrement is carried in pails balanced on shoulder yokes and slopped on the streets in cesspools—a breeding ground for disease. On the streets lumbering water buffaloes pulling heavy loads add to the excrement and the smell. This is the childrens' playground. Some of the boys, when they're five years old, set up shoe-shine boxes and plead with G.I.s to have a shine. I'm sure many a G.I. stops to oblige for how can one resist a child?

Driving through Kunming's narrow twisted streets in a Jeep is a slow risky experience. There are few small buses that operate on the main streets but otherwise I saw no cars except an occasional Jeep. Many of the Chinese are not yet accustomed to this magical machine that moves without having to be pushed or pulled. They stare at a Jeep but don't move. I wonder what's going on in their minds. There are streets for jewelry, for beggars, for shoes, for fabrics, for prostitutes, for pig auctions, and for rickshas to be hired. Men who are knowledgeable say that shops sell the latest American products that are scarce in America and all at exorbitant prices in U.S. currency.

I asked to be taken to the Thieves Market. I was determined to find my cosmetics and pictures, explode with anger, and demand that my things be returned. The place was large and unbelievable in its array of offerings that were somewhat displayed in an unorganized manner. It would be like the proverbial searching for a needle in a haystack. My blood boiled a little hotter. All I found out is that an American lipstick costing us ten cents would sell here for $2.50. I bet my cosmetics brought a small fortune. And pictures of Americans sell for such high prices that I was utterly amazed. What on earth do they want with pictures of Americans? I tried to glare at the Chinese vendors as if each one were the thief who had robbed me but they only smiled back begging me to buy. Infuriating! Maddening! Enraging! I wanted to scream at them.

My health is good though my disposition over the thievery is not so good. So far I've escaped malaria, dysentery, typhus, and every other thing that besets our Americans (as well as the Orientals) I seem to be immune to bugs. I guess they know how I despise them and don't dare enter my body. Some girls have had malaria a number of times and it is definitely weakening. Tonight I'm in a mixed mood of being lonely without my pictures and being in a state of wonderment of what awaits me. So now goodnight. I'll write you from my new post . . . Much love, Eddie

18

Arriving at Yunnanyi Air Base

Dearest Mom and Dad:
    To: Edna May Rawson
    From: Stanley Wilson
    Subject: Special Duty Travel Order

In compliance with the Directive issued by command of General Stilwell under subject:

"For Air Transportation within the CBI Theater" reading "American Red Cross Personnel who have competent orders from American Red Cross Headquarters APO 465 and are authorized to travel by ATC air transportation within the CBI Theater." You are directed to proceed from APO 627 to APO 488 via air reporting on arrival to the senior ARC representative for permanent assignment.

With the above proper form, necessary from now on every time I fly from one place to another, I arrived here at Yunnanyi's Air Base mid all these wonderful planes and surrounded by men, men, men. That may not sound unusual but these men are "OUR MEN," the men Tommy and I will be serving in "OUR CLUB." That's the big difference. Can you feel my excitement? This is a most challenging spot to be in. We're by ourselves seemingly apart from the world. We have the worst food, the greatest scarcity of supplies, and the longest wait in getting needed supplies. But I'm in China and someway, somehow I'm going to see the China and the Chinese I've dreamed about for a long time.

The days are so full from the time we rise till late at night that letters don't get written. I write Dick each night and that is difficult for by the time I write it's very late. The lights are off and I have to write by flashlight and I'm tired and cold. It's frightfully cold here. I wonder how I ever dripped with perspiration in India. Dick's daily letters are very precious to me. He said he has written you, Dad.

Tommy (Naomi) and I have a small building to ourselves, two rooms. The smaller one is our bedroom with two army cots having four posts each that hold up the necessary mosquito netting. The larger one will be our living room which in time we hope to fix up attractively. We've already hired an amah who is a jewel of a Chinese girl and are paying her 5,000 yuan a month. She's worth it. She cleans the place, washes our clothes, shines our shoes, and brings us breakfast in the morning. We buy our own eggs and she prepares them at the dispensary. She's also been bringing us lovely flowers from the hills. They're so delicate and unusual such as I have never seen. Next door is another very small building that serves as our washroom and storeroom for Red Cross supplies—when we get them.

There's one BIG drawback to the lovely picture I've drawn. We have to share our quarters with RATS, some of them so large that I swear they're the size of small pigs. They eat right through the mud foundation of our building which is continuously repaired by the Chinese. I'm too scared to set a trap at night or release it in the morning. GIs or the Chinese do it for us. We lie in bed and listen to the rats chase each other. As soon as one gets caught he drags the trap around. My mosquito netting already has holes. A few nights ago I eased out of bed, flashed my light inside and there were three mice all curled up asleep. The mosquitoes can buzz ferociously and not get through the netting (for any holes are sewed up when they appear) but the rats—well, that's a different horror story. I get so tired that I eventually fall asleep and let the whole tribe romp but my hatred for rats grows.

Our club is a large barn-like building with two wings. The left wing, for the present, is a reading-writing-game room with a few bare tables and chairs. The right wing is our potential canteen which we hope will be ready to open before too long. The bare hall for movies (though they never get here), church services, lectures, etc., have ping pong tables set up near the front entry. As soon as the chapel is opened and the hall is available we'll make it into a lounge and game room. We're "sweating out " our supplies. Everything has to come over the Hump and, of course, war supplies including gas for the bombers have priority. Next, Kunming has priority over us who are "out in the sticks." Meanwhile we're becoming acquainted with the men and pouring out our dreams for the club, beginning what work we can, and making friendships.

On the subject of food, it's not good. We eat out of troughs with a scanty amount of cutlery. Most of the forks have only two tines and often we have to eat with spoons or knives. But what we need most is good cooks and good food. Though the U. S. Army has had a school for training cooks and bakers none of their graduates have arrived here. Our Mess Hall staff men are local Chinese absolutely untrained for this job and the food is all purchased locally. We eat rice, potato, bread (the Chinese bread is awful) and tough meat noon and night day after day. Lately they've been serving us red peppers each meal, so hot that just a look sends me into convulsions. Food is pushed aside by the men, who have lost weight terribly and are likewise losing their hair. Dick has sent me high potency vitamins from India that should help. Our club staff from Kunming are well trained and wonderful to work with.

BUT I'M IN CHINA AND AFTER ALL THIS IS WAR . . . Love, Eddie

19

The Air Base and Surroundings

Dear Mom and Dad:

When the sun rises here, it's setting at home and I realize the great distance between us. I very much appreciate your letters, Dad, though I'm very concerned about you, Mom. Do take good care and follow instructions. I'll be home soon.

Last evening I walked from the club to our quarters to get something I needed. It was the twilight hour and I walked slowly for I was overwhelmed by the beautiful colorful enveloping sky, the red soil, the green terraced rice paddies in the distance, the black hogs driven by the coolies in their blue outfits, and the planes, planes, planes standing, taxiing into position, coming down for a landing or taking off for a mission. I can't get my fill of these huge, wonderful, powerful creatures that man has made. I now can recognize all of them and they thrill me to the core.

I was told how our airfield was built, all by hand. The process is similar to the road building in Assam (that I've told you about) but here the airway has to be smoother and deeper and solid enough for the safe landing of the heaviest planes. Rice fields had to be drained and stones quarried. The two enclosed snapshots are small and one is not too clear but I'm grateful to the GI who gave them to me for they help greatly in telling the story. Foundation stones are the largest and over them are spread cobblestones and finally smaller stones form the crust. Work animals hauled the largest rocks in two-wheeled carts. The other stones had to be carried in baskets on shoulder yokes or pushed in the wheelbarrow rickshas. I have bought a miniature ricksha for a souvenir. The stones for the surface layer are chipped to uniform size and then laid by hand. The enclosed picture of the thin, shaved-headed Chinese boy seated on the ground crushing stone is a pitiable but common sight. Over the top stones a glue-like mud is poured to fill the cracks. This is dried in the sun binding the stones together, keeping them from shifting.

The second picture shows scores of Chinese (about 200 men) dragging a ten ton roller back and forth until the surface is fairly smooth (never really smooth enough). Whole families, including women and children, have worked and continue to work keeping the airway in top condition. Hard work doesn't seem to faze these Chinese. The finished job is 6,000 feet long and 20' deep so that the 100,000 pound B29s can land without damaging the planes or the airway. During the building and the follow-up repair work, the workers seem to sense the approach of Jap air raiders even before they're warned.

I've learned some interesting things about Yunnan which means "South of the Clouds," a name given it by settlers from the lofty cloudy north. As I think I've said before this is a red-earth area with an endless expanse of blue sky and a few cottony white clouds. The Province, mostly covered with forested mountains, is surrounded on the south and west by Vietnam, Laos, and Burma. It's a self-sustaining area obtaining almost nothing from the outside world. Actually it's rich in natural minerals, copper, iron, etc. but retarded because there's no machinery for development. For centuries Yunnan was considered a penal colony—China's Wild West. Enemies of the war lords and political despots were banished to this remote area. These barbarians, former criminals, and undesirables from all over China became farmers. It was that or starvation. In 1914 the people declared themselves separated from the rest of the country and called themselves "Free China."

Yunnanyi, our nearby village, is about 135 miles from Kunming, Yunnan's capital. The people who live in the village are also predominantly farmers whose land is held in small parcels, cultivated by the family members and passed down from fathers to sons. Fortunately, Yunnan is most favorably situated for farming weatherwise though very little of the area is flat. The Chinese were among the first people to develop terraced farming which reduces soil erosion and increases the amount of available land for cultivation. Here in Yunnanyi we see these wonderful terraced rice fields on such steep hills it seems impossible that a human could stand and work without falling over. How do they keep their balance? To develop the fields and sustain them with almost no equipment takes incredible energy and patience but the Chinese seem to have both in abundance. They seem resigned to a life of drudgery but happy and content in producing good crops and plenty of children who are an insurance as future farm workers and caretakers for the elders in their old age. Nowhere does old age command more reverence and honor than in China. The family is a solid organization consisting of all the descendants of a common male ancestor together with their wives. Imagine Americans fitting into this pattern! There'd be "hells a poppin'" in no time flat.

The village homes are either of wood with straw and bamboo thatched roofs or they're constructed of red mud brick. The norm of rooms is two for a family. In either case they have to put up with rats and for that I sympathize with them muchly. The furnishings—tables, chairs, bowls, cups—are usually made of bamboo. The Chinese love walls and use them like we use fences or hedges.

I've been to the village a number of times to buy a few necessities but also just to mix with the people for I find them so very delightful. They thoroughly enjoy bartering whether purchasing or selling and like taking time for the deal but I can't barter. I hate to spoil their fun but I'll either pay the price asked or leave with a smile. Here and in Kunming I've been interested in the waterpipes that are seen everywhere smoked by both women and men. They're in different sizes—large and small and in between. I had to buy a small one for a souvenir. A real photographer gave me a good-sized picture of an old man with a wonderful face smoking a large waterpipe. I wish the photographer had put his name on the back for I'm very grateful for that picture.

The young male Chinese are almost all gone from the area—drafted into the army, working in Assam or fighting in Burma. Of the people left, since most of them wear blue tunics and trousers, it's often difficult to tell women from men.

Dick has sent me five snapshots of himself in different settings and a sixth one showing a lineup of tents with an X marked on the tent where he proposed marriage. They made me very happy since the large picture of him was stolen by that miserable thief. I wonder what Chinese girl bought it and is at this very moment admiring it. I wish I could find her and snatch back my possession.

I've not mentioned what's happening at the club because I decided I'll send you a copy of my August 1944 report so you can see the form I have to follow in reporting to Kunming headquarters each month. I've already sent in my July report. The copy on thin paper was not readable.

20

China-Burma-India Command

To: Regional Supervisor, APO 627
Attn: Alma B. Kerr, Club Operations
From: On-Post Club Report: Gremlin Hall, August 1944

I—General

I have been at APO 488 six weeks today, feel very much at home and find myself thoroughly in love with the job. There is a large amount of work to be done and the hours extend from 10:00 A.M. to 10:00 or 11:00 P.M. with no days off but I never in my lifetime have found keener appreciation on the part of recipients or finer enthusiasm and interest in what is being planned.

The attendance in the club continually increases. Part of it, I know, is due to our program for we have something each week for everyone's interest. But I also know that a large part of it is due to the informal contacts made on the Base—a chat with a fellow we haven't seen before, a friendly acquaintanceship established by interest shown in him, an invitation up to the club to a show or a game night or to read a new book that just came in or to listen to a new record or to join the band or chorus or to just chat. I have found that many of the men I've visited at the dispensary knew almost nothing about the club. Now they're some of our most loyal friends and eager volunteers in the planning and working. Tommy and I feel that individual human interest is our most important job in or out of the club. Consequently, we become stronger like a real family as the men know that the club staff can always and ever be counted on for sympathy, kindliness, due praise, companionship in fun, and well planned offerings for their leisure time.

The first hour of the morning is, and I guess always will be, spent in making the main room attractive—placing the chairs at inviting angles, tables in attractive positions (we can't teach our Chinese staff that American homey touch), checking in returned library books, arranging newspapers and magazines (we're trying to train the men to keep them in order so that their wives will be evermore grateful when they return to the States), placing fresh flowers and leaves in vases.

Our library is USED. I'm proud of my system of cataloging and cross-cataloging of our books but I'm not proud of the caliber of our books. There's a lot of trash with an occasional light from heaven found in a classic novel or an outstanding nonfiction book. And if those few gems are out in use, I stand in shame before the readers who want better material. There are men here taking education courses in their leisure time and would be grateful for reference books on science, arts, etc. The other day a man asked me for poetry, works of Byron, Browning, Keats, Shelley, which he needed for a literary course he is taking for college credit but I had nothing to offer him.

I requisitioned records last month from APO 627, a long suggested list from Bach to Wagner. APO 465 came through with a group of classics this last week. Heaven be praised! Many, however, were vocal numbers from operettas with John McCormick's voice stuck in on too many of them. The men weren't too pleased over these. Even the jitterbugs and jive hounds go for Rachmaninoff, Chopin, and Beethoven. One of these jazz lovers (I love good jazz too) who attended our Classical Hour last week spoke to me the next day. "Eddie, tell me, what is a sympathy—I mean a sym . . ." I corrected him and gave him a quick idea of the construction of a symphony. We ended by his saying: "Gee, Eddie, I enjoyed last night by candlelight." I felt tears of gratification that men over here in the demoralizing atmosphere of war could also be gaining a knowledge and appreciation of great music that could make their future lives richer and fuller. I've cataloged what records we have and separated them into groups so the men can easily find what they want.

Vocal harmonizings and hillbilly groups and jazz band sessions are heard more and more around the edges. We sing on Sunday evenings after church before refreshments are served. An enthusiastic GI leader, a few instruments, and a lot of good old harmony. We sing if the lights go off, and they do, when small groups are together. Singing Americans forgetting temporarily that they are far away from home in a remote area. Lt. Lawrence is going to produce an excellent band here or bust. He won't have to bust except for pride. The response has been thrilling. If two or three are together they start and call for me to play a jazz accompaniment on our small reed organ. Full rehearsals are scheduled for Monday and Thursday afternoons. We now have a bass fiddle, traps, guitar, banjo, accordion, and a privately owned trumpet. Those without instruments literally drool wanting to give release to their pent-up emotions. The long awaited piano came today. I haven't played it yet. Am trying not to expect too much. But the fact that we have a piano sends chills up and down our spines. Special Services is pulling for us to get the instruments we need.

Our TRUTH or CONSEQUENCES Night was one "rolling in the aisles" success. The M.C. and the members of the ATC and 27th T.C. teams were wound up as was the audience. I wrote the patter for the consequences to which the M.C. ad libbed and with help from the enlisted men we got together complete and startlingly effective props. We gave a small prize to each member of the team, the M.C., the scorekeeper, and to the best performer of the Consequences. As a result of that night, some men are working on their own for a new and novel quiz night with no consequences but with a hundred gags and laughs. So far it sounds very clever.

Our DUPLICATE BRIDGE TOURNAMENT was so highly successful that we've been besieged with requests for another. Tomorrow night is the night. We learned a few things from the other one. We will have a typed copy on each table of Contract Bridge Rules for overtricks, penalties, and game bonuses. Even good bridge players make mistakes in scoring from memory when they haven't scored for some time. We made the duplicate boards out of old cartons, numbered them, and stated on each one the Dealer and whether the players would be vulnerable or nonvulnerable. After the last tournament we posted the master score sheets for E-W and N-S on the bulletin board and the players swarmed around highly amazed at the variety of scores resulting from the different biddings of one hand. For days they discussed the results and studied the possibilities of certain hands as they recalled them. A Colonel and an enlisted man helped me in making the tournament a success.

We use the SNACK BAR room for various activities but as yet it doesn't deserve its name. No food, no coffee. We've worked hard to push the work along and a lot has been accomplished. We get discouraged with the slowness of it all but still persist. The food! Will that ever arrive so we can open? These men are always hungry. So am I. We eat the same tough meat, potatoes, rice and gravy every noon and night out of troughs in the Mess Hall. The men get to the point where they can't look the stuff in the face. They push it aside and lose pound after pound. They long for good sandwiches and sweets.

Tommy found a very talented fellow among the enlisted men who is now painting murals on the walls of the big hall depicting the activities of the various units on the Base. I have four good pictures given me. I would prefer scenic murals rather than planes—a diversion for the men. At least these give the room more interest and character. It's a joy to watch the project grow. We badly need material so that I can start making the draperies for the hall as well as for the wings. The bright colors will give the men a lift when they come in to relax from their day's work.

A PING PONG TOURNAMENT has been lined up for the men. A large group have participated and we are about ready for the finals when the winner of the officers' team will play the winner of the enlisted men's team. Our three ping pong tables are always in use only our balls are practically gone. It's good exercise for the men and so will be the tennis and the badminton courts when they are completed.

II—Problems Encountered

There are no baffling problems except lack of supplies which I already commented on in July's report. We have a good building for a club. We have men with their enthusiasm, interest, and helpfulness. We have a program they like. We have their respect. All we need is materials and THAT IS A PROBLEM.

III—Activities of Volunteers

There isn't a thing we do that isn't to a great extent a result of helpful suggestions and work on the part of the men. I am recalling my only attendance at a Red Cross meeting during my four day stay at APO 627 (before I came to Yunnanyi) where it was advocated that the men do all the planning, if possible, and hold their meetings without Red Cross personnel being present. That doesn't work here. The men are busy and can't assume too much responsibility in carrying on program planning and furthermore they want us in on everything. They want us there— period—looking as pretty as we can. They want our suggestions and ideas. It's their club, their program but we belong to them. I'm so glad we do.

IV—Program

I gave a complete schedule of our program in my July report and have already commented on our additional activities in Section I. There is nothing to add except that as before we have used the nights for meetings, special rehearsals, and small groups down at our quarters for social evenings which the men seem to appreciate very much. It's more like home.

V—Future Plans

To have a big carnival on the evening of September 6th which will include all the units on the Base, each unit being responsible for a particular activity.

To increase our Men's Chorus which has been running successfully.

To complete the work necessary for opening our Snack Bar.

To complete the decorating and furnishing of the main hall.

VI—Human Interest Stories

I already mentioned two of these in Section I. Similar Interesting incidents arise continually but they are hard to recall unless written down at the time.

VII—Changes from the Normal Trend

The coming of a Special Services officer who is enthusiastic and ready to give the needed help.

An increasing attendance at the club for all activities including just coming in to talk or read or play games or write letters.

A short time after my arrival I was invited out to dinner by three men who are stationed in a remote area with a special secret military assignment. I was met and taken in a Jeep. They had prepared the food themselves, typed the classy menu, and planned the entertainment. I was requested to "dress up" for the occasion. It was really fun and, of course, I was treated like a queen.

* * * *   SUPPER MENU   * * * *

TUESDAY NITE, 25 JULY

* *

TOMATO JUICE
COCKTAILS

* * *   *   * * *

CHICKEN STEW   * *

CORN ON THE COB   * *

PEACH COBBLER   * *

****

PLANTERS PEANUTS * *   ENGLISH WALNUT FUDGE

* * * * * * * * *

DINNER AT 7:15 P.M.   DINNER MUSIC

* * * * * * * * *

CHINA

21

Chinese Deaths and Funerals

Dear Ones:

I'm famous (?) I made the China-Burma-India Theater Paper—a military paper. Quite exciting but what a way to receive publicity. The article follows:

Slick Salween Horse Trader Gigs U.S. Vet

HQS, CASAC... Chinese livestock merchants of the Salween country never heard of David Harum, but when it comes to "slick horse trading" they are hard men to "beat," says Capt. Bert Reinow, base veterinarian in the area.

Reinow, veteran of 23 months in Asia who speaks Mandarin, woke one morning with the bright idea of buying a donkey as a pack animal, in lieu of the always-busy Jeeps. He repaired forthwith to the local market.

There he found a toothy merchant who had not one but two donkeys for sale, twins in fact, a jack and a jenny. Reinow glowed at the news, well knowing he could easily sell a jenny when and if Ol' Man Rotation touched him with the magic wand. He knew the beast was worth about 3000 CN; the merchant asked 4000, so of course Reinow bid 2000.

After the customary smiles, retiring for tea and taking up the offer again, the deal was clinched for 3000, an hour and a half later. The Chinaman loaded the animal on the American's trailer cart and departed with his other donkey.

Reinow arrived at base, all smiles, and announced his good luck. "We'll call her Edna" he said, thus bestowing high honor (for the Salween country) on the local Red Cross girl. A friend took one look and said: "I think you better call it Ed."

The Captain winced, conducted a clinical experiment, then screamed. "And me a vet, too!" His Chinese friend had slipped him

113

the jack and shuffled off with the twin jenny towards the terraced hills.

Bert Reinow gave me two pictures to remember him and the thwarted honor. In one (which I'm enclosing) he is posed with a Chinese watercolored paper parasol over his head and in the other he is posed with the jack that should have been a jenny.

I am so charmed by these Chinese peasants that it bothers me greatly how their lives are so much controlled by superstitions. The temple priests help keep the superstitions strongly rooted. There are evil spirits everywhere. Sometimes they're frightened away by large bunches of loud firecrackers but that rids them only temporarily. A number of times I've seen a Chinese run in front of a plane as it's starting down the runway. If the man times it rightly he escapes while the evil spirit following him is killed. You can imagine how this irritates the pilots.

Baby boys, so very highly prized, are often given feminine names and put into feminine apparel. Thus evil spirits are deceived mistaking them for girls who are not worth molesting. At a certain age (I'm not sure when) a silver yoke is sometimes placed around the boy child's neck for safety from these spirits. From it hang two overlapping circles bearing seven engraved Chinese characters standing for happiness, prosperity, productivity, etc., and from the circles dangle five little bells to scare away the evil ones. I was so fascinated by them that I bought one to wear when I get home. I wouldn't wear it here and offend the people.

A number of times I've heard drums and sounded gongs and noise makers of varying sorts circling a house driving out a devil that had taken possession of a family member and caused serious sickness. The member usually dies in spite of this careful precaution, but before I get into deaths and funerals, I'll refresh your minds as to the background.

In China's early history when a king or a man in a lofty position died, it was the custom to bury with him his wives, concubines, servants, chariots and horses, and all possessions which he had found useful and might need in the next life. Thus many lives were sacrificed. When the first emperor to rule over China died in the 3rd century B.C., the human sacrifices numbered into the thousands. His tomb was so elaborate that stories traveled far and wide and even became the plot for one of the tales in the "Arabian Nights." Feelings of the public gradually became more and more aroused in horror at the great slaughter of their fellowmen and finally this period came to an end.

However, the thought of leaving loved ones alone in the world beyond was unbearable, for Paternalism was strong and worship of one's ancestors was of the utmost importance. So small clay images were substituted for the living and for the needed conveniences—wives and servants, tables, chairs, waterpipes, opium pipes, clothing, wash basins, chamber pots, etc., etc. Later these were replaced by paper replicas.

Both in Kunming and in Yunnanyi I've seen where they make and sell these tissue paper articles for the world beyond. It's a thriving business in every Chinese city and village. The paper articles are important and necessary presents which any deceased person would be glad to receive. They are transferred to the Chinese heavenly sphere by burning them before the tomb or the ancestral shrine of the deceased and when they are fully burned and disappear in the flames, they immediately reappear in the other world in a live or real substantial form. The manufacturing job is important, for the more flimsy and wholly inflammable the ghost figures are, the surer they will be fully burned. If a table intended for Grandfather Cheng was burned all except one leg, his dishes of food would slide off onto the floor. He would be terribly angry with his family on earth. His spirit could make life miserable for his descendants. Of course, paper money can be purchased and burned so that the loved one can do his own shopping but this is not so common.

The Geomancer sets the exact day and hour for the funeral, as well as for all important occasions, for he is skilled in divining the lucky time by means of some aspect of the earth. I've seen numerous funeral parades. In Kunming I saw one that obviously represented a wealthy family. There was a brass band, large banners and paper lanterns on bamboo poles carried by hired natives, paper figures galore and hired mourners to moan and sob. Families put on as big a display as they can afford and too often more than they can afford. That's no different from the elaborate weddings and sometimes funerals put on by low incomed families in America. "Keeping up with the Joneses" or "saving face" is so stupid. I'm enclosing the only snapshot I have showing a paper "house-coffin" in the lead with other paper figures following. Incense is usually burned at the shrine of the deceased.

Aside from paper funeral presents, lovely watercolored parasols also are made of paper. It's a common sight on a bright sunny day to see many of them in the village. Fans are made of paper as well as from silk and dried palm leaves and are used to dust off furniture, to blow up fires, to cool tea and food or to shade eyes from the bright sun.

This has been a longer letter than I intended and I must quit . . . Much love to you, Eddie

Crossing the Equator.

Initiation on *Ship Mt. Vernon*. Everyone was doused.

Dorothy viewing one of the sad results of Hitler's ceaseless bombing of London.

Yunnanyi Air Base, my first assignment in China.

A child is crushing rocks into small pieces for top layer of runway.

Our delightful kitchen staff.

Bert is with the jack that should have been a jenny, named Edna.

Ann Sheridan, the Sweater Girl of Hollywood, with her Interlocutor.

U.S.O. crew ready to leave with Ann smiling, so anxious to get out of this rat world.

Men from the wet, cold hangar jammed into our club with welcome dryness, warmth, and food.

The Sgt. did so much work for our club.

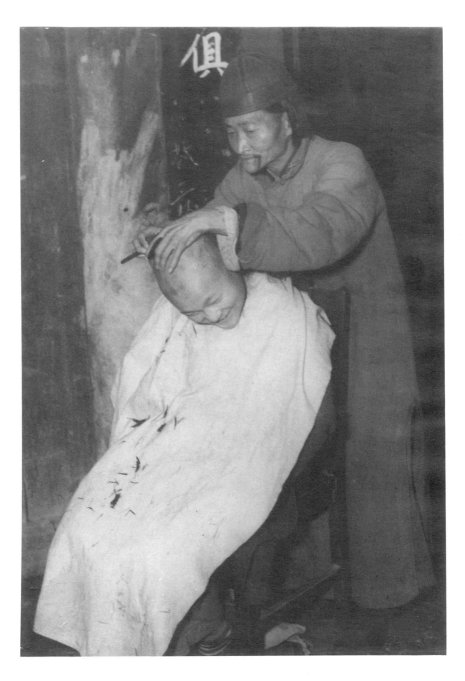

No hair styling needed—it's just shaved off without the aid of soap or water. *That's the style!*

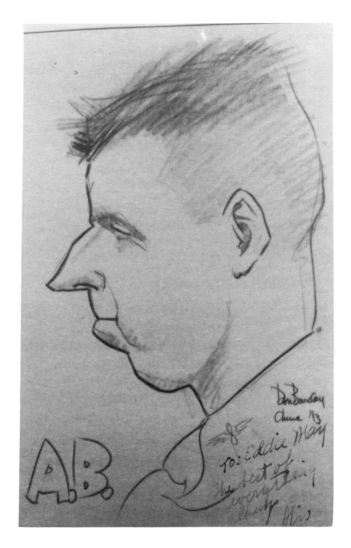

A laughable caricacture of fun-loving A.B.

Scenes in Yunnanyi Village. A family cooking their meal in the street. Daily chore of carrying slops, which always spill over, breeding disease. Yunnanyi woman with her grandson in front of typical mud-brick home.

Bill with his glamorous collection of beauties—an inspiring sight for our fighting men.

Liege, Belgium—Dorothy in her Red Cross Field Director's office. The beautiful desk is from the German Gestapo headquarters, as is the bronze statue of Mercury.

In a sampan, off on another trip.

A wonderful walk in the hills with my good friend, Nathan.

A wide street in Chengtu, Szechwan Province. My second China assignment was on an isolated air base removed from the city.

A shoreline jammed with shabby dwellings and sampans which are the permanent homes of families.

I was the first American woman these villagers had seen.

A father teaching his son the fine intricate embroidery stitches for which China has been famous. They're smiling, but many a Chinese person has become blind in this eye straining work.

A Pagoda "High on the Hill" was entered in our Picture contest by Wm. Dorfmeier.

EDNA RAWSON

The "Sampan with Coolie" was entered in our Monogram contest. I don't have the name of the clever creator.

Our first trip to the Buddhist temple.

I was asked to pose while
the camera took shots.

That shoulder yoke was *heavy.* I managed a few steps for the camera.

With two sober faced orphans from the temple orphanage.

My darling Frances Chen.

Betty Hu, the Chinese General's daughter.

One of the Belgium, 1944 Christmas cards. In color, it looks like a watercolor painting.

Dorothy in Loch Lomond posed in Scottish garb before sailing for home.

The winning crew at the exciting Dragon Festival.

22

Sheridan, Movie Star, and Those Miserable Rats

Dear Mom and Dad:

Am enclosing a bill for four dinners at the one and only restaurant in the village of Yunnanyi. We eat here quite often though I always feel guilty having the men pay for it but they insist. I'm their invited guest. The prices are ridiculous. You can see below how rapidly the rate of money exchange is rising. The men drink the Chinese wine. I've smelled of it—the smell is terrible.

4	Chicken and walnuts	1000
2	Egg foo yung	240
2	Chicken fried noodle	300
1	Pot of coffee	250
2	Grange wine	1400
1	Pot of coffee	250
		3440

Below this all was written in Chinese characters. Some American had evidently furnished the owner with English names to oblige the men on the Base. By the way, I've become adept at using chopsticks and enjoy it.

I had a long walk up in the hills today with one of my good friends, Lt. Col. Nathan Ranck. We picked the most unusual flowers like nothing we have in the States. I wish I could bring seeds home but it's forbidden. The Chinese were all so friendly along the way. I've learned a little of the language so that I can carry on a sketchy conversation and they manage someway to get what I'm driving at which is a lot to their credit! The children are perfectly darling but quite dirty. Each one sticks up his thumb and calls out a cheery "Ding Hao." They have so little in food, clothing, and real pleasures. Such young children trudging along the road bearing heavy burdens both to and from work. Almost all of the adult Chinese we saw were coolies. What a tremendous task China faces in her future raising her people to a higher level. Nathan and I sat for a long time on a bank near a bridge and talked and talked. It was a memorable afternoon. I'll never forget the good friend he was to me. One of the enclosed pictures is of Nathan, two are of me, one of both of us and one of the arched bridge near the bank where we sat and talked and talked.

Through Social Services we've had two U.S.O. entertainments.* Pat O'Brien came first and put on an act. He was well oiled with liquor and I was disgusted with him. Later when I heard that Ann Sheridan, movie star, was coming I was both excited and curious. Just before the war Sheridan, wearing a close-fitting sweater, was on the cover of *Life Magazine*. She was known as the "Sweater Girl." I was really curious to see what was so remarkable about her breasts that gave her that distinguishing title.

They came, the whole troupe. With the star were two attractive girls who were kept somewhat in the background, along to dress Sheridan's hair, wait on her, do odd jobs, I guess, and there were a few men necessary for some purpose or other, probably keeping the wolves away from the girls. The whole troupe ate in the Mess Hall where the GIs swarmed around and looked on agog at this queen from Hollywood. I'm sure she didn't eat much of that horrible food.

The show was primarily a prepared dialogue between Sheridan and the male interlocutor. It was quite ordinary, I thought, and somewhat coarse. Following the show, the three girls were brought to our quarters for we were to have the honor (?) of bedding them. In our living room we already had two cots that served as 'sofas'. One more had been brought in and the three made up. After some artificial conversation between us—for ordinary Red Cross girls are not on a high level with a glamorous

*These were the only U.S.O. shows we had while I was in China.

138

movie queen and her attendants—we all retired to our cots in the two separate rooms.

Shortly afterwards there were screams. Tommy and I jumped up, ran to the door, opened it and stared out into the living room. Sheridan was standing on her cot, nude from the waist up, with a horrified expression on her face. Likewise, the other two girls were screaming. Rats, Rats. Taking full advantage of this unexpected situation, I carefully examined the queen's breasts. Hmm. They were no different from any normal breasts except that they were a brownish shade around the nipples as if they had been colored. I knew girls were beginning to paint their toenails though I hadn't had time or interest in that pursuit, but painted breasts? It puzzled me. Were they painted or was that natural? If natural, would that be a positive asset that would earn her the title of "Sweater Girl"? Still puzzled I looked at Tommy, and receiving a nod, I closed the door. We went back to our cots where I discussed this serious matter with my roommate. The screams continued. With no compassion and with no guilty consciences we fell asleep. Tommy and I are darned nice people but we're not perfect and anyway what could we do? Rats are rats. I'm enclosing four pictures given me as momentos of the occasion: (1) Ann and interrogator on stage facing the audience of men (2) Ann seated on stage with part of the audience showing (3) Ann signing her autograph (4) the whole crew in front of their plane before leaving—8 men, two girls and Ann who was smiling broadly, so glad to be leaving this rat world.

Following the Sheridan episode I feel I should write a brief essay on Rats being somewhat of an authority since they've become my nightly companions. You recall, I'm sure, the legend of the Pied Piper of Hamelin who, while playing magical notes on his flute, lured all the rats in town down to the river and into the deep waters. The piper, then cheated out of his promised reward by the stingy town burghers, began to lure away all the children. Of course the burghers were forced to pay up and the children were saved. But what happened to the rats? Was that really the end of them? Ah, the legend doesn't go that far but I will. Rats can swim and tread water. I'll bet they all returned to the town of Hamelin and that the burghers were ready to hang the piper with his magical flute but the clever piper had already skipped town with his rich reward.

I had heard much about rats in India where they destroyed a large proportion of all food crops including the much needed rice, depriving the hungry people who often starved as a result. Each year rats in Asia consume at least 48 million tons of rice—enough to feed a quarter of a billion people. But in India the rats—like those dumb cows and infernal cockroaches—are welcome as sacred creatures. In the Hindu religion even the elephant-headed god Ganesha, symbol of prosperity, was traditionally carried by rats. Someway rats never bothered me in that country. Evidently I got out before they discovered I was there or maybe they never had a chance since I was always surrounded by cockroaches.

It was here in China I learned that rats bite human beings. Quite often I hear a man complain that a rat had nibbled on his toes while he was asleep. That's how treacherously underhanded and sinister they are, attacking a man when he's defenseless. Since they can gnaw through pipes, gnawing through mosquito netting is nothing and it's mere "child's play" gnawing through the mud and dung foundations of our quarters.

Few rats live more than a year. Now that's jolly good news—but—the females bear their young at two months and produce seven pups each time. Rats increase so rapidly that a pair could have 15,000 descendants in one year. It isn't that male rats have amorous feelings for the females or that they're desirous of having children for they have no hearts or souls. What they have is lustful savage sexual urges that result in brutal rape of every she rat within sight or smell. However, the shes don't warrant our sympathy for both shes and hes are mean and nasty. Maybe the shes lead the hes on, I don't know.

Rats eat almost anything and live anywhere. There are more rats on earth than any other mammal group and they are the most destructive. They spread diseases like mad. I'm absolutely certain God didn't create rats. If there is a Devil or Satan then undoubtedly he, through magic, produced these pernicious beasts to bring misery to human beings. As much as I hate war, I firmly believe that when we've won this WW II—and we will have won very soon now—there should be a WW III on RATS.

So much for Ann Sheridan,
the Sweater Girl from Hollywood
She flew in, She screamed, She flew out
But the rats we have ever with us

I've had word to report to Kunming for a few days. This should be a nice break from the pressing schedule here and I'm looking forward to it. Will write you when I get back . . . Love, Eddie

*   *   *

An After-the-War Follow-up on Ann Sheridan

I had read Dr. Gordan Seagrave's wonderful WW II book *Burma Surgeon Returns* and was greatly amused that he and his brave Burmese nurses also had an interesting experience with Ann Sheridan when she and her group came to Burma for a show. Soon after their arrival, a Special Services officer called the famous doctor saying that Miss Sheridan would be coming to the hospital at 11:00 to be photographed with the Burmese nurses. Would he please have the girls dressed in their best Burmese costumes? Seagrave comments that the girls loved to dress up occasionally for men but definitely not for a woman. The girls protested but the good doctor persuaded them: "Publicity for the CBI theater is important. We need supplies." The girls put on their beautiful silk longyis and sheer jackets and sat for two hours with their hands folded but the glamorous movie star never came.

Much later the SS officer called to say that Miss Sheridan had been too busy to come but would be brokenhearted if she left CBI without a picture of herself with the famous Burma surgeon. Would the doctor please go to the strip and meet the "great lady" (Seagrave's words with tongue in cheek) at 4:30. The doctor didn't dare express his feelings out loud but he went. A battery of

141

cameras arrived and finally Sheridan herself appeared along with the troupe. It was quite obvious that the star didn't know the doctor from Adam and cared less about meeting him. "After all," says Dr. Seagrave "movie stars aren't interested in missionaries, medical or otherwise." The photographer said: "Miss Sheridan, please shake hands with Dr. Seagrave for the picture." "She looked around to see whose hand was extended and seeing mine she held her hand out rather limply." Dr. Seagrave graciously said: "It's a shame you are forced into this." "Oh," shrugged the 'great one.' "It's all part of a day's job."

23

To Kunming for a Four-Day Break

Dearest Mom and Dad:

I'm back from Kunming, was there four wonderfully full days. I guess Mrs. Kerr thought I needed a break. I really had fun and feel better with renewed energy.

In all the spare time I had there I was with Lt. Col. AB (his nickname). We had bushels of fun together and felt we had known each other for ages. He was intelligent and excellent company. I actually rode in a sedan—a great rarity in these parts.

Kunming lies on a high fertile plateau surrounded on three sides by the rolling mountains. Southwest of the city is beautiful Lake Dian, twenty-five miles long where flowers grow profusely—jasmines, primroses, geraniums . . . The city has grown and moved fast from a primitive city before the war to the unofficial military capital of Free China. Since I was last there the streets seemed more crowded, more noisy, more confusing with more rickshas, more buses and cars and Jeeps and every driver blasting his horn at the pedestrians who ran this way and that paying no attention to any other moving thing. And the ricksha coolies were no more careful than the pedestrians. They trotted through any opening without looking to the left or to the right. Using peripheral vision was not a part of their makeup. I rode in a ricksha once and that was sufficient. I gave the coolie more than he asked. He whimpered so against my better judgment I gave him another large yuan bill. I could have stood there for an hour handing out yuans and he would have still whimpered for more.

I hadn't realized there were so many Chinese from minority groups in Kunming. Their varied colorful costumes added greatly to the scenes. I'm told there are about twenty-five minority groups in Yunnan Province, each with its own culture, costume, and language. Shaved heads of male Chinese seem to be the fashion, though I don't know why, so the barbers always have a waiting line. Even children have shaved heads with a bit of black tuft in the back. Since the barber shops are open for all passersby to watch, I also stood and observed the process. The barber I watched used no soap and only a bit of water. Viewing the scalping job I knew I would never allow the barber to touch my glorious brown tresses. I'll let them grow and grow. I've been given an excellent photographer's picture in which the barber is seriously involved with his job while his client has a broad smile as bits of his hair fall down on the cloth covering him. It's a wonderful human interest picture.

The dentists also work in shops open to the public. On shelves behind them are displayed various sets of false teeth from which they select a set for each client. For those who can afford luxuries, the dentists have gold teeth and jade fillings for sale.

I wanted to see the United Nations House. It wasn't quite what I expected. There was a large dance floor with tables around the sides, a not too good sounding orchestra, and plenty of Chinese girls ready to flirt with or entertain any American men who entered.

In a shop I purchased six watercolor scrolls—four of exotic birds and two of Chinese in mandarin coats with scenic background. I also bought a blue hanging with a colorfully embroidered phoenix in the upper left and a brilliant dragon in the lower right, both contending for the celestial pearl in the center. The phoenix has the head of a pheasant, the beak of a swallow, the neck of a tortoise, and colorful plumage of red, green, yellow, white, and black. It conveys uprightness, sincerity, justice, fidelity, and benevolence. Chinese consider the phoenix the "Emperor of the Birds" symbolizing the sun and its warmth. The dragon has the head of a camel, eyes of a rabbit, neck of a snake, horns of a deer, stomach of a frog, and claws of a tiger. It's regarded as the guardian of treasure, a symbol of strength, justice, and authority. It guards the temples from evil influences. The dragon always seems to me the primary symbol of China. The celestial pearl represents the sun with the rays of fire appearing as a blazing pearl.

I was taken to the top restaurant in Kunming for a very special dinner but it was more like a feast. The room was large with many tables and many customers. At the very beginning each of us was given a steaming hot towel for face and hands. It felt so good. Since I had no makeup I didn't have to worry about smearing. In front of each of us was a bowl, red lacquered chopsticks, a China ladle and a saucer. We dipped each in boiling water that was brought to us. In the middle of the table were bowls and more continually being brought in—so many I lost count—each filled with either vegetables or chicken, walnuts, sweet-sour pork, shrimps, fish, pigeon's eggs floating in bird's nest soup, funny little cakes which looked and tasted like potato cakes, fried duck livers, bamboo sprouts, dried grasshoppers. A great deal of oil is used in the cooking and the dishes were rich. We dived into these center bowls and put a little from each into our individual bowls that meanwhile had been filled halfway with rice.

I have been taught that the secret of eating with chopsticks is to keep the lower stick very firm while the upper one is manipulated to grasp the morsels of food between them. I've developed the technique and am quite good but still sometimes I wait in suspense while hastening to get the food in my mouth. It's maddening if the sticks are empty by the time I reach that waiting cavity. Quite maddening but loads of fun. It's hard work to keep the sticks going as it should be done. If I take my bowl up in my left hand and shovel the food into my mouth, as I do with our kitchen staff at the club, it goes quite nicely. Many of the Chinese make noises while eating showing how much the food is being enjoyed. Those Chinese who have had more contact with foreigners and have progressed "socially" according to western standards would not react that way. It's said the Chinese almost inhale their food.

At intervals during the feast a servant brought in more steaming towels sweet with perfume added to the water to bathe our faces and hands. Quite often Chinese around us rinsed their mouths with hot water and spat it out on the floor. I wanted to try that little trick and was dared to do it but I couldn't quite make it. Thoughts of it broke me up in laughter.

For dessert there were plates of walnuts candied in honey, peanuts salted in shells by being soaked in brine, blanched almonds, melon seeds, black dates...The final bill was high, high, high.

It was a real treat seeing city life for a change, dressing up, going to a dance, etc. A.B. is on the 14th Air Force Staff so one night he took me to the headquarters of General Glenn and General Chennault to see a movie. Imagine me, an ordinary Red Cross girl from the backwoods of Yunnanyi, relaxing in a large comfortable chair in a decorated generals' quarters seated beside General Chennault of the original famous "Flying Tigers." A.B. was at my right. There were fifteen people present—all high ranking.

When I left Kunming, A.B. took me to the plane. The plane ride to and from Kunming was tremendously beautiful from the view up in the skies—the terraced rice paddies in intriguing patterns and varying shades of green and the fascinating contours of the mountains. I was the only person with the pilot on the return flight so I sat in the co-pilot's seat feeling very important but if the pilot had suddenly collapsed I'm not sure what would have happened. Back in Yunnanyi I later received a package from A.B. containing a beautiful Chinese silver bracelet and two silver pins. He also sent me a caricature of himself to remember him and our four days of fun. I have no idea who did the caricature but in a far-fetched way I can see that it's A.B.

Yesterday I spent two hours at the dispensary where there are a lot of malaria patients. And that reminds me that I must get fresh shots for I've had none since leaving Washington.

A few nights ago I spent a whole evening with Col. Kennedy and Major Gibbons, son of Floyd Gibbons, war correspondent. Major Gibbons was born in Istanbul and later lived twenty years in France. He told me all the latest happenings in France and gave me some exceedingly interesting information. It brought me much closer to Dot and somewhat eased the loneliness I've had for her.

146

So now to bed and to sleep while the rats enjoy their nightly frolic . . . Love, Eddie

*   *   *

1997 Footnote on Chennault and the Flying Tigers

As of 1996 I found the reading of war activities in the CBI theater fascinating and marveled at our successes with so many conflicts between all the leaders in command positions—General Chennault, General Stilwell, Chiang Kai-shek, President Roosevelt. At this point (since I sat next to Chennault watching a movie) I'll enjoy reviewing a few highlights about him.

Japan began taking over China bit by bit dropping bombs on city after city. Chiang hired Chennault to develop a China Air Force. Chennault found very few of the Chinese planes fit to fly and Chinese air pilots were an even greater problem, especially in their takeoffs and landings which resulted in great wreckage. As sons of wealthy families they could not be dropped out of the training program or they would lose face—a thing no Chinese can endure. Chennault said they could be trained to fly in fair weather but in bad weather or in emergencies they easily lost control. They were certainly no match for the large number of Japanese pilots and their superior planes.

The summer of 1940 Chennault longed for American pilots and American planes and Chiang knew they were needed. Chennault sought help from Madame Chiang. Her brother, China's chief lobbyist in the U.S., pulled strings and received President Roosevelt's reluctant permission for Chennault to hire American volunteers from the army, navy, and marines. This would be all undercover for America was not at war. Pilots jumped at the opportunity of combat fighting and adventure. 112 were hired under the guise as workers for an Aircraft Maintenance Co. So in the summer of 1941, Chennault made this American Volunteer Group (AVG) into a fighting unit, teaching them to fly in pairs, dive at top speed from great heights, bomb, and break away never engaging a Jap plane in a one on one duel.

Chennault's group became known as the "Flying Tigers" and

their successes became like fables to be told and retold. Each pilot was paid $600 to $700 a month with a $500 bonus for every Japanese plane destroyed—high pay in those days but they were worth it and it's said that the pay didn't interest them so much as the adventure and excitement. Seven months later the U.S. entered the war. In July 1942, the Flying Tigers were re-formed into U.S. Army Air Task Force's 23rd Fighter Group and in March 1943 they were made part of U.S. 14th Air Force, still under General Chennault.

The goal of America's chiefs of staff and President Roosevelt was to keep China fighting the Japanese for China was needed as a base for future bombing of Japan. Thus America gave China about two billion dollars in Lend-Lease aid besides the American pilots and one hundred P-40 fighter planes. Chiang was not fully cooperative. He expected the Allies to defeat the Japs, oust them from his country while he hoarded Lend-Lease equipment to fight the communists when WW II was over. By the end of the war, the Flying Tigers had downed 1200 enemy planes and a possible 700 more.

24

September Program Report to ARC Headquarters

My dear Parents:

I'm sending you a copy of my September report as it will save time in writing.

On-Post September 1944 Club Report to Regional Supervisor

I—General

This has been a month of dreams come true. A large amount of supplies came over the Hump the first of the month. The pilot who deserves the credit for getting them here has since then been killed and we were deeply saddened. He was a fine, clean-cut youth way above the average.

Mrs. Thompson and I unpacked and stored the food in our storeroom and stood back and grinned. We knew it wouldn't last the duration but it was a goodly supply of food and we were grateful. Now the men will have some surprise treats.

The second big surprise package came while Mrs. Thompson was on leave. It was brought back from Kunming by Lt. Ankrim, our Special Services officer—about sixty nonfiction and reference books covering a great many subjects—a large theatrical box containing wigs, costumes, and make-up—musical instruments: trumpet, E flat sax, clarinet, violin, and guitar—transcription machine—a box of transcription records of U.S. radio broadcasts—three boxes of playing cards—and some athletic equipment. I practically tore myself to pieces in my excitement.

Needless to say, the supplies are now being fully used. From the material sent from India I've made sixteen pairs of burnt orange draperies for both wings, all by hand. The color, both inside and out, is invigorating. I'm sure Mrs. Kerr would approve of the Snack Bar. We had talked of color schemes when she was here. It has been done in burnt orange, blue, and Chinese red. After burning all the furniture with blow torches we painted the paneling of the Snack Bar itself a lovely bright medium blue with Chinese red trim on the inner edges of the paneling. The nine table tops and thirty-six chair seats are painted the same blue with Chinese red on the sides—the thickness of the wood. All this has been varnished. Six coolie hats have been painted blue with a wide Chinese red border and inverted over the light bulbs. The coffee container was painted brown. I'm also making small fringed doilies of heavy grayish white material for each table to hold a vase of flowers, salt, pepper, and sugar. It's a colorful room and yet masculine. At present it is used as much as the other wing for general activities and for the time being it is graced by the piano.

With the books Lt. Ankrin brought us, our library has now taken on an imposing appearance. We have a full bookcase of mystery and detective books with the complete list arranged alphabetically by authors posted in view, a full two-sided bookcase of fiction with the complete list posted on the side of the case. The posted list shows them grouped under types: adventure, biographical, classic, romance, sea stories, short stories, travel, western, plays, etc. There's a whole bookcase of nonfiction and reference books with a posted list according to subject: geography, music, education, military, religion, poetry, etc. The books on all the shelves are arranged by authors and each book has the author's initial painted in white on the binding. But how does one teach men to put books back where they belong? I'd give my last bottle of perfume if someone would tell me—a rather rash statement but I guess my perfume is safe.

We have a new Sgt. lined up as Chairman of the Skit Committee. We're searching out theatrical talent on the Base and hope to put on a number of good skits on the future Wednesday nights. With our large theatrical box we have an extra incentive.

The new instruments have given our jazz band additional impetus. Already we have discovered some men who were big time players back in the States. They're breaking in the instruments and likewise strengthening their embouchures which have become flabby with nonuse. We're all looking forward to the super band that will result.

I have been very tired this last week from the strenuous month we have had and yet so terribly happy and satisfied with the development of the program due to the new supplies.

II—Problems Encountered

Many men recently have asked for a log book to check on men from their home states and towns. We started ruling sheets of paper but before we continue with this big project we are wondering if Red Cross has a book we can use for this purpose. It would save us time and provide us with a better book than we could make.

It is difficult keeping our classical records from being broken when they are used daily and kept in cardboard boxes piled one on the other. Does Red Cross have any albums they could send us? Even if we have a filing cabinet built, we still would need albums. And speaking of records, are we allowed any more?

The jazz band is trying to get going with no music. Bert Schaefer from APO 465 sent us 24 copies of popular sheet music which the men have enjoyed tremendously. But what are the chances for some standard orchestrations, and also manuscript paper for orchestrating our own? Is there a chance for a bass drum, a tenor sax, a trombone, and an accordion? We have excellent players for these instruments. Could a piano tuner be sent over to tune our piano and put it in better shape and also fix our reed organ for chapel services? We have no one on the Base who can do that. The C.O. has checked carefully. I've never learned how to do this and furthermore I don't have the time.

The men long for more magazines. Could more be sent and a greater variety of them—especially the kind men like?

Could any suggestions be sent on making cushions for our chairs before I cover them? Mrs. Kerr made a good suggestion of using burlap stuffed with straw but we can't get straw. Would newspaper wadded into burlap work—if we could get enough old newspapers? I did that with two hassocks in the States and it was very satisfactory but, of course, they weren't sat on daily by muscular men.

III—Activities of Volunteers

Two of our enlisted men borrowed blow torches and burned all of our furniture including the Snack Bar.* One of them worked for three days with Wing (a Chinese man) painting the panels of the Snack Bar, the table tops, and chair seats and coolie hat lamp shades. After the paint had dried, they varnished all the furniture.

Four enlisted men worked one night from 8:00 to 11:30 painting the authors' initials on each of our newly acquired reference books, filing the new library cards as I typed them, helping in rearranging the whole library.

Cpl. Young is teaching the Chinese class.

A Sgt. is orchestrating music for the jazz band.

Another Sgt. has volunteered his services in heading up a Skit Program Committee for Wednesday nights.

Two different enlisted men work behind the Snack Bar each Sunday night helping with the refreshments.

Enlisted men and officers have furnished music for us each Sunday night while refreshments are being served.

Men have volunteered to go with us to the Base Dispensary once a week to carry the necessary equipment and set it up for the transcription Broadcast Programs we are giving there.

Men have taken pictures of our activities, made equipment

*For those not familiar with this process it sounds as though we were bent on destruction but we were really creating a more ritzy effect. Blow torching the wood brought out the grain and, when done carefully, created a two tone effect of light and a darker tan in varied interesting patterns.

152

for our Snack Bar and wooden dice for Monopoly and Football Games—original dice had been depleted.

IV-Program

Monday—CHINESE CLASSES from 7:00–8:00

Cpl. Young has proven to be a most capable and likable instructor and class attendance has consequently increased to over 50 men. We have the Victrola records that follow the *Chinese Phrase Books*. These are used both during the lessons and available for the men at any other time. The textbooks and guidebooks are kept on top of the bookstalls with a "Help yourself" sign. They go like hotcakes. Beginning next Monday we're using the last ten or fifteen minutes of the class for questions from the men on phrases they want particularly to say in Chinese.

MENS' CHORUS—8:00–9:00

The men are working on a program to be presented in the near future on a Sunday evening after church. New voices have been added every rehearsal night. They are singing a variety of music—sacred, folk songs, popular, and ballads.

Wednesday

Sept. 6—MONTE CARLO NIGHT—Every unit was represented and the hall overflowed with men and excitement

Sept. 13—The hall was to be closed for quartering new men. Plans were changed late in the day so we simply had Open House

Sept. 20—BINGO PARTY—The lights went off but everyone present—about 125—participated by flashlight. Lt. Jones and Sgt. McMorrow assisted in the distribution of material and calling off numbers. There was much humor and many side jokes which kept the evening alive. We used 25 Red Cross Christmas boxes for prizes.

Sept. 27—BRIDGE TOURNAMENT and Reading in the Left Wing. Jazz Band and Letter writing in the Right Wing. GAME NIGHT in the hall—the men making their choices of Pinochle, Hearts, Chess, Checkers, Dominoes, Monopoly, or Football Game. Red Cross Christmas boxes or cigarettes were given to all winners.

Friday—LECTURES 7:30–8:30

Sept. 1—"War Theaters" presented by Major Gibbons, Captain Marshall, and Captain Bass.... Sept. 15—"Snow Mountain," experiences in the Salmon Campaign presented by Major Hockley.... Sept. 22—"War Theaters" continued.

CLASSICAL MUSIC HOUR—8:45–10:00—One of our men designed and built me a candelabra so we have extra candle light and also the light, warmth, and cheer from our fireplace. I give a brief intro before each composition. Interest has increased so that more and more we hear the men playing classical records during the day in the Rec. Hall. Friday night is a relaxing and soul refreshing hour of the week for me as well as for the men.

SPECIAL PARTIES and MEETINGS ... Sept. 8–27th Troop Carrier Squadron meeting and party with the Rec. Hall closed to all others. Mrs. Thompson and I were guests of honor and were extremely moved by the evening's events. The party brought us closer to all of the men ... Sept. 22–25th Fighter Squadron meeting from 9:00—10:00 ... Sept. 29—25th Fighter Squadron meeting and party with the Rec. Hall closed to all others. Mrs. Thompson and I were guests of honor.

Sunday—JAZZ BAND SESSIONS, and FREE REFRESHMENTS served in the Snack Bar following church. Each Sunday these have been highly attended. There has been a grand spirit and a better opportunity than any other time in the week to meet more of the men personally.

DAYTIME UNPLANNED ACTIVITIES—There has been tremendous use of our library—of newspapers, magazines, writing tables, records (jazz and classical), games and athletic equipment, a soaking up of heat from our two fireplaces which have been kept going each day since Sept. 9th during the cold, chilly, rainy spell, use of the piano almost continuously (even though it needs tuning badly—it drives my ear a little wacky) and also the other instruments which have come to us, spontaneous jam sessions ever so often.

MUSIC HOUR at DISPENSARY began Sept. 27th to be continued weekly. Three of us carried the amplifier, transcription machine, records, and plug-in board over to the Base Dispensary to play broadcasts of Bob Hope, Harry James, Spot Light Bands, etc. We visited with each one of the twenty patients. They welcomed the broadcasts heartily.

V—Future Plans

To open the Snack Bar as soon as the Resident Engineers (who are terrifically busy at this time) can install the water system and drain pipes and as soon as we get the material Dr. May promised he would send us.

To complete the Left Wing by making new chair seats and back cushions covering them with our new material.

To complete the murals on the walls of the Hall and make new draperies when the dark green striped material comes.

To complete all our courts for all outdoor activities.

To visit the Task Force and men in remote areas. Now that Mr. Ginsburg is here and now that a good Special Services man has been assigned to the Hall, it looks plausible. We could use a Chinese girl.

VI—Human Interest Stories

On the morning of Sept. 10th I rode in a Jeep down the field to Hangar 2 taking with me books, stationery, and games. It has been raining continuously and the air was chilly and penetrating. My heart ached for the men, most of them young boys, when I saw them just over from India and living in that open, cold, and muddy hangar. There was no other place for them on the Base. It had rained so steadily that every man had wet feet and a damp disposition. I wandered among them—most of them were in their cots trying to keep warm—and promised I'd bring them hot chocolate in the afternoon. We made a large supply in the Mess Hall and took it back to the hangar. I served many men in bed, chatted with them, and told them to come to the Rec. Hall (a mile away) as soon as they could. I promised them a fire. Later the Hall was crammed with the men pouring in. I have a picture of them crowded like sardines in a can. They sat on the floor. We had fires in both wings all day and night. The men took off their shoes, dried their feet, and reveled in the warmth of the rooms. Our Rec. Hall never gave greater service or was more appreciated than during those five cold, rainy days.

A Staff Sgt., of his own free will, spent the better part of three days blow torching, painting, and varnishing in our Snack Bar. I was so grateful that I invited him down to cook dinner with us over our small stove in our quarters. I suddenly realized that though it was a nice gesture, I had no food. I told my plight to four other men who graciously came to my rescue with supplies. We had a delicious supper cooked by ourselves. He left at 11:00. It sounds as though it were a romantic night and he the envy of the men on the Base. Well, it *was* romantic—our own peculiar and particular kind of romance here in this barren place where we long for some beauty. We made five pair of drapes for the Snack Bar. He measured and pinned and I sewed.

VII—Changes from the Normal Trend

An increase of men to the Rec. Hall so that suddenly the building seems too small to accommodate them. More transients than usual have been using our club and unfortunately they don't have the same concern for the facilities as the regular Base men. It's not their building.

The increase of supplies we have received has made for an increased program.

P.S. I still feel most fortunate to be stationed with Naomi Thompson (Tommy). She is wholeheartedly concerned for the welfare and happiness of the men and gives unselfishly of her time and energy to the job.

25

An Ode to China—One Time

The following "Ode To China—One Time" was written by a GI who presented me with a copy. I neglected to have him sign it and can't remember his name, which is unfortunate. It's a dismal picture of a country of warm loving people and yet wartime doesn't help one to see the rosy side of things and much of what he has pictured does bring back the dirty, dreary, and pitiful side. Many times we saw the worst and not the best. Like him, in his closing lines, I'm glad I was there. I would give so very much to look at the faces of the Chinese who meant a great deal to me, who worked with me, and struggled with me for the happiness of our men away from home. I wish I could hug those Chinese once more—men and women.

AN ODE TO CHINA—ONE TIME

If I were an artist with nothing to do
I'd paint a picture,
A composite view
Of historic China in which I'd show
Vision of contrast,
The high and the low.

There'd be towering mountains, a deep green lea,
Filthy brats
Yelling 'Ding hao' at me;
High plumed horses and colorful carts,
Two toned tresses
On hustling tarts.

I'd show Chinese coolies, seemingly merry,
Dejected old women

With too much to carry;
A dignified gent with Fu Manchu beard,
Bare bottomed children
With both ends smeared.

Temples and graves and houses too,
Houses on mountains—
A marvelous view;
Homes made of wood, bricks made of mud;
People covered with scabs,
Scurvy and crud;

Poverty and want, a man practically nude,
Searching through garbage
For much needed food;
Stately temples with high toned bells,
Covered shelters
With horrible smells.

Mounding catacombs—a place for the breeze,
Goats wading in filth
Up to their knees;
Revealing statues, all details complete,
A sensuous beauty
With sores on her feet.

Creeping roadways—a spangled team,
Alleys that wind
Like a dope fiend's dream;
Rice paddies set on the side of a hill.
A sidewalk latrine
With privacy nil.

Two by four shops with shelving all bare,
Gesturing merchants
Flailing the air;
Lumbering carts hogging the road,
Old nondescript trucks

Frequently towed.

Diminutive donkeys loaded for bear,
Man-drawn taxis
Seeking a fare;
Determined pedestrians courting disaster,
Walking in gutters
Where moving is faster;

Chinese drivers all accident bound
Weaving and twisting
To cover the ground;
Homemade brooms tied to a stick,
Used on the streets
To clean off the bricks.

Rickshas and pushcarts blocking the path,
Street corner sloppies
Needing a bath;
Soldiers galore with manners quite mild,
Prolific women
All heavy with child.

Arrogant wretches picking up snipes,
Miniatured flats
Of various types.
Listless housewives with tiny bound feet,
Washing and cooking
Right out in the street.

The family wash of tattle-tale gray
Hangs from a cord
Blocking your way;
Native coffee, ugh, what a mixture,
Filthy buildings
With nary a fixture,

Chinese zoot suiters flashily dressed,

160

Bare footed beggars
Looking depressed;
Mud smeared children clustering about
Filling their jugs
From the community spout.

A dutiful mother with a look of despair
Picking the lice
From her small daughter's hair;
Capable craftsmen, skilled with the art,
Decrepit old shack
Falling apart.

Intricate needlework out on display
Surrounded by filth,
Rot and decay;
Elegant caskets carved out by hand,
Odorous shops
Where leather is tanned.

A shoemaker's shop, a black market store,
Crawling with vermin,
No screen on the door.
No mention of war scars visible yet,
These are things
We try to forget.
I'm glad I came but am anxious to go;
The Chinese can have China,
I'm ready to blow.

26

Progress, Slow but Sure

Dear Mom and Dad:

This is a follow-up letter from the last club report I sent you—a few odds and ends that might be of interest and some pictures the men have given me.

Tommy's and my living room pleases us immensely. I've made covers and colored pillows for our two army cots turning them into real sofas, also draperies for the windows that have Chinese window screens, and cloth covered backs for our four chairs. On the floor we have four rugs from India, white background with colorful Indian figures. Our walls are covered with all sorts of interesting things we've purchased in the markets. We're crazy about the room and the men who come here for meetings etc., say it's like home.

For the club, I've finished making cushions and backs for the sixteen lounging chairs in the Left Wing and all by hand. I made the cushions out of burlap stuffed with cotton I purchased in the village. I had to tie off each cushion in a number of places to keep the cotton from bunching up through many sittings. It was a big job for the cushions measure 23″ by 20″ and are 3″ deep. The backs are 36″ by 23″. When I finished I sent them to the area tailor who covered them with the new material that had been sent from India. They are fairly soft and colorful and truly make a big difference in that wing.

The Reading Corner has improved greatly since we've received more supplies. There's a reading table, chairs, magazine racks, newspaper table, and lounging chairs. On the walls I've hung scrolls and Chinese figures and on the shelves everything Chinese I could find in the Yunnanyi market to fill in the empty spaces. The men like the womanly touch.

I'm sending you two pictures of our staff sent to us from

Kunming Headquarters: 1st and 2nd cook, dish washer, accountant, and a cashier. As you can see I'm pictured with them or have I changed so much that I look like the Orientals? They are a sweet group, well trained and easy to work with. The second picture includes a woman we had to hire for laundry and for cleaning.

Our Snack Bar is beautiful and the men love it and so do I. I described it quite fully in the report I sent you but you'd have to see it to appreciate it. Unfortunately I have no picture that really shows it. One enclosed picture shows me smiling proudly in front of the bright colored striped drapes I made and behind a high stack of doughnuts. In the second I'm standing in front of a window drapery that shows the varied stripes running horizontally but you can't enjoy the exciting colors in black and white photography. In the third the Staff Sgt., who did so much work blowtorching and painting, and I are having a cup of coffee and chatting.

Bill, who did a lot of work around the club, has signed his name, Bill Humence, on the picture of his precious collection. Don't you love it? It's a masterpiece display of over one hundred beauties—actresses and models in bathing suits or other scanty costumes—covering a large wall. What an inspiration for all the men who've seen it—something to fight for.

I have only one picture to send you of two Chinese soldiers who appear in much better shape than most soldiers I've seen. I see them again and again in long straggling lines appearing sick, thin and worn, their clothes in rags, thin sandals on their feet, and with scanty equipment. It's a sad and discouraging sight.

I have been in on some of the Chinese class lessons and have found them enormously helpful for I have to communicate with our Chinese staff. I blurt out words to them feeling quite proficient and then they laugh at me—all in good humor. It's a darned hard language to deal with.

I'm thoroughly proud of my Classical Music Hour by Candlelight, delighted at the men's response. In the beginning I expected about fifteen but one hundred plus turn out each time. When the first fireplace was built, we had the fire burning which added to the relaxing, the comfort and beauty of it all. The Men's Chorus has been real fun, singing everything imaginable. We've sung for church services occasionally and expect to sing in the big show the men are writing and staging. On Sunday nights we have spontaneous programs and singing is always a part of those.

I have my picture taken constantly alone, with someone, or in a group but almost never see the developed copies. I suppose they're sent home for development. I'm lucky to have the pictures given me though most of them are unsigned. In one enclosed picture I'm wearing a pair of lovely white sandals a man brought me from his last flight into India. He'd take no money for them. In the second picture he's clowning as he hugs me saying: "I'll take my pay in a big hug." Another does have writing on the back: " It's been wonderful knowing you. Thanks for making life here more bearable. Hank" I'm grateful for the picture of those men from the hangar 3 jammed into our Rec. Hall without even an inch between them. They're all grinning so I guess they've already felt the heat from the fireplaces (our men had built a second one) and dryness of the room. Blessed dryness, out of the rain and mud and dampness, and blessed warmth, out of the miserable chill. I'll see you in my next letter. Take awfully good care for I'll be home before very long . . . Much love, Eddie

* * *

A corporal handed the following to me at the club. He was leaving the next day on his way back to the States. I was delighted and grateful for the tribute. I wish he had signed it.

MORALE
What is this thing they call Morale?
Is it a book, a game, a gal?
Is it soft music by candlelight?
Is it a smile to set things right?
Is it a song to fill the air?
Is it a ribbon in soft brown hair?
Is it a friendly word to all
To amuse us, thrill us, and recall

A bit of home in far-flung places,
A little love in friendly faces?
Is it a slice of chocolate cake,
A cup of coffee that they make?
Is it a chair with cushions soft
Wherein we're wafted to clouds aloft?
Or is it just a friend, a pal,
That we call our Red Cross Gal?

*   *   *

Yunnanyi (8)

My dear wonderful Parents:

I've been so busy at the club that letter writing has suffered. I apologize. I can't even send copies of my last two reports for they're unreadable. My copy paper is so very thin and my carbon paper is worn beyond any valuable usage. I'm enclosing some more pictures given me by the men for your interest and to save for me when I arrive home.

I wish I had good pictures of the planes that I've lived with at Yunnanyi and especially of the pilots who flew them, but am grateful for the pictures given me. I've known many of the pilots well and we've become friends. When one has become killed on a mission or flying over the Hump it has been almost too sad to bear. Fine young men, their lives cut short in the horrors of war. Most of the enclosed pictures are unsigned, which I regret . . . However, one says on the back: "I'll never forget your lovely self. Bew." Two were taken by George Clayton "photographing movies of air dropping missions over northern Burma." One by Claude Hockley shows "a large parachuting scene over Burma."

Other enclosed pictures show glimpses of Chinese and our surrounding area: a well dressed man (belonging to a minority group) with his arm in a sling, a village gateway with a three tiered roof top, a woman bent over with an enormous load on her

165

back, a boy carrying buckets of slop on a shoulder yoke, a group of children in front of a mud brick building, a grandmother with grandson, a family cooking their meal out on the street, two men and a young girl, a street scene in Yunnanyi crowded with Chinese (many of them holding the lovely watercolored paper parasols to shield them from the sun), a woman of one of the lesser minorities, a woman weaving in the street, a swaying bridge (I stepped on one and was sure I would tumble into the water far below), a coolie leading an oxcart with a very heavy load (far better than hauling the load on his back), and men taking care of their precious baby boys.

On Thanksgiving Day, Congress promised that every U. S. soldier in the world would have turkey for dinner. It didn't happen at Yunnanyi but, of course, we're out of this world. Sometimes we're not exactly sure where we are. So for Thanksgiving we had the same old hog's feed in the Mess Hall.

A few nights ago I had ICE CREAM. I don't know who made it but a pilot had frozen it up high in his plane and brought it to me. What an amazing surprise and treasurable gift. I closed my eyes and with each taste I thought I was in heaven.

Tommy and I are with men almost constantly—men walk us home from the club, take us on trips, come down to our quarters for special meetings, or even come in small groups uninvited. It's a natural part of our lives. It was through music that Tommy and I fell into a special friendly relationship with two pilots. Barney (alias) had a glorious baritone voice and Ted (alias) a beautiful tenor voice. Tommy sang soprano and I alto. The four of us began singing music we had on hand but discovered that the three of us could improvise so there began music sessions at our quarters after the club had closed and at times when there was no conflicting activity.

Our improvised singing was amazing. We became so sensitive to each other that if two, especially the inner tenor and alto, began on the same note one would quickly shift to another pitch so as to preserve the four-part harmony. There was no audience and no recorder so the world will never know what it's missed. But it wasn't for the world. It was just for our exquisite pleasure. I have a picture of Barney and me taken on a long Jeep ride trip visiting some of the villages where Americans were really strangers. On leaving one village we were followed by a crowd of kids who were determined to get on our Jeep and go with us. It was a day of warm enchanting encounters and also delightful laughter. However, Barney's emotions began to need release beyond singing and the strain on me became too great. I was relieved when he was sent to India for a long overdue leave. It was shortly after he returned that he flew a mission over north Africa. His plane was shot down and he was killed.* I love you both and miss you greatly, Eddie

*At Christmastime 1946 I received a surprise card from Ted: "Thank God for the American Red Cross and a girl like you. I once again thank you for all your work in making life bearable in China. I'll never forget your undying efforts to show us all a good time." Enclosed were two pictures. One of him with his seven-member crew and the other in his plane waving.

27

Arriving at Liège, Belgium, Combat Zone

Dearest Folks:

We are now in Belgium, bag and baggage. It was a lucky break for us. We, along with another hospital, managed to get into permanent buildings for a change. The others will have tent setups. We are located in an old Belgium Cavalry Post recently used by the Germans for Prisoners of War, so I'm told. Our area covers much space but is compact and the buildings are in good shape. We are going through the process of drawing appliance to convert the building and horse stalls on the ground floors into wards, clinics, Red Cross etc. It looks impossible at a glance but our engineers will soon have this Cavalry Post torn apart, the horse stalls all out, new floors and partitions laid and no one will know the old place when the Americans get through with the process. It will be a glorified hospital fully equipped and again the 56th will have a show place as a side line to operation.

It's so wonderful to live in buildings again, have feet on wooden floors, have electricity, running water, and toilet facilities all inside for the winter months ahead. We have a very attractive fireplace in our room but it's closed off and we use a small stove for heat with compressed coal for fuel which is plentiful. The nurses have a large building for their living quarters with wide spacious halls. The rooms are lovely. Ours overlooks the street corners with plenty of traffic going by and people to watch and is the nicest, we think.

We are in a large city of about 400,000 so there's much of interest here. Already I have had a free tour in an army Jeep all over the place going out on business to various sections of the city. The shop windows are full of amazing things but prices are high according to the value of the money exchange. The U.S. gov-

168

ernment discourages buying and really gyps us in rate of exchange of money. We pay four times what things are worth as a result. Ice cream is advertised everywhere. Some of the girls have tried it and say it's similar to American sherbet. The Belgians use skimmed milk and the ingredients are poor but it's called ice cream. Fruit and vegetables in the markets are plentiful—large bunches of grapes, huge grapes, and not too expensive. We're careful about eating food outside. We wash fruit with chlorinated water. Flowers and plants are gorgeous and plentiful. Chrysanthemums are beautiful. It's so good to be in a city again and yet sufficiently removed from the main section.

This week I expect to go to Paris on business. Our C.O. will give me a Recon and trailer to bring back supplies. Getting supplies through Red Cross is quite a problem and we never seem to have adequate supplies. Red Cross buys through the Army Quartermaster but transportation has held things up. While in Paris I'll do the town. It will take several days away from here.

Two nurses, my secretary and I live together and are congenial. We lived together in our tent before. Our room has two large double French windows, a large marble fireplace with mantel and huge beveled framed mirror over it. The two doors have padded red leather lining inside. We sleep on steel cots with real springs. What a change! Also we have a lovely large desk in the center of the room which is certainly an incentive for writing letters—much easier than writing on a cot in a tent with poor light. We have a gorgeous chandelier over the desk in the center high ceiling, paneled walls and clothes closets and small stands with shelves for extra belongings. All we need is a radio and a plant with flowers. The latter is possible but I'm not sure about the first.

Our Mess Hall is in another building across from us. At first we had to eat out of our mess gear but now we have cafeteria service and sit at tables with dishes. What luxury! At night, for a pastime, we turn off the lights and watch the buzz bombs from our windows—an interesting sight spitting fire. They travel fast and don't stop here so don't worry. They go over all the time.

I got a permanent before leaving France, only $5.00 and it was a really good one. My hair is real short now. I just comb it out and I'm all set. It looks good.

We have beautiful tiled showers available every day for us. It's going to be easy here to keep clean and keep our clothes in condition. We were issued another combat suit recently. Imagine all that has been given to us—free sightseeing and our meals at 25 cents each. And think of all the interesting experiences we are getting and sights we are seeing. I'm afraid it's going to be dull returning to the States after all this. Yet we're anxious for the war to be over and to be able to see our families.

Don't overdo, Dad, save a bit for us when we return. I'll watch eagerly for the Christmas package and the fruit cake you're sending. Thank you so very much for all your efforts in keeping us three kids supplied and happy during this period of separation . . . Love, Dot

*　　*　　*

1998 Notes

Liège, Belgium, bordering on Germany, was Dot's last "stamping ground." I'm adding some information that was not mentioned in her letters.

Belgium is a small country about the size of Maryland, inhabited by the Flemish who live in Flanders along the North Sea and speak Dutch, and the Walloons who live on the southern plains and speak French. There's also a small eastern section of German speaking Belgians. Brussels, the capital, is bilingual. Though speaking different languages, all the Belgians resemble each other in appearance and in their efficiency and hospitality and mania for cleanliness. Liège is especially famed for hospitality as Dot mentions. It's a strange combination forming a country that became an independent nation in 1830 set up by the great powers as a buffer nation at the heart of western Europe. It's bordered by France on the south, Netherlands on the north, Germany on the east, and England on the west though separated from England by the North Sea.

Belgium is the second most densely populated country in Europe, Netherlands being the first. It was in this country that

Napoleon met his Waterloo in 1815. In WW I it was in Flanders that multitudes of Belgians were killed and homes and buildings destroyed by the Germans. As Dot writes home in December 1944, Paris has already been liberated and since December 16th the Germans have been heavily bombing this area of the Walloons. Hitler hopes to break through and take Antwerp which is not only the fifth largest port in the world but is also the fastest turn-around-time airport in the world and, at this time, the Allies' most important port.

The buzz bombs Dot refers to were inaccurate and often terrifying because there was no way of knowing where they would land.

*   *   *

Belgium (2)

Dearest Eddie:

We're in Belgium back in combat zone. The buzz bombs are a curious sight with the flare coming out behind and fascinating to watch. So far they're flying over us and not aiming at us.

Our engineers are doing an enormous job converting this old Cavalry Post with its horse stalls (recently used by the Germans for prisoners of war) into a hospital but nothing is impossible in the American Army.

Today is Election Day in the States. I sent in my vote and am wondering how things are going. Though we're still in early November the main shops are full of all kinds of toys, since St. Nicholas Day is Dec. 6th—Children's Christmas. Then everyone celebrates Christmas on the 25th. Most Belgiums don't send Christmas cards but the stores are full of New Year's cards. I bought three Christmas cards for souvenirs and they were very hard to find. They're strange, very different from ours and colored more by the war than the spirit of Christmas. Paper and envelopes are scarce and expensive.

Ice cream signs appear all over the city but their ice cream is more like our sherbet. People here eat ice cream in the middle of the afternoon like the English drink their tea. In some places sundaes can be bought with a choice of syrups, nuts on top and a wafer for decoration. They're real fancy looking but disappointing in taste.

Today was Communion Sunday. I've persuaded the chaplain to let me play hymns softly during communion. He loves the old evangelistic type songs but I manage to get in some good music in between. I guess some of the men like the other kind so who am I to decide. The chapel, when finished, will be the old horse stalls converted. A bunch of Belgian civilians are now cleaning up the place.

We're beginning to get green salads served in the mess now. Tonight we had a raw carrot and celery salad—the first celery since leaving the States. We all went a little crazy in our pleasure over it. We've missed green stuff so much.

A few days ago we got mixed up coming home from the center of the city. Using my best French accent I asked the way to our location and as a result we had a personal escort to our hospital including two small boys who insisted on going the full way. Everyone is anxious to help us. My French has been coming back to me and now that we have the people so close my speech should improve rapidly. We can stay out till 9:30 P.M. and are taking advantage of it while our hospital is being set up.

Yesterday Fran and I returned to the center of the city and surprisingly we found that we could ferry across the Messe River which cuts the city in half rather than walking down to a bridge and back on the other side. We were directed on to the ferry without purchasing a ticket—Americans can travel free. The array of things in the stores was utterly amazing—anything you might want and plenty of it. But we understand that the Belgian people have to have coupons for many items. The store people seemed anxious to sell to the Americans. We've been told not to buy clothing, shoes, or food.

Disobeying orders, on the way back we bought lovely tomatoes. There were gorgeous bunches of celery. When we tried to buy a bunch, the storekeeper insisted on giving it to us. We also insisted on paying. He won so we ended up by giving him one franc which is worth about two and a half cents. Ridiculous! We bought some apples, and pears and lettuce. Last night we toasted bread (from our Mess Hall) in our room and had toasted tomato and lettuce sandwiches with crisp celery on the side. Delicious! How I'd love some Hellmanns' Mayonnaise and pickles and olives. We don't lack for food by any means for we have wonderful food in the army but it's heavy so we go after fresh fruit and vegetables like starved people.

This is such a change from being out in the wilderness of Normandy, at least it seemed like wilderness living in tents out in cow pastures and clay mud with towns around us in ruins and the peasants in that section attempting to live in their ruined homes. This is a modern city with all conveniences. Children of the middle classes and up wear fur coats as do the women, and the women even carry fur-covered shopping bags. Tell me what you want and I'll send it but don't ask for a Belgium Draft Horse though there are plenty here . . . My love to you, Dot

Belgium (3)

Dear Folks:

We were enjoying a relaxed life and seeing the city when all of a sudden we were told that patients were arriving at our hospital. The engineers had just begun the construction and everything was in a mess but all went to work concentrating on one building. Debris was carried down one side of the stairways while cots, bedside tables, medical equipment, etc. were brought up the other side. I've never seen such fast action. The rooms were made ready. A temporary operating room and clinics were set up and the patients arrived—numbers of them. Along with them came the robot bombing which you probably read about. In two days' time we suddenly received more patients who were evacuated from another General Hospital here which was hit by one of the bombs.

Two other buildings were opened and there was no time for cleaning or scrubbing. The cots were barely put up before the patients arrived and were put in them. That first night I was on the wards helping calm the patients and covering them with blankets as the nurses and ward men were taking temperatures and doing their routine work. For a whole week we were in a hubbub.

We of Red Cross found a little room where we placed a cabinet for our comfort articles and necessary supplies, set up small tables and chairs for the patients to write letters and play games and a place for them to read and listen to the radio. Patients swarmed the place but most of our work has been on the wards. Our hospital had been operating as a holding point but many of the patients remained longer than we expected and also we are getting new ones.

Now as I write you the engineers have practically completed the hospital and have started on the Red Cross area. Hopefully we will be able to move in the last of the week. We were given two large ground floor rooms which were full of five-foot horse stalls when we first came. You should see them now—the two rooms 60' x 80' in length and 30' in width. An archway has been cut in the wall connecting them. We have half of one of the large buildings. From the large archway in the center of the building we have a large entrance with double doors. Inside along the wide corridor are offices built in, a storeroom, two latrines for staff and patients, then a large space to the rear of the first room that will be a writing room and a library. The next room will be an open recreation room except for one room to the rear which will be a craft and carpenter shop.

The Belgium Red Cross have been wonderful to us. They're getting furniture, desks, billiard tables, ping pong tables, easy chairs, etc. They already have brought us fresh fruit, flowers, Belgium tobacco (we can't get American cigarettes) and English books. They're helping us get Christmas trees and evergreens and holly and decorations. We're planning a big Christmas celebration for the patients with individual gifts furnished by the Belgium Red Cross and American Red Cross, Christmas cellophane stockings containing candy, cigarettes, etc., a Santa Claus, special refreshments, and, of course, caroling. Belgium youngsters are coming to sing. There will be Christmas trees on each ward and a prize for the ward having the best trimmed tree. Christmas is near and we want to be in our new quarters by then but it will take tall hustling.

I haven't heard from Eddie or Vint in ages. I wish we could all be together at this time. I'm getting more and more lonesome for the family as Christmas approaches...All my love to you, Dot

Belgium (4)

Dearest Folks:

I hadn't heard from you in over a month and a half and I've been worried. Then last night your letter of November 18th arrived and I was so grateful to receive it. I resolved I would answer immediately but writing has been difficult for there's so much happening all the time.

We have been in the midst of things here with buzz bombings. Our men began reconstructuring this place into a hospital and suddenly patients arrived. Soon we were flooded with them, every nook and corner became occupied. Construction has continued, with work being carried on around the patients. Then the back part of our hospital was hit by a buzz bomb. Fortunately no one was killed. I came out of it with a few cuts from flying glass but it was nothing. What is sad, so very sad, is seeing patients with amputations.

What a mess that buzz bomb made. It held us back in the construction, plaster and glass down all over, some of the beams were moved out of place and roofs blown off or wavy. We're still repairing from that. Other hospitals were also hit. Some had to close out but the 56th is a persistent bunch. Between the constant flow of patients in and out and the strain of uncertainty of these buzz bombs we have all become very tired. Yet everyone carries on and with inconveniences. This is an exceptional group of people I'm with.

Our Red Cross quarters are as disorganized as the rest with construction here too. Our offices, storeroom, latrines are built but the electrical fixtures and plumbing still have to be done. We have lights but they are inadequate for our needs. We haven't been able to get all the furniture we desire as yet and we haven't set up our library and writing room or craft shop. However, we do have plenty of small tables and chairs in our large Recreation Room, a borrowed piano from the Belgiums until ours has been renovated and a radio. The ambulatory patients certainly use our quarters fully. Belgium Red Cross personnel have been wonderful to us bringing us apples and other items for the patients and offering help. They are real friends.

Christmas was lovely in spite of the strain and confusion from bombs. We brought in local entertainers, had a big Christmas Eve party, gave out Red Cross Christmas boxes, had two patients dressed as Santa to take the boxes on the wards for bed patients, sang Christmas carols and were entertained by Belgium children. Our own personnel had a Christmas tree, bending every effort into making it nice for all. Everyone had a good turkey dinner, a real treat.

I'm afraid the people at home were too optimistic about this war ending. We have patients direct from the front so we get some first hand information. In fact we've been practically on the front ourselves. These men have been through hell and there isn't anything I wouldn't do for them during their stay with us. They are most appreciative and have fine spirits.

I must stop and get to work. I got my office partially set up yesterday but the stove isn't in yet. At least I have a table to work on until I get a desk and with my coat on I keep fairly warm. Things come slowly but we're adjusted to that. I haven't heard from Eddie or Vint in ages so I'm glad to get word of them through you. I didn't get your Christmas card sent nor your package. I long for the time when we'll be all together. Hold On Tight...All my love, Dot

28

Rest Camp at Kwabsiany, China

Dear Mom and Dad:

It's almost Christmas, Dec. 19, and I feel so apart from those I love. I'm among strangers and have received no mail for a month. Lately I've been thinking of our Christmas holidays—our lovely tree, the unwrapping of gifts, caroling all over town, parties.

About a week ago I received word to pack my luggage and report by the next plane to Kunming and that from there I would go to my new assignment to set up a club at APO 210. I was shocked. I didn't want to leave. I had become attached to all the men. I had accomplished wonders in the club and as I looked around the club I felt as though it were mine. I notified all the pilots to have all planes "fully loaded" for the next few days for I still had a few dreams for the club that I wanted to bring into reality. The pilots were more than agreeable.

In five months I had made so many wonderful friendships of men who were still there, although other men were coming and leaving constantly, it warmed me through and through to have them pour into the club and into our quarters to express their regrets. I felt more than repaid for all that I had done.

Before leaving APO 488 I had a thorough examination by the doctor. Generally speaking I'm in excellent condition but he said my blood pressure was down and I showed every evidence of fatigue. He gave me iron and ammonium citrate tablets to take and also high potency vitamin tablets and some tablets to quiet my nerves. He suggested I take off a few days in Kunming for sleeping.

So I finally left my old stamping ground where I had experienced my first bombings, life in a slit trench, and scores of new adventures and flew to Kunming. We arrived too late that night to get transportation for my luggage. The next morning I found that the ever present Chinese thieves had gotten into the plane. My barracks bag had been mostly emptied. The most important things taken were my blue wool bathrobe and two wool sweaters. How I will miss them and all the things taken from me. Those lousy thieves! And darn that Chinese pilot who left the plane unprotected. If this continues I may be leaving China in my PJs.

I reported to Headquarters and was told I was being shipped immediately to the one and only Rest Camp in China. It didn't take me long to pack a few things rolled up in two blankets since my musette bag had been stolen. I was driven to camp in a Jeep and it's here I am now as I write you.

Kunming, that I have mentioned so often, lies on a fertile plain in an amphitheater of mountains and is north of Lake Tien Chih. It's on this blue, blue mountain lake where I'm recuperating. Beyond are the ever fascinating terraced rice fields. I'm a mile and a quarter above sea level in a most healthful climate with marvelous sunshine. A high ranking Chinese General loaned the area, known as Kwabsiany, to the U.S. Army for the convalescence of selected Americans. Kwabsiany is beautiful beyond my ability to describe. Buildings are scattered up the hillside with charming stone paths and flowers galore—jasmines, red geraniums, primroses . . . Three of us have a building nearest the lake all to ourselves with separate bedroom for each and a living room with fireplace. The food is wonderful. We can be alone to sleep, read, write letters or walk outside. Already I feel like a new person and am very grateful to whoever was responsible for sending me here.

I was just called up to the office to answer a telephone call from Headquarters. They had received a radiogram from you inquiring about my health and welfare—said you hadn't heard from me since October. I can't imagine where my letters have gone and am sure you must be worried since I'm told that lately the U.S. headlines have been plugging China. Mr. Taylor said he would radiogram you immediately for that would go faster than a cable from me. I have written regularly. I'll be here till Dec. 23rd and then return to Kunming to await transportation to APO 210, an entirely different section of China where I'll again be on an airfield base and have to start from scratch in a new club to be opened. With a little more sleep I think I'll be ready to tear the place apart and reconstruct it.

I'm trying hard to forget Dick for I know my free-thinking religion is too strong to let me change to his church and he would not be changing to mine. Just before leaving 488, one of our officers, Claude McCarty, flew to India. Claude censored all our mail and knew more about me than anyone around. While there he looked up Dick and spent three hours with him. He came back and reported to me that Dick is deeply in love with me and Mac said: "Eddie, he has so much on the ball that you two would be foolish to break up." His letters have helped me to keep going. His mother wrote me a very beautiful letter: "I have such respect for Dick's judgment that if he loves you I know you must be a very fine person." I guess it's over but I'll always treasure the love we've had . . . . .My love to you, Eddie

The following letter came months later but this seems the appropriate place to insert it. I was deeply appreciative and perhaps more so because it came so long after my leaving Yunnanyi.

HEADQUARTERS 69TH COMPOSITE WING
Office of the Commanding General

APO 627
6 April 1945

Dear Miss Rawson,

      This is a fine time to express our appreciation of what you did, 4, 5, 6 and more months ago. So many times have the personnel of this Headquarters, not to mention the other units referred to the good work you did at Yunnanyi that every few days, I have intended writing to you but always delayed. I wonder how many have received as genuine praise so long after their departure as you have. The officers and men both apparently miss your kindness, spirit, enthusiasm and conscientiousness very much and seem to hope that you will be at a Red Cross Club near them again sometime.

      We all hope that you have a pleasant place and appreciative personnel where you are now and send our continued best wishes.

Sincerely,

J. C. KENNEDY
Brig. Gen., USA

29

Arriving at Chengtu, Szechwan Province

Dearest Mom and Dad:

I had my longest plane ride in China from APO 627 here to Chengtu and arrived December 23rd. My heart sank when I landed. It was as cold as Iceland, bleak and dreary as a magnified picture of my worst dreams. I expected to be stranded for the night and possibly days in that strange area away from nowhere. However, about 9:00 P.M. I received a telephone message that a bed was available for me at the Air Base and that transportation was en route.

On arrival, the sight of the room that would be mine did nothing to raise my dejected spirits. The room was very small, like a prison cell with a cement floor, bare crude looking walls, and one window. An extra cot had been brought in for me which crowded the small space. A nurse (I was surprised to see a female) who was preparing to leave in a few days had her side cluttered with her locker, bedroll, duffel bag, suitcase. When my luggage was dumped beside hers it was a depressing sight to behold. We huddled over a small charcoal brazier fire and stared at each other. At that point my artistic soul was weeping buckets. I missed our Yunnanyi quarters that Tommy and I had made so attractive. I missed Tommy. I missed our Yunnanyi club that I had made homelike. I missed the men who were my friends.

Though the Chengtu club building was already open for use, it was quite barren. The formal opening would not be till February 3rd and there was plenty to be done. I soon discovered that the personality of our club director was going to be worse to cope with than the cold and barren atmosphere. She is childish and petty in her make-up resenting any original ideas on my part and any indication of initiative and yet she doesn't seem to have much of her own. No day goes by that I'm not hurt. I was told at Kunming Headquarters when I left that if I were not happy with her to tell them and they would remove her but I hesitate to make an issue of it. I just hope and pray daily that someway we'll arrive at a harmonious coworker relationship.

Eventually the nurse sharing my room left. I got rid of the extra cot and proceeded to unpack, hang my Chinese watercolor scrolls and my phoenix, dragon, celestial pearl blue hanging purchased at 488. Since then I've bought some matting for the cement floor, made draperies for my window and a cover for my army cot from left-over material I had brought from 488. As my small room begins to look more livable my spirits have risen a few degrees—but—it's *cold*, so very cold here. Charcoal is scarce and I either have a scanty fire in my brazier or none at all. My brazier is a round metal receptacle about 15" in diameter and rests in the center of my floor.

Every morning I have to go to where the charcoal is deposited and, if I'm lucky, I come back with enough charcoal balls to start a fire and heat water in the tea kettle I had purchased in Yunnanyi. I've learned how the balls are made. Powdered charcoal is mixed with water, molded by hand into balls, and dried in the sun. I've discovered that they burn slowly, throw off an offensive smell, and literally toss dust out into the air. You have no idea how dirty one becomes from that charcoal dust. I bathe in a basin of water and by the time I get through the homely task and start washing my feet, the water looks quite impossible. I've washed underclothes by the same process and hung them in my room but since there's no ironing facility I'm not wearing blouses.

I live in wool army slacks and a sweater with all the wool underwear available. I also wear GI shoes—not a real glamorous outfit. Occasionally I become very brave and put on my uniform with a sweater underneath. I left the States with three sweaters but have only one left. The others were stolen along with my lovely blue wool robe and other warm things. Everyone suffers from robberies and there's not a darned thing one can do about it. Someone said: "Oh well, I still have my identification tags," which aren't exactly attractive jewelry hanging around one's neck. After having had a few thieveries, I've now learned how to travel in China. It's best to sit on your luggage (sleep on it, if necessary) until it's delivered to your quarters and never let it out of your sight while it's being delivered. When it's safely in your quarters be sure it's not near an open or screened window or an unlocked door. In fact, it's better to nail your windows shut. It's your choice; fresh air through an open window, or losing all your possessions or . . . If my luggage weren't so cumbersome I'd hang it around my neck.

I sent money to Dorothy (Vint's wife) over two months ago for a black sweater and black shoes but they haven't arrived yet.

This is a mournful letter to send following the usual joyous Christmas season and I should apologize but I can't seem to prod my spirits to a higher level. I miss you greatly. I'm sure my next letter will be more on the up . . . Love to you, Eddie

Chengtu (2)

My dear Mom and Dad:

I received the fruit cake you sent and the Kleenex stuffed in between. Bless you, I shared the cake with a number of the men. It was so good. We lingered over each mouthful and ohed and ahed. Thank you muchly.

Now for some good news to make up for my last gloomy letter. I acquired an old sewing machine from a missionary who is returning to the States. What an asset that will be. At present I'm in the throes of making twenty-four pairs of draperies for the club, also cushions and cushion covers. Thank heavens Aunt Em taught me to sew when I was a small child. She would have been amazed if she could have foreseen my wartime sewing projects. More good news. Headquarters has sent us a staff of well trained men for the kitchen. The First Cook was a Head Chef in one of China's best hotels. Isn't that marvelous!

In your last letter you mentioned food experiences of the fellows on the various battle fronts. I'm afraid I can't group myself with those who brag about food. Food in our Mess Hall is terrible. In Yunnanyi it was bad enough but here it's sometimes impossible. I eat because I have to. Vegetables, if we have them, are ruined. I've lost weight and hate to lose more. The U.S. Army has had its own training school for cooks and bakers but here in our Mess Hall we don't have trained Americans. We have Chinese who obviously never prepared anything but rice—plain rice, no fancy stuff. I wouldn't risk going out in their kitchen. I'd be shocked. So if our Club First Cook is really tops, all of us, in turn, may get a "good food break" occasionally.

Our club program is on its feet and has taken a few steps forward. We're beginning my Classical Music Hour and a Men's Chorus and have already had various kinds of game tournaments. I'm supposed to sing in a February show but have had a cough ever since I arrived.

Haven't heard from Dot in ages. I wrote her a long letter from the Rest Camp but sent it to the wrong APO so I guess she'll never get it. Am enclosing a one yuan note which is worth exactly nothing. The money market keeps changing and the Chinese value of a CN goes down and down and down . . . My love to you, Eddie

Chengtu (3)

My dear Parents:

This will be a brief letter to tell you that the BIG BOX arrived while I was in the club. About forty men stood around while I opened one package after another. I was like a kid at Christmas time. The jewelry is perfect. I love the long strand of pearls and wore them last night wound three times around my neck. The earrings are lovely, lovely. They make me feel feminine. The stockings are the first sent me overseas and how I need them! Mine are beyond repair. I try to dress up a little at night though it's terribly cold here. And white shoe polish! All the shoes I have left are white though white sandals aren't very appropriate for December. Dates and figs are delicious and the vitamins much needed. The perfume came through perfectly and the men raved over it when I wore it last night. Everyone wanted to smell it. The nail polish bottle leaked a little but didn't hurt anything. I was glad to get the polish remover. Thanks for the needles (I guess you realized I need them for all my sewing) and for all the Kleenex you stuck in. I know it was a JOB PLUS getting it all assembled and packed but if you had seen my joy and the big kick the men got out of watching me unwrap each item, I'm sure you would have felt repaid. THANK YOU, THANK YOU. You've been so good to me.

I've received two packages from Florence Borst Ives and three from Margaret Tunney as well as boxes from other friends. Flo and Margaret have been sweethearts in writing. I miss them both. Flo has a small baby girl, Betsy, and is justly proud.

I know how you feel, Dad, about my marrying Dick but I do wish you had answered his letter to you. His mother's letter to me was lovely and warm. Since our religious backgrounds differ, I question marriage and I think in time he will too. It's really utterly stupid that Christians have divided themselves up into so many different branches, denominations, and sects when basically our faith is the same—a love of the one and only God who loves us and the example of how we are to love mankind as shown through the life of Jesus. It would be a great day to be all united. What a powerful force for good we'd be in the world! Dick's letters have meant a great deal to me. I'm thankful that we have loved each other. I'll never forget him.

My deep thanks to you for loving me and for letters sent and boxes sent. I in turn love you fully . . . Eddie

30

To Paris on ARC Business

Nationalsozialistsche Deutsche

Dear Folks:

This is some German paper I picked up in Paris at Headquarters—some that was found in the building. I finally got to Paris and am still thrilled over the experience. I went in on business but after a couple of days I realized how tired I was. I had been talking and acting in double quick time. So I decided to take a little time to relax. I'm so glad I did for now I feel so much better and am back at the old grind with much more enthusiasm. My nervous system has calmed down immensely.

Paris is so different from the area I'm located in. One wouldn't realize there is a war on there. I took a half day trip to Versailles, visited the buildings and gardens. I also took a Red Cross tour of Paris with an English interpreter, visiting many points of interest: the Dome with Napoleon's Tomb and Notre Dame and driving past more places than I could mention. We walked through the Arc de Triumph and up and down the historic streets. I ran into Major Ellis Bonnell of the 108th General Hospital who came overseas with us. He is a psychiatrist and a very fine person. He took me to a famous nightclub with floor show of practically nude women and also to a Ballet at the Paris Opera House. It was wonderful.

The shops were full of things but everything was sky-high in price. It was hard to find the kinds of perfumes I wanted since so many Americans have been there buying but I did get a few bottles. I found a new frame for Eddie's picture. It was all grand and relaxing and one more interesting experience to add to the many others. I thought of you, Dad, as I walked around seeing the many sights, of when you were here at age nineteen although you visited the Louvre and I didn't get there. The weather wasn't good. It was penetratingly damp with little heat in the buildings.

I prefer Belgium to France except for the buzz bombs but the bombing continues and that makes us extra weary. The Belgians are very friendly and the Belgium Red Cross workers have been marvelous to us. We've been having a lot of snow the last few days and the countryside is beautiful with the snow-laden trees. I bought myself a good pair of fleece lined boots in the Army clothing store—sold only to combat groups. They're the warmest things I've had in ages. Now my feet are nice and toasty.

I received many Christmas cards and packages from people I didn't expect to hear from. Your package came yesterday. The shampoo is wonderful and extra Kleenex appreciated. We get some through the P.X. but never enough. I loved everything you sent. It's the first nuts I've had in ages. We don't get them here. Also the figs and dates, Fannie Farmer Candy, silk stockings. I've received so much from you and also much from so many.

Now I'm tired and must quit. Do take care of yourselves and don't worry about me. I'm safe. I've seen a tiny bit of Germany and Holland. The scenery is beautiful . . . Love, Dot

31

Much More on Chengtu and Szechwan

Dear Mom and Dad:

I had forgotten to mention something of real importance to me. At the beginning of February, Headquarters sent me a Chinese girl, Frances Chen. She is darling and I love her. She's not only been a female companion for me (which I badly needed) but has helped me in the program tremendously. As I look back, I don't know how I would have managed without her or endured my female loneliness without her.

Tensions have eased up greatly. The club director I had complained about was ill this whole month and I became deucedly tired trying to carry on her work and mine too. I still haven't finished straightening out February finances. I've been assured she'll be replaced. I do need another girl, especially to help with cashiering. Frances has been teaching two classes a week in Chinese but I haven't had time to sit in on them. Since I've been working more fully with the men in the kitchen I have to attempt the Mandarin to get my message across so I cope with it amid howls of laughter. The kitchen staff are absolutely wonderful and cooperative. I love them and I know they like me. I've been having lunch with them each noon as we discuss business. It's always rice fried in olive oil with bits of hard boiled eggs and bits of ham. Delicious.

The carbon copy of my February report is too faint to send you. I expect to be getting new carbon sheets very soon so I'll send my March report which should give you a fairly complete picture of what's been going on. I can say only that I've been very busy and things are moving forward.

It's been terribly cold and I've been fascinated as to how the Chinese cope with it. They've been looking stouter and stouter and I was quite sure they weren't putting on weight and growing fat. Frances informed me that as they get colder they add more cotton padding under their top garments with more high collars around their necks. I hadn't realized that wool is not available here. There is no animal product out of which wool clothes can be made. There are no sheep for there's not enough fodder to feed the sheep and also no leather for shoes for there aren't enough animals to provide the leather. Demands on the fields are tremendous. All arable land is needed for growing rice and wheat. Thus the Chinese adjust to the cold by padding themselves with cotton giving a deceptive appearance of stoutness. Cotton needed for winter is raised by the northern farmers. Lucky are the people who are wearing my stolen woolens.

The babies too look overly plump like overstuffed dolls. When the baby cries the mother puts on another suit of padded cotton. The suits on a baby can be counted by the number of high collars showing at the neck. Six inches of padded cotton will keep out the cold. Since mothers carry their babies in a wide cloth sling on their backs, the whole combination of mother and baby is a very bulky unit.

Frances Chen is in a higher social status so she wears the long Chinese gown lined with soft fur and her slippers are lined with fur. A little fur peeks out at the high neck and at the bottom of the sleeve. This is a wonderful idea for she looks no bigger and yet is softly warm. I should have one.

Be good to yourselves. I'll be coming home before long . . . Eddie

Chengtu (5)

Dear Parents:

The new club director arrived at the beginning of March—Margaret Thompson (no relation to Naomi)—and I like her very much. She believes in getting things done but not in breaking our necks. She should be good for me. I need someone to slow me down.

The main problem right now is supplies. It's maddening waiting when I'm itching to get things moving faster. Of course, supplies that come from America come slowly for a freighter takes two months for the trip to Calcutta. From there they are railed 800 miles north to Assam, then flown over the Hump in the freight planes to Kunming. When sent from there to our Air Base they come in either trucks or carts over exceedingly rough roads. War supplies have priority. Kunming Red Cross comes next and we're last but distance is the major factor. I understand all the reasons why our supplies don't come "flying through on a magic carpet" but it doesn't alleviate my impatience.

Slowly I've been gathering information on the background of this area so that you as well as I would have a clearer picture of where I am. Chengtu (pronounced CHUNGDOO) is capital of Szechuan province (pronounced SECH-WAN) and regional capital of West China. Szechuan has had centuries of isolation due to the rugged high Qin Ling mountains that separate northern and southern China and form a natural barrier for the province. I was told a charming folktale of how the mountains came into existence. Ten large dragons were flying over the area and became so overwhelmed with its beauty that they decided to stay here. They settled down and slowly turned into mountains. The first of these mountains the people named Wolong, the Reclining Dragon. Until WW II this province, which is only a little larger than France, could be reached only by mules or sedan chairs (hanging from poles that rested on the shoulders of the coolies who carried them). Regarding its isolation and inaccessibility, I've heard two varying interpretations of a quote by an 8th century poet: "It would be easier to climb to heaven than to walk the Szechuan road" and "It is more difficult to go to Szechuan than to get to heaven."

In the latter 1930s as the Japs bombed eastern China's cities causing enormous destruction, killing thousands of civilians, capturing all of the eastern seaports, Chiang Kai-shek moved the Nationalists' capital to Chungking in this province. He had a road built from Chungking to Chengtu. In 1937 the University of Nanking and some eastern colleges moved here for safety. Safety? No place is safe from the Japanese. Chungking is the mountain city gateway to the Yangtze River. It sits on a rocky promontory with spectacular scenic views. The towering mountains drop almost perpendicularly into the river "as though" someone said "they had been chopped with an axe." The grandeur of these and the swollen roaring river have been an inspiration of China's poets and painters for centuries.

In the NW part of Szechwan is a smooth plain 70 X 40 miles. The even surface contrasts greatly with the rest of the mountainous area. Chengtu is in the center of the plain which is about 2000 feet above sea level but lies in a sheltered position and yields heavy crops. Farmers owe thanks to Li Ping who, in the 3rd century B.C. planned a marvelous irrigation system which was further developed in later periods so that the river's waters were led off at Kevan-hien. At the lower end of the plain the channels were drawn together and became two rivers—the Min-Hi and the Chung-Kiang.

Szechwan has been called the "heavenly Kingdom" because of its fertile soil, its flowing rivers, beautiful green foliage, dense bamboo forests where the pandas live in happiness and roam the area, fields of yellow rapeseed which yields an excellent oil, and golden brown wheat. The lush rice fields are separated by rows of mulberry trees where silk worms flourish providing the source for silk thread and silk material that the Chinese embroider with such fine stitches. I hope to buy some of their work before I leave.

Chengtu has over one million people. For over two thousand years it has been the economic and cultural center of the province. It was established as the capital of the state of Shu in the 4th century B.C. and became widely known all over China for its lacquerware, gold and silver handicrafts, and brocades After the fall of the Han Dynasty it became the capital of the Kingdom of Shu. It has now lost some of its former splendor. The Jin Jiang River (often called the Brocade River) in which silks were washed has turned gray and muddy. Ancient walls still stand though some have been destroyed in old wars.

It's been said that China has the greatest number of tea houses in the whole world and that Chengtu has the most tea houses in China. I've seen a goodly number of these open on to the streets. It's here where the Chinese, mostly elderly men with furrowed faces, sit and smoke their waterpipes, drink tea, spit on the floor or the ground, and chat and chat for hours. There are many small restaurants that serve excellent Szechwanese food. The food is quite spicy having the ingredient "Jagara" or chini pepper. Nearby is the colorful marketplace—always an interesting spot to visit and be among the people.

Though naturally our airfield is outside the city, I am grateful to be in this area rather than near a city influenced by foreign countries. I, and the men too, hope to see and experience much while we're here. Kunming, though we would call it primitive, is somewhat more progressive due to the influx of so many refugees from the east and the influence of the American military who named it the Military Capital.

Wish you were here . . . Love, Eddie

32

Liège Hospital Damage
Being Repaired

My dearest Eddie:

Do you remember the pilot I dated in France who painted "Dotty" on his plane? I received word that his plane was shot down. He was a grand person and I felt very saddened. I also learned that he didn't have his own plane that day so the plane painted "Dotty" still flies over Germany with a different pilot who has undoubtedly painted over Dotty and a new name now appears.

We're all getting very tired at this point and wish that the war would end so we could go home. It seems as if we have been here for ages but we'll have plenty to think about and remember in the years to come. This has been an unusual experience. I get depressed with all I see but I love my work and enjoy getting on the wards helping to cheer up the fellows. We have quite a number of PW patients right now and many are severe trench foot cases that will require amputations.

When the damage to our hospital has been repaired and the construction completed it will be a beautiful compact and very convenient hospital. I hope we stay long enough to enjoy it. Now we can walk under cover to all the wards in the three large ward buildings, the Operating Room, and adjoining rooms which are really show places. Every day brings more changes for the better.

Our Red Cross area is taking real shape too. The plumbing and the wiring are complete and we await a paint job. It's hard to recall that this place was full of horse stalls with a strong stench when we first came in November. We're proud of our Red Cross setup for we planned it ourselves and it's working beautifully. In the large Recreation Room we have two ping pong tables and a billiard table. The horse troughs along the sides have been covered with plywood and make excellent shelves or even seats for shows. We have a Belgian carpenter working for us who is very clever. He's made bookcases, waste baskets, wall shelves, framed mirrors, racks for towels and toilet paper, mended broken furniture. The hospital assigned him to us. He'll be helping in the Craft Shop as soon as it's set up. I had to move out of my office for a week while the plumbers drilled another hole through my office walls for pipes. The plaster kept falling down but now they're finished. When the walls are painted I'll be quite swanky. We now have pot belly stoves for heating.

Tomorrow we'll go for fresh fruit which a Liège organization has for us. People are always giving us apples which the patients love and they've given us some books. They are grand to us, so friendly and sincere. I think the Belgians like us better than the French or English did. I've had many invitations to Belgium homes but as yet haven't been able to take time to go. I hope to make time for it would be a good experience. I still want to go to Brussels and Antwerp.

We haven't been getting so many buzz bombs lately which is a relief. I'm wondering what the end of the war will bring to us all. I wish I could look forward to a settled life with a husband and children but I haven't met anyone I deeply care about. Social life here seems so artificial and somewhat silly but I've managed to have good times. I don't frequent the Officers' Club except for dancing. I've become quite adept at jitterbugging at the enlisted mens' dances. But the dances are a workout with men constantly cutting in.

As to the matter of love, Eddie, it is better for both of us to wait till we get back to the States, meet the mens' families and see the men in civilian lives before we make great decisions. Overseas during war is far different from civilian living in our own country. We've both had several proposals from fine men who seemed sincere. And yet I haven't been strongly interested. You'll always be solid, Eddie, so don't worry about being abnormal. Take it in your stride and wait. Have fun. Generally I get disgusted with the "play love" life but still I smile and go along. A group of us are going to Holland this week. One of the nurses has arranged it and I have a date with a general. I hope it will be pleasant.

Your letters take a month en route and they are so few. I wonder and worry about you. I was upset when I heard you were in a Rest Camp. You must learn to take it easier. There's always more to be done than one can do and there's five of us here to do the RC work. Still the nervous strain gets us down and occasionally one at a time each of us has to take a break. I dream of coming to China and seeing you. One never knows . . . My love to you, Dot

33

Chengtu March Program Report to ARC Headquarters

Anyone who has had any part in transforming a drab barren "army issue" building into a stateside club knows the resulting thrill when men enter, grin appreciatively and make comments like one man who said: "Miss, do you have a room in this hotel that's not too expensive?" It does sort of resemble an expensive hotel lobby (if you stretch your imagination to its limits) and we're proud of it, proud too that the room looks bigger, less crowded, and comfortable, and that during all the time work was, and still is, being done the club was actually closed to the men only one day and night with the Snack Bar remaining open.

I've finished nine pairs of draperies—fifteen more to be done. GI lights were installed. New furniture arrived. An outgoing group gave us a large information desk and a filing cabinet. We had a conference with one of the new GIs who was an Interior Decorator in the States. His ideas for the room were so full of imagination and color that we immediately swung into a fast pace for their fulfillment. Sketches were drawn up for a new entrance door with windows, and for a round table to fit around our central post in the room, for coffee tables to set in front of our settees, for a staggered bookcase arrangement at one end of the room which would give us both height, interest, and a place to display pottery, vases, and Chinese relics.

While Miss Thompson approached our resident engineers with the sketches and the paint and materials needed and sold them on our ideas, I began making the straight chair back covers, long cushions for the settees, and cushions for the wicker chairs. I made the cushions out of burlap and stuffed them with old mattresses I obtained from army supply. The lovely green material with stripes of rose red, purple, blues, and greens sent by Red Cross made up beautifully. I'm so grateful to the missionary who left me her sewing machine. In Yunnanyi, I had to do all by hand.

While waiting for the paint to arrive we got some men busy making new lighting fixtures out of metal. But we need sixteen lighting fixtures and metal is scarce so temporarily the job is at a standstill. The 1st Photo Group gave us pictures for our walls which we've framed.

REORGANIZED ENLISTED MEN'S COMMITTEE had its first meeting. We served them delicious pie, made by our super First Cook, and coffee, gave them copies of my typed weekly program to post on each unit's bulletin board, exchanged ideas and received important information.

CLASSICAL MUSIC HOUR has had a rough row of it. We've been shifted from Special Services Annex to Red Cross Annex (an annex given to us and then very shortly taken away) to Mess Hall to Snack Bar where men were constantly pouring in for food and chat. Every week I have to look for transportation to get a record player from Special Services on the other side of the field and then when I get it I cuss the old machine with its wobbly disk. I have fifteen records of our own. At the beginning of January I sent a request to Headquarters for a machine and classical recordings but have had no word. With the innovation of coffee hour on Sunday afternoons in the Lounge, I jumped into a new approach where we could have quiet and peaceful listening. At noon I drew the curtains in the Snack Bar, pushed back the tables, brought in a few lounging chairs, set up a head table with flowers and candles, and at 3:30 Sunday the classical music listeners moved in for Chopin, Bach, and Mendelssohn. HOWEVER, we need a good machine and more records and also a machine for the jazz record enthusiasts, and a piano in the lounge for every possible occasion.

MENS' CHORUS I made a big mistake and feel sort of angry inside. I had lined up forty some enthusiastic men. I had arranged popular numbers for future anticipated shows and had made folders for each two men to share the "handwritten" music—a job that took hours of work. I learned of a GI who was a music grad and music teacher so I asked him if he would like to direct the chorus which pleased him. At the first rehearsal I was shocked at his dry approach with no enthusiasm, no smoking, no talking, just plugging on parts. Attendance dropped off fast. How much I wish I had taken it myself. Now it's hard to start again.

CHINESE LESSONS From March 1–20 Frances Chen has taught six lessons on "Dining Room Service." Nineteen GIs have come faithfully to her classes for they've found Frances an excellent teacher not only in drilling them carefully and thoroughly but in coloring the whole hour with her humor and charming personality. I typed the complete series she had set up and gave a copy to each man. All nineteen graduated with honors—so dear Frances said. We rewarded them with a CHINESE DINNER on March 22nd at 5:30 in the Snack Bar—the dinner planned by Frances and prepared by our outstanding First Cook. As we enjoyed the eight different dishes in the center of the table, from which we dipped out a fair amount into our own individual bowls of rice, Frances instructed us in the etiquette of using our chopsticks and our bowls as well as general courtesy at the table. She laughed at us heartily as we threw our English out the window and jabbered away in her native tongue. She told us Chinese jokes, the best of which was the "Bishop's Soup."

SUNDAY AFTERNOON COFFEE HOUR has had all the earmarks of a party. We've covered a long table with a white cloth, added flowers and candles and decorations in keeping with a holiday or season of the year. "We women" have dolled up in civilian clothes, one of us seated at either end of the table to pour coffee. Special delicacies have been prepared for each Sunday. The men have come especially groomed with grins on their faces and have seemed to enjoy this rare bit of culture midst an often drab life. When I began the Classical Music Hour in the adjoining Snack Bar, many moved on into that peaceful setting.

BINGO PARTIES—the second of our series was held on March 4 and again on the 18th. The prizes were written invitations to a Stateside Dinner and gifts from India. Bingo has been amazingly successful with almost every man in the lounge participating and dropping whatever he had been involved in. No wonder! With a chance to get some good food, what regular client of our Mess Hall wouldn't want to participate! There was good humor galore. I wonder who named the armies' eating place the "Mess Hall." It's very fitting here for the food is a mess.

ST. PATRICK'S DINNER in the Snack Bar was for the thirty-five winners of Bingo and a few guests of honor. The week before, the Lounge had been decorated with green hats and shamrocks but for the dinner the decorations surpassed those of the Lounge. The lights bore two-toned green crepe paper shades. On the walls were hats and shamrocks. Tables were placed in a U-shape covered with white cloths and sprinkled with shamrocks of various sizes. Three bowls held graceful sprays of mustard blossoms and yellow candles sprang out of green paper clusters. Our First Cook is invaluable and the men did the honors due him. We had chicken croquettes with cream sauce, baked glazed potatoes, baked carrot and peanut dish, fruit and nut slaw salad, fresh rolls that melted at a glance, apricot jam, orange pie, and coffee. The men, ironed out in their best clothes, were quite agog.

BRIDGE TOURNAMENTS were held on March 1st and 11th for there seemed to be a large group of bridge enthusiasts. Sgt. Fagen, who has played with many of the experts in the States, has been in charge and has a point system for judging the winners. I made duplicate boards from cardboard and covered them with green construction paper.

LIBRARY—Through January and February I had catalogued hundreds of books given us by men on the base but due to insufficient staff to cover the club, books gradually disappeared. Beginning in March our Library procedure has changed for the better. We've left the older and more used books on the shelves for more general use but have put others under lock and key in a cabinet to be signed out only from someone on duty. A list of the locked up books is posted on the bulletin board along with a display of paper covers. We need magazines badly, men continually ask for them.

The paint arrived. Carpenters and painters had already been lined up and waiting so the job began with the accelerator way down. One man mixed the stain and a few of us armed with three brushes, ranging from a 4" to a watercolor size, tackled the woodwork. The next day the resident engineers sent us a coolie to assist with the painting. We stained the ten game table legs, the four writing table legs, the information desk, bulletin board, magazine rack, two long benches with backs and ran out of blue paint for the stain. It's on its way and we're waiting longingly to paint the lower sections of the thirty-six straight back chairs. The game tables and writing tables, three cabinets, and filing case were all painted a cheery deep yellow. The tables are trimmed with a narrow scroll design and the panels of the doors painted with graceful spraying bamboo trees. The interior of the stained staggered bookcase will be painted red.

Our goal had been to complete our plans for Easter. The night before Easter there were still details missing but we set up the room. The yellow game tables with blue trim surrounded by chairs with the green striped back covers looked mighty attractive. We arranged the settees bearing their new cushions. The staggered arrangement of our office equipment added grace and interest to the room. We bedecked the place with bowls of orange and yellow flowers. Our full job would not be finished till along in April but the results of what we had done so far were overwhelming. As the men entered on EASTER MORNING we were repaid for our work. The sounds of surprise, delight, amazement bounced around the Lounge like instruments of a symphony orchestra tuning up before the concert. A wonderful cacophony of praise.

Chengtu (6)

Dear Mom and Dad:
    It's so beautiful today that I feel guilty for ever having complained about cold and bleakness. We didn't see the sun for a long, long time but now he's back blessing us with his warmth and cheer. I've sent you a copy of my complete March Report so you'll know what's been going on at the club and I won't have to comment further. I now have new carbon paper, thank heavens.

Now that warmer weather is coming I have to be careful what I do in my small room quarters with the window drapes open for all too often someone astride a water buffalo is standing outside my window peering in. Since I charge no admission fee the word has spread. I'm happy to provide entertainment as long as I'm not bathing in the nude. Often "the peerer" is a child. It amazes me how companionable they are—the buffalo patient, gentle, obedient—for the buffalo can be moody and dangerous when not wallowing in the cool mud of the rice fields. Yet that seems to be characteristic of so many animals, the sensing of a child versus an adult, and so becoming docile.

Here we don't wait till the 4th of July to hear the exciting sound of firecrackers. They can be heard at almost any moment when some celebration demands them. I have learned how they are made, at least the simple ones. Tiny paper tubes are wrapped with red paper. A handful of these are stood on end and tied together with a string. White paper is pasted firmly across the top and bottom so that none of the openings are exposed. The tops of the tubes are perforated with a bamboo punch to admit to each tube a layer of clay, then the powder, the fuse, and another layer of clay. Whatever number of these tubes is required are strung together and wrapped in a package. The ones I see more commonly are in long strips attached to poles. The Chinese have been making these for centuries but it still takes time and patience. It's a shame they are gone so fast when they are lighted.

The other day I rode on two different ferries. Each one was propelled by an enormous paddle handled by six blue-clad Chinese. A resident engineer had to buy lumber and took me with him. While he bargained for over an hour (the necessary drawn-out procedure that the Chinese love) I strolled through the village stopping at various small open sided shops looking at articles of interest and smiling at everyone. I was constantly surrounded by Chinese. An American woman is a novelty in this province. When the engineer came looking for me, he took the enclosed shot. Although just my back and profiled face are toward the camera I'm easy to be seen for I'm the only American in the crowd and I'm wearing my light gray uniform with my left hand raised in a greeting gesture. At 5′7″ I appear to be taller than many of the Chinese seen around me.

Along the river sides we saw crowded areas of the poor—

some living in dilapidated looking small dwellings jammed together on the edge of the river and others in their house boats which are simply sampans with a crude roof. Thousands of poor Chinese live in these crowded and shabby homes. Some Chinese are born, live their entire lives, and die on sampans. It's hard to believe what a limited life they live and evidently not aware of anything better beyond them. A sampan festooned in red means a wedding is taking place in that small dismal area. No honeymoon. No privacy for the newlyweds. If white is shown, it indicates mourning.

Recently news was exciting hearing that northern Burma and Mandalay had been recaptured from the Japs. But in southern Burma the fighting continues. Our pilots are taking off or landing day and night. I don't know where they go or much about what's happening "out there." Naturally they can't talk about it unless free to do so and I can't ask questions. But news of Mandalay spread with no restraint and lifted our spirits. A pilot took me in his B-29 bomber at nighttime to the very spot. While he had the plane refueled I stood someplace in Mandalay in black darkness and full voiced sang: "On the road to Mandalay where the flying fishes play and the dawn comes up like thunder out of China cross the bay." I couldn't see a darn thing but my feet were on Burma soil and I was thrilled to pieces. Kipling who wrote the words of that famous song never set foot in Burma . . . Love to you, Eddie

*　　*　　*

1998 Notes

In 1996 I read every book shown on Internet that dealt with war in the CBI Theater. I am grateful to the authors for giving me a clear insight of what happened with our fighting men throughout the theater including Burma, of course. Winston Churchill said: "I regard Burma and contact with China as the most important feature of the whole eastern theater of the war."

The fighting throughout the country was fierce under almost impossible conditions but it seems to me, as I've read, that the worst almost anywhere in the world was in the dense, impenetrable jungles in the mountain range along the western frontier. Fighters up to their calves in mud, mud, mud, suffering from typhus, malaria, dysentery, rotting feet, blood-sucking leeches, body sores, dengue fever, vicious rats. I shuddered as I read in different sources what our men went through in Burma's jungles they called "Green Hell." Many died there.

One great tragedy was the country of Burma which had nothing to do with these great powers. As someone expressed it "innocents in a giants' battle." Their country was ruined with cities, towns, and villages burned to the ground, every railway destroyed, the people impoverished and cut off from the world. Their wooden buildings with thatched roofs blazed like matchsticks. In Mandalay life almost ceased. Killed Burmese were thrown into the moat surrounding the magnificent palace of the last Burmese King and the palace buildings destroyed.

In the 1970s my sister and I had seven days in Burma when the military in control opened her doors for a one-week visa. The city and important seaport of Rangoon, on the Irrawaddy River, looked like a primitive overgrown village. In great contrast the Schwedagon rose in all its magnificent and costly glory, its slender spire encrusted with almost 8000 diamonds, rubies, sapphires, and topaz and at the very golden tip the 76 carat diamond.

Everywhere from south to north we saw the aftermath of the war. Mandalay, where I had sung with joy and thrill on that black night, had no cars but did have army Jeeps given them by the Americans. We climbed Mandalay Hill, 934´ high and 1,724 steps, with its hundreds of pagodas—a holy hill that became a bloody battleground in the final phase of the war. Before Mandalay could be taken, our troops had to storm this hill and following the hard won vantage point came the siege to the mile square area of the last Burmese King, King Thibaw, who was deported when the British took over Burma in 1885. Within this area had been a great highly carved teak palace surrounded by 50 beautifully carved teak buildings. Around the outside area were brick walls 26' high and 30' thick backed by an earth embankment 70´ across which was protected by a broad 225´ moat. 2,000 pound bombs had skipped off the surface of the moat and into the walls. After exceedingly long, heavy fighting, Mandalay fell. August 1st General Mizukami apologized to the Japanese Emperor for his defeat and committed harakiri. Almost 600 Japanese tried to escape but were caught and killed. Only one carved and decorated teak wood building remained of the original fifty.

We fell in love with the Burmese, delightful and charming victims of that wholly destructive war.

*   *   *

34

Cristalleries du Val Saint Lambert

Dear Folks:

The painting has been completed and we've arranged things attractively and now our building looks lovely. It's full of patients and we're all busy. I spend a lot of time on the wards writing letters for incapacitated patients and also send cables to Home Service Chapters in the States for health and welfare reports. My hand gets so tired that at the end of the day when I want to write you, it's quite an effort.

Our Red Cross Recreation Building is used by all our unit personnel as well as the patients because all other space had to be turned into wards. Even our enlisted mens' dances are held here. It's thrilling to work for these boys who give their all to the cause. They are wonderful and have the most marvelous attitudes, even those who have had amputations. I don't know how they take it all so well. Ambulatory patients come over to help us take supplies to the wards, help with work in the building and even help in writing letters for the bed patients who can't write.

In the city a Protestant church has been released to the army for GI services. I play there for the 9 A.M. service on a large reed organ with a group of stops. It has a nice tone and I enjoy playing. Today our choir sang "The Palms." Last Sunday I played for three services. From the chaplains' fund they spent $50.00 for flowers—white lilacs and calla lilies. Flowers are very expensive. I now have three large brass shells brought in from the battle fields, cleaned and polished to use for vases on the altar at Sunday services—thanks to two GIs. Two of the bomb shells are the same height and size and the third taller and larger. From the battle field to the church! That's quite a good switch. You know me, I'll always be able to find flowers for those 3 "shell vases."* So Easter was lovely.

Last week 2 workers from Paris Headquarters came for a joint meeting of all the AFDs of surrounding hospitals—the meeting held here at our Red Cross Building. It proved most worthwhile. The meetings were ordered by our own Colonel Hill who is in charge of all the hospitals. He came in yesterday to see me—expects me to check up on all area hospitals and call meetings for discussion, etc. Looks as if I've gotten into a big job. Today I received a copy of a notice sent by Col. Hill to all the hospitals and certain departments stating that I am coordinator and authorized to visit all units as deemed necessary. It made me happy for the American Field Directors (AFD) had already appointed me to that position. As a result I went with one of our workers to visit all the hospitals this week. I got some good ideas but came back feeling that we have the best setup of all. We really have a beautiful building and everyone raves about it. Right now it's peaceful here.

A group of us were entertained by two generals in Holland. A car was sent to the plane for us, the first time I've ridden in a civilian car since I left the States. We stayed overnight at their headquarters. Talk about luxury. The guest room two of us slept in had twin beds placed together making a huge bed, though the beds were made up separately. The bathrooms were also beautiful in colored tile with equipment to match—two sinks rather than one—with modern lighting. The hotel was more modern than I've seen in the States. The two dining rooms were beautiful with chandeliers and palms. The generals were very busy but they were wonderful to us. I came back with three gifts: a bracelet of tiny silver coins, a nylon silk scarf all hemmed and a tiny silver spoon.

I've just discovered why I haven't been getting your letters. You must put on 56th General Hospital. That's more important than our APO number. This is March and I just received your December letters. I long to hear from you.

*Of the numerous souvenirs Dot brought home, these three bomb shells are especially treasured by me, for they have double significance. They not only went from the battlefield to the church's altar, but they also represent Dot's contribution through her organ playing and decorating for all the chapel services.

Today I went to a famous crystal factory outside Liège—Cristalleries du Val Saint Lambert, Marcel de Fraiponts, Directoire. I was completely thrilled over the display of crystal glass and lingered a long time looking and admiring. I finally couldn't resist buying, and bought twenty-four gorgeous crystal goblets, three kinds in a set of eight each—champagne and two sizes for wines. They're for Eddie in case she decides to get married. I raised one of the crystal goblets filled with imaginary champagne and drank a toast to my beloved sister in China, Land of the Dragon. I also bought two vases for myself—one large and one small. They were all expensive but very beautiful. I'll send them home when I get them packed. Let me know immediately if they arrive okay. Belgiums excel in the making of crystal and in the manufacture of colored glass for stained glass windows.

In a shop in Liège I also bought three pieces of Belgium lace—a handkerchief that is mostly lace, a large double lace butterfly which can be worn on a black dress or a dressy suit, and a small lace doily. Handmade bobbin lace is a Belgium specialty. The lacemakers start their training early in life. Burges lace is made of linen thread from Flemish flax. My third purchase was a pair of bookends in black lacquer with a brass Belgium boy on one and a girl on the other. Both are dressed in old time Dutch costumes. They bear brass yokes with small brass buckets on their shoulders.

I'm going to send a cable through Red Cross in regard to Eddie. I haven't heard from her since December. I worry for fear something has happened. If you learn anything let me know immediately.

I have made several trips into Germany to get things for our Red Cross building, having obtained permission from the Military Government to go into certain places. It's amazing the things I've brought back from bombed-out areas. Our building is now furnished beautifully. In my office I have a large oak desk which came out of the Gestapo Headquarters in Cologne. Our PW has refinished it and it's a beauty. All around the edges of the room are knickknacks which I've accumulated in my wanderings—a regular museum.

The war news is good so we wonder what will happen next. We're among the older hospitals here so we may go home—that's MAY GO HOME—for a short period provided our unit holds together and is routed to the CBI Theater. If our unit splits up, we Red Cross will be sent to Paris Headquarters for reassignment and then what? Everything is very unsettled at this point. In some ways I'd like to go to CBI and hopefully see Eddie and also see that part of the world.

Joe Chiott, an AFD who was in Washington with me, drove up for a dance party last night. He's now quite near at Namur. It was good seeing him again for he's a grand person. I spent two evenings with a captain of the 83rd Division before he was sent into Germany. (The 83rd Division has made real strides all along in this last push, as you've probably read in the papers.) I thoroughly enjoyed him for we seemed to have much in common. We've written a few letters to each other but letters can't be too frequent either way as we've both been very busy. He was wounded and hospitalized for a short time but nothing too serious. I'm concerned about him as he's been in such dangerous spots—but haven't they all! . . . My love to you, Dot

*   *   *

1998 Notes

The Ardennes district covers about one-fourth of Belgium and lies about forty miles south of Liège. It was in the Ardennes hills and forests around Thanksgiving time 1944 that the Germans launched a desperate counterattack isolating a U.S. detachment under General McAuliffe. The Germans called on the General to surrender. He replied in German with a loud strong voice: "NUFS" ('nuts' in English) and went on fighting. What a funny but marvelous sharp retort that has become legendary. Eventually General Patton arrived to relieve the besieged garrison which had suffered terrible losses. The Allied

Forces checked the attack, regained the initiative and obliterated the "Bulge" defeating and ousting the Germans. The Allies then crossed the Rhine and into the heart of Germany. V-E Day arrived May 8th 1945.

35

The End of the War with Germany

Belgium (8)

Dear Folks:
    THE END OF THE WAR OVER HERE HAS COME.

We weren't too excited for we had been expecting it. But we did join in a bit with the civilians in celebrating. Two of the officers drove a couple of us over into the city. Everyone was out on the streets, mobs of them. It was like 42nd Street in New York City on New Year's Eve. So many young fellows piled on top of our Jeep that we were afraid the Jeep would nestle into the ground. We drove around for awhile with them hanging on and yelling their heads off till finally our driver stopped and told them to get off. At that point the fellows turned to me and asked in French if I would give them two kisses for the Liberation, one for each cheek.

    For the first time in years the streets and buildings were illuminated with bright lights, Neon lights prevalent. It was something to see after all the blackouts we've been through. Almost immediately the windows in the city were decorated as though the people were prepared for the occasion. All sizes and kinds of the Allies' flags were displayed everywhere and the narrower streets were truly festive with flags. Crowds of young people and old people formed chains and skipped along singing lustily blocking all traffic. We finally parked the Jeep and joined the mob. Crowds congregated in the cafés. Street cafés were filled and tables were brought out into the road. This went on for a full week, the people jubilant and bursting with happiness.

Now broken windows have been replaced and the shops are in full swing. But for us the war isn't over. We still have to work for there's much to be done. We have mixed feelings at this time and await plans that will be made for us.

I had a real thrilling experience last weekend. Twenty-five nurses including myself were invited to dinner and dance at an air strip in Germany. They sent down five B-26 Bombers for us and then detoured a bit so we could see the countryside. I crawled up into the nose of our plane where all the Plexiglass is with my feet extended out into the glass. I had a wonderful view all around and up and down. We saw a number of the cities that had been bombed out, crossed the Rhine, of course, and could see the zigzag lines of trenches, also holes where the artillery had been and marks on the fields where tanks had moved back and forth. We flew at about 600' so that everything was clearly visible. I looked out in the distance with field glasses hoping to see Berlin but couldn't quite make it. We flew over some of the same territory I had covered previously in a truck when I went over part way into Germany for things we needed for our Red Cross building. I must say it was much easier traveling by plane than in a truck and interesting looking down on things that I had looked out at before. We flew over Cologne a number of times and I had a good look at the Cathedral from above. It isn't too badly damaged. We wore the complete paraphernalia of the fliers including parachute and it was heavy. The trip was the highlight though we did have a wonderful time at the party, stayed overnight in a German hotel where the fliers have their quarters, and then came back the next day.

Before I tell you about an unexpected thing that happened, I have to remind you that we workers in Red Cross are neither man, fowl, nor beast but a breed unto ourselves. We are with the Army, under Army orders, but not of the Army. We are grouped with the officers but we hold no rank. We receive no honors and can wear no medals or ribbons. When we leave the service we receive no pension as do the military personnel. So the following was a great surprise.

The Army gave us Red Cross workers in the hospital a campaign ribbon with three stars on it. We are to receive another star soon for the Battle of the Bulge. The Army feels that we should wear the ribbon. Maybe someday Red Cross will get around to authorizing the wearing. We're proud of the ribbon for it was wholly unexpected. I should have acknowledged the cuts I received from flying glass from the buzz bomb that hit our hospital and I might have been given the Purple Heart!?!

This past week one of our workers and I were invited to a Belgium home for dinner. Several of their Belgium friends also came and there was one man who could speak a little English. Fran and I taxed our minds trying to hold conversations in French and felt that we did quite well between the two of us helping each other. We were at the table from 7 to 11 P.M. We were the first Americans they had entertained and they really did the thing up brown with their best china, silver wear, crystal, and linens. They are florists and you know me always making friends with the florists. The place was decorated with all kinds of flowers. The centerpiece was made in two sections with sweet peas. On one side was the American flag and on the other the Belgium. In the goblets were large linen napkins (I had almost forgotten how to use a napkin) and there was a corsage for each of us made of a pink carnation and fern wired together and wrapped with tinfoil around the stems.

Wine was served throughout the meal and there was one course after another until I thought I would be woozy. They expected we would eat plenty to acknowledge the good food so I couldn't let them down. We started with fresh asparagus soup, then there were beaucoup hors d'oeuvres which I thoroughly enjoyed. The meat course was wonderful roast beef with new parsleyed potatoes and creamed cauliflower with cheese, and hard rolls. There were two desserts—the first a carmel pudding covered with large red strawberries and the second a liberation cake of three layers with mocha frosting. Both were served with coffee. This was all topped off with a Liqueur Eau d'Or which tasted like licorice and had flecks of gold in it. When we left we were presented with bouquets of flowers. We thoroughly enjoyed being there with the people. One man had just returned from Germany where he had been a PW for five years.

It was in the period when our area hospitals were more or

less alone in working out their individual problems and Red Cross had no field supervisor here in Liège, that I was appointed Coordinator of all Red Cross activities in the hospitals . . . Now a Field Supervisor has been sent here so I am relieved of that job. From the first our Red Cross unit seemed to be the clearing point on everything pertaining to Red Cross. I enjoyed the job for I could get around to the other units and see what was cooking with them which was an asset to our own program.

Though now we don't have so many patients or such a turnover of patients, there still is plenty to do but we can give more individual attention than before. We make ward visits regularly, carry on a recreational program both in the wards and in our Red Cross Building, write lots of letters for those who are incapacitated, talk over their problems with them, send communications to the Home Service Chapters when problems at home are pressing, and take care of a multitude of sundry things for them. Yesterday most of our ambulatory patients were taken by boat (rented by the Red Cross) to an island where they spent the day. I went down to the river to see them off. Two of our recreation workers went along in charge of the trip. It took one and a half hours one way. We now have the boat for our patients every Saturday. They all returned very enthusiastic.

An officer and I went to various nurseries and brought back trees, shrubs, and plants which we set out in our hospital area. It is a confined area with little space between the buildings for any landscaping and there wasn't a thing growing here. The place was full of cobblestones and stone walks. I missed plants so much that I asked our Commanding Officer if I could do something about it and he agreed. We had to dig up the stones around the building and put in dirt before we could plant anything but it was well worth the effort. We now have many blooming flowers.

I found the Military Government American officers in Germany very cooperative. So now our Red Cross building is lovely. We have all kinds and descriptions of furniture and knick-knacks. In my office I have a lovely large rug which I had the PWs wash. My desk is a solid dark oak which I personally picked out in the Gestapo Headquarters in Cologne and which the fellows about broke their necks carrying it down two flights of stairs. It was somewhat damaged but the carpenters of our hospital really fixed it up like new. I have a bronze statue of Mercury which I grow fonder of each day. I also have several upholstered chairs, Bavarian china, Dutch china vases, some German silver pieces and other odds and ends—some I got and others were brought in. My office is a regular museum, and interesting to all who enter. A Colonel whom we had here as a patient came to my office quite often and always remarked how feminine my office was. At first it bothered me for fear it didn't look official but he said the feminine touch was what the boys who came here from the front needed. Patients continually come in and look at everything with interest.

Have no idea when I'll be getting home but I'll be coming sometime so hold on . . . Love, Dot

36

April Program Report to ARC Headquarters

Warm weather has taken everyone out of doors and the club is strangely quiet with only a few letter writers and readers. Yet the men are still hungry for a snack and in the evenings they still yearn for something to do. In their yearnings most of them don't want to exert effort to obtain entertainment. I have to do all of the planning and most of the enactment in bringing them some happiness. They want to go home more than anything in the world and it would be easy to slip into their attitudes for I too want to go home.

We had hoped to complete the Lounge decorations by the middle of April but as we've well learned in China one doesn't snap his fingers and get what he wants. So we're waiting impatiently for paint. Meanwhile we've had fun doing detail work. Our walls are all decorated with Stateside scenic painted pictures. We had to give up our original idea of metal light fixtures due to the scarcity of metal but have purchased hats of bamboo shoots for the lights. The hats look as though they've been varnished. We obtained our four coffee tables and have accomplished much in our Chinese Display Corner. We framed our enlarged Chinese pictures and obtained nine Shadow Play Figures that we arranged in a scene from the story which they represent—romantic love crushed by a villainous government official. The bamboo matting behind our staggered bookcase has now been painted red. But the climax is the purchase of a beautiful yellow and white canary in a cage. His remarkable repertoire of song with its endless cascades of trills brings bright cheer to the club and the men love him. Who could not help but feel joyful hearing such merry carefree sounds.

SUNDAY AFTERNOON COFFEE HOUR has continued

and is enjoyed. Cigarettes have been sent us so we've placed these also on the table.

SECOND SERIES OF CHINESE LESSONS taught by Frances Chen has been as successful as the first—the subject this time being "Shopping." The men have met every Monday and Wednesday at 7:15 in the Lounge and have already signed up for the third series. They love Frances. She has also given them good ideas of things to purchase to take home.

BINGO, though I think it's a stupid game, remains popular with the Lounge full of participants and their wonderfully good humor. It's most certainly the prizes that entice the players. April 11th the prizes were invitations to our Spring Dinner. Twelve prizes admitted one each and four admitted one each with his buddy. There were also small gifts from India. On April 22nd the game was played again with much spirit, for the prizes were invitations to a stateside picnic. Other prizes were cigarettes and cigars. The men have been low on smokes and appreciated a chance of getting some.

Our SPRING DINNER was attended not only by the April 11th winners of Bingo but also some men who had helped us greatly in the decorating of the Lounge. The long table with a white cloth had a wide patch down the center of finely cut up pine needles and over the top were scattered varied colored blossoms. Each place had a name card with a picture of a comic character buying a new hat, going golfing, etc.—all done in watercolors. I had fun making half of them after being taught by one of the GIs. The dinner was super as always.

Most of our bridge enthusiasts have left the base. We're dropping the tournaments until more interest pops up.

CHAMPION GAME NIGHT—the poster announcing it was very attractive. Players of Cribbage, Pinochle, and Hearts would compete for beautiful gifts from India. Thirty-six men participated, stopping first at the Information Desk to pick up their numbers for Door Prizes, their tally sheets, and Rules for Playing. On each table was a dish of candy. Small prizes were given to each table winner and larger prizes to the champion of each game. Even those who didn't win said they enjoyed it.

EASTER EGG SCAVENGER HUNT was a HOWLING success. The club was a madhouse that Easter night with so much noise that if the end of the war had been boomed out over a loud speaker, no one would have heard it. At 7:00 P.M. I had placed nests of green paper in various spots of the Lounge, each nest holding bright colored eggs (real ones hard boiled) lettered in black to spell a unit's name. In each nest were seven duplicate copies of instructions as to what must be brought into the club to earn all of the eggs in the nest. The first winning unit would receive a huge plate of chocolate fudge made by our First Cook. That unit could then immediately start work on the climactic nest that rested on the information desk, the nest holding six eggs each bearing a letter of the word EASTER and the list of instructions showing the necessary articles needed to win the nest. The final prize for the winning unit was an enormous chocolate layer cake which our cook had decorated beautifully with Chinese characters meaning "This is your happy day."

The Lounge was soon startled with live cackling hens and quacking ducks along with a steady flow of sixty-some items. Two units won the cake simultaneously and had to split it. Later in the evening when all were lounging back comfortably munching fudge and cake—for the winning men generously shared their treasures—and while they were still roaring with laughter over the obtained articles, one fellow yelled: "Hey, Eddie, do you suppose I should go untie that Chinaman?" "What Chinaman?" I asked. "What Chinaman? How do you suppose I got that ricksha in this desolate place?"

I had intended using the nests of colored eggs as decorations on the Snack Bar tables for the coming week. At the end of the night there wasn't an egg in sight. They must have eaten them all—shells included.

The men long to go home. They—and I too—feel that China has been the forgotten theater. We've lost so many men in air missions. Some I knew quite well and some just slightly. Worse still I've seen planes burst into flames and have been sick at heart. I've danced with men or played games with them or sat and talked with them and a few days later have gotten word that they were shot down. Sometimes I've lost control but I try hard not to. I worry about the men and some of them so young.

217

Chengtu (7)

My Wonderful Parents:

For the first time overseas I'm writing a letter in the club. Frances is cashiering, Margaret went home (her quarters) and I'm in no mood to find work to do. The weather has suddenly become very warm and the shift was too sudden. We're all suffering from spring fever. We're told the weather will gradually get hotter until it approximates the heat of India. Heaven forbid! My mosquito netting, which had been taken down during the cold weather, was put up two days ago but our screens aren't up yet and the mosquitoes are coming at us full speed. I escaped malaria last summer and hope to escape again this time though I've had no shots since leaving Washington. Must get them very soon.

Though speaking Chinese Mandarin is something I'll never accomplish, I do stumble along mixing everything up like goulash and highly entertain the kitchen staff with my noble efforts. To me the written characters look like some signals from outer space but, at my request, Frances had my name painted in those puzzling strokes, also Dot's name, and names of a few close friends back home.

There is no meaning to the name as a whole. Each name has to be translated from the English sound into a corresponding Chinese sound. Where there is no corresponding sound, an approximation is used. The name is read from the right column down, then the left column down. It's written with a camel's hair brush and ink. There's no punctuation used in Chinese writing of phrases or sentences. Just one word can be extended to a phrase making the character for the word involved. Here's an example: Two characters give the meaning for "to ask"—(1) gate 尸 and (2) mouth ～ or "mouth at the gate" 尸～尸

You probably wonder why I haven't mentioned rats. Either they're not so bad as at Yunnanyi or my room foundations are better. But they're still my undesirable companions. The other morning when I woke a huge rat was crawling up the wall just a few inches away. My cot is next to the wall so that there was nothing between us but the mosquito netting. I lay horrified at its closeness. He crept on up the wall and disappeared. I don't know where he went. For a few minutes I couldn't move. I hope to heavens he went out—out of my room—out of my life.

I sent you my April report which I hope you've received. The Scavenger Hunt brought forth so many funny, wild, riotous items that I wish you could have been there—though the noise would have deafened you—for I can't possibly relate it in detail. Many of the requested items were farfetched, of course. A Dagwood sandwich was two cans of tunafish in two layers between crackers. One brave man turned himself into a " blond ballet dancer" to help his buddies win the prize. They all strained their imaginations to the limit and again I was amazed at our marvelous American men. The good-sized Buddha that was brought in upset the kitchen crew but Frances and I calmed them down and assured them that it would be returned.

My original drab dinky room has become quite charming. One of the GIs and I whitewashed the walls and burned, with a blowtorch, the wide crude pieces of lumber that divide the walls into panels. The room now is quite wholly Chinese with odds and ends of things I've picked up here and there. The cot covering and the window drapes I made from the orange striped material I had brought from Yunnanyi. One of the men made me a "coffee table" to place in front of my cot. My locker, setting on boxes to give it height, is in front of my window covered with a skirt I made of the green striped material. My very few books are kept there. Over the window are Shadow Play Figures. On the side panels are masks—rather cheap but effective. On the wall at the head of my cot is my precious Marriage Ceremonial Group of three separate pieces. It's at least one hundred years old and I should imagine it was very meaningful to the Chinese family who sold it. I feel very privileged to have it but also ashamed as I realize Chinese are selling heirlooms in their desperate need for money. Someone purchased this for me or I'm sure I couldn't have taken it. Of course, my sewing machine, a most valuable possession, has found a spot. So I have created my home away from home. But I'm grateful it's not forever.

Frances took a small group of us to witness a month-old baby boy's first major celebration. He was dressed in red silk with red silk slippers on his feet. All his grandparents and his uncles were there for the momentous occasion along with "all his aunts and his cousins whom he numbered by the dozens, all his sisters and his cousins and his aunts" (apologies to Sullivan and his "Mikado"). Quite an audience! The baby's head was shaved except for one little tuft of hair in the back. Following the shaving, the priest rubbed the inside white of an egg over the baby's head and gave a blessing (so Frances told us) that the baby might become a great man of learning. A large silver yoke bearing symbols representing health, happiness, etc. was placed around his neck. From the yoke tiny bells tingled to scare the devils away and protect the infant. Do you remember I had purchased one at Yunnanyi? Later I also bought two silver ornaments like the one that the baby wears on his forehead. A GI is making them into earrings for me. There were slews of hard boiled eggs dyed red for happiness. So the baby was off to a good start. For Chinese older people, the end of the decades are politely ignored while the beginning of each next decade is highly celebrated. We Americans cling to the end of a decade and dread entering the next decade, a sign that we're aging. An interesting contrast of conceptions.

Recently I had a trip "off the beaten track" to where two men live all alone running some important piece of war equipment. I was met and taken in Jeep style. They had notified their neighbors days in advance that a real American woman was coming out to the area. A short time after my arrival Chinese began to appear—women trudging up the hill with their babies, men too and children. What a royal reception I had! They looked me all over, admired me (at least that's what the men said) and chattered midst themselves until finally the men told them in Chinese that we were ready to eat dinner. They left reluctantly. I was amazed and delighted at what the men had done. They had prepared a complete duck dinner with dressing and vegetables. It was really good. I was invited back there again but was told to wear fatigues and GI shoes for we'll spend the whole day touring the surrounding area on foot. They said it's beautiful with bridges, temples, and pagodas. If I can get enough transportation I'd like to take some of the men there . . . I must quit. Love to you, Eddie

Chengtu (8)

Dear Mom and Dad:

Gradually, since I've been here, I've purchased some priceless embroidered pieces over one hundred years old. Of course, I have feelings of guilt that Chinese are selling these things to make money but Frances says if I don't buy them someone else will. I will always treasure them and display or wear them for other Americans to enjoy. I have two Mandarin coats. One is a marriage coat of red silk with gorgeous embroidered flowers and panels solidly embroidered with gold thread. The other is a beauteous blue brocade with black satin borders. I will wear these for evening wraps or for special occasions. I also have two wedding skirts. One is a red silk wedding skirt of one hundred pleats that is spoken of by Pearl Buck in one of her books. There are fifty tiny pleats on each side with a straight embroidered panel in the front and back. The second skirt is a lovely soft green with embroidered flowers and black satin borders. I have worn these a few times with a white blouse (all I had for a combination) for dress up at our Sunday Coffee Hour. I have an embroidered wedding collar with three-inch green fringe. This will be hung on the wall at home. And lastly I have a very large embroidered red felt hanging.

The workmanship of these treasures is so exquisite that the wrong side is almost as perfect as the right side. Children are taught at an early age by their fathers or mothers and often work over the intricate patterns with the exceedingly fine stitches in dimly lighted dark back rooms of small shops. Over a period of time their eyes are damaged. If spectacles have to be worn they are usually chosen from a pile of cheap handmade ones after a number of them have been tried on. The Peking stitch is called the "blinding stitch" for eventually the embroiderers go blind. Beauty for people to enjoy at a terrible price to the creators!

I purchased a white silk large scroll that hangs from ceiling to floor. In the center is a Chinese woman of high class painted in watercolor. Very lovely. When I get home, I'll have the plain top and bottom of the scroll cut off and the middle section of the lady framed. I've also purchased three pair of scrolls that were gorgeously embroidered cuffs of Mandarin coats, removed and mounted on rice cloth—one pair in light blue background and two in white background. The stitches on the small faces of the figures are unbelievably tiny. How on earth did these embroiderers do it and so perfectly and marvelously beautiful! Every stitch done by hand and the product sold for way too low a price. But these things are priceless.

Yesterday some of us hitch-hiked to town. I tried to buy some ceremonial masks better than the cheap ones I already had, but I had waited too long. It was well past the Chinese New Year and no masks could be found. We stopped at a candy store to buy some candy for the children who were always greeting us. The candy was fascinating. We watched the man blow and spoon the melted sugar into all sorts of shapes: a dragon with horns, a lovely flower, a frog, etc. The children we met along the way were delighted with our hand-out treat.

The highlight of our trip was stopping at a Chinese Middle School where all the girls between ages eleven and sixteen were dressed alike in full black skirts and green blouses with a red tie. Each girl's hair was cut slightly below the ears in a short straight bob. They all looked attractive and neat. The recess bell rang just after we arrived and was followed by a bedlam of noise. We drank tea in the teachers' room and the 250 girls draped themselves all around the open windows and stared and chatted. I wish I could have known what they were saying or maybe it was well that I didn't know. We received an invitation to attend a big entertainment they're having next Saturday afternoon. The invitation was painted beautifully in Chinese characters on rice paper and placed in an interesting Chinese envelope. I'm looking forward very much to their singing. They have asked me to sing also. Maybe I'll sing Brahms' *Lullaby* and rock an imaginary baby in my arms—I dunno. I'm going to try to arrange for some of the girls to be brought to the club to entertain our men with dance, singing, and one of their plays. I think the men would enjoy it.

On the way back we passed a pagoda, white with very ornate red decorations. Pagodas vary from three to thirteen stories or levels but the ones I've seen have been either seven or nine. Pagodas were regarded by ancient Chinese as objects having mystical and geomantic powers. They were often built at temple sites to help guard the premises from evil spirits. The curved roofs are both beautiful and functional. They keep out the high hot sun of summer and admit the low summer sun. Wherever the pagodas are, they guard the people against evil spirits and their influence. The stairs to the top were very steep and narrow but the view on top was exceedingly beautiful with mountains in the distance . . . Much love as always, Eddie

Chengtu (9)

My dear Mom and Dad:

With years of Latin and Greek in your background, Dad, plus Aramaic, Hebrew, and German I think you should add at least an introduction to Chinese to your list. I'm picking up more and more bits of the language and managing along with hand gestures and facial expressions to get my message across to the kitchen crew, though I doubt if the Chinese agree. I love to hear Frances speak it. It's a musical language so once I get the proper pronunciation I let my voice rise and fall and slide as I would feel it in English and I don't worry about whether I'm rising when I should be falling; I don't have time for that. I have fun with it and hope some of it makes sense.

Mandarin, I've learned, is the everyday language of at least three hundred million Chinese but is pronounced differently in different parts of the country just as English is in America. The high percentage of the people can't read but they venerate learning and respect any piece of paper that has writing on it. In the latter 1920s some missionaries and progressive officials were responsible for developing a phonetic system of thirty-nine symbols evolved from the thousands of Chinese characters so that all over China the people would be pronouncing the Mandarin the same way and those who spoke dialects could learn Mandarin. From what I've heard, it's not been so successful as anticipated.

The vowel sounds are so important I'll start with them:
A as in father
E as the oo in look except when followed by n or ng when
    it's pronounced like u in sun,
I as in teen
O as aw in law,
U as in prune but when the syllable ends with n the sound
    is like in pudding

I have a restricted CHINESE Phrase Book put out by the War Department. It gives phrases that are most important for the men serving in China, with only a few phrases pertaining to food and drink. Phrases I've listed below are written in phonetics as we would sound them in English. Small letters mean low voice level while capitals mean high level. An exclamation point (!) means to start high and slide down, a curved line means your voice slides up, etc., but I will not add the inflections. Rise and fall as you please.

Here are a few to play around with:

Hello	NEE-E na OO
I am hungry	waw UH la
I am thirsty	WAW kuh LA
Please give me tea	ching GAY-EE waw CHAA
Please give me food	ching GAY-EE-waw CHER sher
Thank you	SHYEH-shyeh

Evidently being thirsty is more demanding than being hungry. Practice on your friends. If you're not perfectly correct, people at home won't know the difference. They'll just be properly impressed . . . Much love, Eddie

37

What Next after Liège, Belgium?

Dear Folks:

I just returned from the chapel where I played for a joint service for our GIs and the local Protestant Belgiums. The Belgium minister gave the sermon and a local Belgium girl interpreted in English. She also interpreted throughout the service. Following was a musical service in which a Belgium choir sang some lovely music a cappella. Our choir sang one number with the organ and our quartet sang a cappella. This was followed by refreshments and I left at that point. For the Belgians meat and coffee are scarce—coffee is almost a minus drink. The people have to shop in the black market to get adequate food.

Since we came to Belgium in November I've been playing for two services—one here at the post and the other in a Liège Protestant church for the GIs. In between I have been roped in on other services in the area by various chaplains. The only chance I've had to sing is when we've done a number a cappella. I've really missed singing.

Today a case consultant came here and read all my records. She asked me to write up some of my experiences with the patients during that hectic period, the report to be sent to Washington. I don't know how I can get to it with all I have to do. I was evaluated by our Field Supervisor who is now in Liège. She's a wonderful understanding person. She read me my Washington evaluation which was highly commendatory. She feels I've done an excellent job in our unit. It's so nice to be praised—sort of an award. I had mentioned an incoming Field Supervisor in a previous letter but I didn't know at the time whether it would be a he or a she.

Now that the war is over we have all the comforts and conveniences that we never had before. I hope to get away for a seven-day leave to the Riviera soon. I have been tying myself down too much for my own good. This period I'm going to get some personal things done for a change. I haven't taken my leave for last year or this year. I want some relaxation. I have promise of a car, a sedan that is to be brought over to me from Germany. One of the Colonels told his officer driver to bring me one of the best cars they have in the parking area, equip it with four new tires, paint a red cross on it and be sure it is in excellent condition. Red Cross allows us to have cars and they insure them for us. I'll get a driver's license and can tear around without having to depend on a Motor Pool. That will be something! We are now getting invitations for plane rides into Germany. I hope soon to get over near Berlin.

I took some time off and went into the center for a permanent. Instead of a machine, they put on heated clamps doing one section of the head at a time, the same system they used in France for my last permanent; the best perms I've ever had, soft and fluffy.

What happens now, I don't know. Things are at a standstill. I could be placed in a Pool in Paris and that I wouldn't like at all. I have asked for a Pacific assignment in the CBI Theater but Red Cross has a way of sending you where "you are needed." The Army has been a great life. I wouldn't have missed this experience for the whole world. It has been good for me to have been with a crowd of army people living closely together. It takes out of one that self-centeredness. From the Rest Camp Eddie was going to APO 210 but I haven't heard from her.

Last night I went to the Opera House with a Colonel friend. It was Puccini's *Tosca*—beautiful. He has taken me to several of the operas. We sat in a box on the side—wonderful seats. People over here attend operas like our people attend movies. So with the beauty of last night still with me, I send you my love . . . Dot

38

May Program Report
to ARC Headquarters

May has been one of those months when we've been assured with no doubt that the Red Cross Club is truly contributing a real service to our men. The club has been consistently filled from early morn to closing hour. Again and again I have felt keenly the harmonious atmosphere in the lounge and many times have marveled at how so many men occupy our one room and participate in so many varied activities with seemingly no interference with each other.

Here in the "wilds" with little material at our disposal for attaining desired effects, we have an attractive and livable lounge that we are proud of. The Chinese Corner grows and affords not only general interest but has been an incentive in starting a small art group. On the walls we've added two large scrolls of birds and flowers and also paper figures which are burned at the graves of the deceased. On the shelves are colored bowls, teapots and vases, fans and coolie slippers, pottery jars—one red with gold Chinese characters and two yellow with red characters—a violin (hope to get a flute and drum soon), a large Buddha that was acquired in the Scavenger Hunt (not yet returned but the kitchen crew seem to have forgotten it), red and green Chinese sewing baskets. A Mess Hall table stained and bearing a runner of green material and a lovely large brown jar with fresh flowers adds a homey touch and, of course, our still treasured singing canary in a cage. We have no piano and I guess will never have one.

Our BULLETIN BOARD is our pride and joy. We glow at overheard remarks: "What a swanky board" and "Clever posters." It changes every few days. Though I've had to develop the art of poster making, a number of GIs have contributed their artistic ability and have taught me a great deal. There is always color, clever variety of printing, sketches in watercolor, silhouettes mounted on contrasting backgrounds and so on.

Our SUGGESTION BOX has brought us excellent ideas and in most cases we have been able to carry them out.

MUSIC—I bless Red Cross for the portable we have at last received. Lest anything should happen to it, I am saving it entirely for classical music. We began our Music Hour again. I blacked out the windows in the Snack Bar, pushed back the tables, brought in a settee, lounging chairs, and coffee tables, set out a bouquet of flowers and candles, and we were set. Following that Sunday one man said to me: "This is the most pleasurable experience I've had since arriving in China." I introduced and gave a little backgound information on numbers heard. Later I found musical GIs who were happy to act with me as commentators. At the same time in the Lounge the jazz enthusiasts were relaxing with the new records you sent us. We didn't conflict with each other.

SUNDAY AFTERNOON COFFEE HOUR still serves many men. The long table covered with a white cloth is decorated with flowers and candles and, using crepe paper, we have a different color scheme and arrangement each week. There's always music, for the record player left us by the 1st Photo Group has been repaired and is in almost constant use.

PICTURE OF THE WEEK CONTEST—Men were given one week to hand in scenic, or human interest, or building pictures of China. May 18th we displayed them on a large board covered with green construction paper, each picture having a number. The men dropped their votes in a box nearby. The pictures created much interest for it was a good opportunity for seeing excellent photography of China. The manner of voting will be improved next month when we have our screen contest. The winner this time received a large album and art corners. His picture held proud position on the board for a week. I was grateful that three of the non-winning pictures were given me.

The BRAIN BUSTER MYSTERIES 1 and 2 appeared on a poster twice during the month. Two packs of cigarettes were given for the first correct solution.

The THIRD SERIES OF CHINESE LESSONS have been held on Tuesday and Saturday evenings and will end June 2nd. I gave each man a folder for his notations and at each lesson I gave each a typewritten copy of the previous lesson with hints in pronunciation. Frances continues to be a wonderful teacher. At the close we entertained the "Chinese Students" with Chinese dishes. This was held in the Snack Bar after closing time.

BINGO was played on Sunday nights, May 6th and 20th, with all the men in the filled lounge participating. Prizes were invitations to a Stateside picnic as well as smaller prizes of cigarettes and a few cigars that Miss Thompson and I managed to secure, also one much sought after corn-cob pipe. On the day of the picnic the Bingo winners set forth by foot down to the river's edge. Sampans carried us across to one of the greenest, most peaceful spots I have yet seen in China. Our staff had prepared a PICNIC SUPPER deluxe for us—potato salad, fried Vienna sausages, pickles, cinnamon rolls with dates and nuts, and lemon pie. We stretched out on the grass to recover from our feast and watched a firecracker display.

VICTORS' GAME NIGHT was held again on May 17th— Hearts, Cribbage, Pinochle. At 9:30 when the playing ceased we went into the Snack Bar for a party of lemonade and frosted cookies. While the men ate I handed out the door prize, the table winners' prizes, and the three champion' prizes for the three games. The prizes from India were well worth winning and the men were as pleased as kids.

The CHESS TOURNAMENT, which took a week to play off, drew only eight men. Chess players are scarce and the eight men seemed to appreciate a chance to compete with each other. A carton of cigarettes was a gratefully received prize.

BUNCO—COOTIE NIGHT was so-so. I was more proud of the clever poster advertising the event than I was pleased over the results of the evening. Eighteen men gave it a try and it passed an evening for them but it demanded no skill or thinking. I'll not try it again.

CHECKERS TOURNAMENT has begun and will be completed in June.

INFORMAL DISCUSSION GROUPS ON WORLD PROB-

LEMS—The first of this series was held in the Chinese Corner of the Lounge on Sunday May 27th led by Sgt. Danchik, a well read and very intelligent GI. About thirty were present and the discussion became heated as they declared what should be done with Germany after the war. Next Sunday's topic on Post-War Labor in the United States is already being talked about. I've started a scrapbook of newspaper clippings given to me by the men. It will be available at the desk for all those interested in outstanding articles culled from a great variety of papers sent from the States.

A MONOGRAM CONTEST was so challenging that it drew few participants but many interested onlookers. The final complete display was fascinating. An animal's face was made from Frances Chen's first name—a human face from Margaret's name and a sampan and coolie from my name, Edna Rawson. A copy of it was given me.

CHAMPIONSHIP GAME NIGHT—The poster was very attractive. Players of Cribbage, Pinochle, and Hearts competed for beautiful gifts from India. Thirty-six men participated, stopping first at the Information Desk to pick up their numbers for Door Prizes, their tally sheets, and Rules for Playing. On each table was a dish of candy. Small prizes were given to each table winner and larger prizes to the champion of each game. Even those who didn't win said they enjoyed it,

TRIP TO A BUDDHIST TEMPLE—This trip with a Stateside Lunch was an experiment that turned out to be a huge success, talked about for days following. Thirty-four men signed up but only eighteen were able to make it on May 19th. Two of the men suggested I wear fatigues and loaned me the outfit. I also wore GI shoes. I looked more GI than the GIs themselves but not very glamorous. I wished later I had worn my uniform which would have been more appropriate.

We left at 10:00 A.M. At the river we obtained sampans with a large crowd of Chinese watching us in wonder. Frances had said a number of times that the Chinese couldn't understand one woman with so many men. I must have shocked them. I have no idea what they were thinking but certainly hope they were not judging me too harshly. Our men showed a real kid spirit by rolling up their pant legs, removing shoes and socks, and jumping in the water to help the young coolies push the sampans out of the shallow area. Later I was given two pictures of me posing in a sampan at the request of the photographers. It was a cool, pleasant trip.

From the sampans we boarded a ferry, then switched again to sampans and finally had to walk. Two kitchen staff men came with us carrying large baskets, filled with our food, hanging from bamboo poles that rested on their shoulders. Yet our men, always thoughtful, also did a great deal of the carrying and even forced me into manual labor. I managed to advance three feet, long enough for all the cameras to snap me. Those baskets were HEAVY.

It was quite a walk but finally we crossed a bridge and on through a moongate that led us into the grounds which were beautiful with flowers, interestingly water-shaped rocks, and a pond with lotus blossoms. The lotus is the symbol of purity for it springs from mud with undefiled beauty. It was quiet and peaceful away from the world. We found a secluded spot in the lovely gardens and feasted on the lunch our First Cook and helpers had prepared for us—turkey sandwiches, Vienna sausages, potato chips, pickles, fruit juice, and fresh apricot pie. While eating, we noted the glazed tile temple roof, three-tiered with three graceful curves tilting upwards.

After cleaning up, we visited the temple which was the climax of our trip and later also visited the adjoining orphanage. We arrived back at the Base at 4:30, tired and happy. I wish I could see all the snaps that were taken that day. I've asked to borrow some of them, when they're developed, for a poster announcing our next trip for those who missed this one.

Chengtu (9)

My dear Mom and Dad:

The May report I sent you should give you a quite clear picture of what's been going on here. The trip to the Buddhist temple was really a wonderful experience. As I view it, there's a puzzling combination, even in the temple, of Ancestor Worship, Taoism that demands superstition and use of the geomancer, Confucianism that stresses ethics, and Buddhism that teaches meditation. The Geomancer, trained in the art of divination, carefully selects the right site for a temple. There must be a hill or elevated rise of land behind and a body of water in front. The temple should face southward. NE and SW are directions of the devil.

The tiered and tilting roof is supposed to signify man's persistent and yet humble efforts to seek salvation and the graces of heaven or Nirvana or whatever they believe comes after death. They seem to believe in life after death which is good but their various conceptions of what that life is like confuse me. However, among Christians I also find strange and confusing differences. The roof is the most obvious and important temple feature. In front of the temple were two stone pedestals, one on either side, bearing two large stone lions with their mouths wide open as if roaring to drive away evil spirits. There are always beggars around and there were plenty there—some of them for real, old and disfigured and incapacitated, in need of help and some were fakes. It's not always easy to see which is which.

Inside straight ahead was a large, well-polished bronze Buddha with extra-long ear lobes, clear-cut features and a peaceful gaze. In front of it a trousered legged worshipper was kneeling and burning incense in a metal receptacle. The smell of the incense was delightful. All around were more Buddhas in various poses and also other statues of his deciples. The temple was colorful—the ceiling, floors, and walls patterned or decorated with figures and animals of good omen. The primary colors were red, green, and blue. Between two large incense burners there was a container of joss sticks—slender sticks of dried fragrant paste. When lighted they entice the presence of the gods and serve as a means of communication with them. There was a live serpent in a silk-lined box and we saw Chinese bowing before it asking for help. Help from a snake! I shudder. It seemed to me that these people were more attracted to the sound of the bells, the odor of the incense, and the vision of all the statues than they were aware of the essence of religion, its true meaning. What was going on in their minds? I wish I knew.

There was an orphanage adjoining. We visited the class-rooms and also the dining room and the kitchen. I was snapped with a boy and a girl. It was sad realizing they had no parents and yet here they were being taken care of but with how much love I don't know. On the way back we walked and walked, took the ferry, and walked some more, dying of thirst for so many had forgotten their canteens. We arrived back at the base at 4:30 tired and happy. It was a day of beauty, of learning, of charm and fascination. I wish I could have seen all the pictures taken that day but am grateful for those given me. There will be a return trip for those who missed it.

We've seen so much burning of incense at temples, shrines, pagodas and at special events that I'll pass on what I've learned from Frances about their production. The incense is made of plant materials, mainly elm and cedar. The limbs, branches, roots, and bark are ground and then sifted to remove any mater-ial not wanted. It's cedar that gives the basic fragrance but the elm powder is the binder giving body to the incense. Powders are mixed dry with added small amounts of orange peel or rose petals or lilac or sandalwood, etc., according to the odor wanted in the finished product. Water is added and the whole is stirred into a dough-like mass. A wooden cylinder, closed at one end except for a hole three-eighths of an inch in diameter for the plunger is filled with the mixture. The plunger operates like a pastry tube so that the mixture is forced out in a continuous string which can be cooled in all sorts of loops on to shallow bas-kets. When the baskets are filled, the wet strings are laid side by side on canvas trays and are snipped off to desired lengths. Over the canvas tray of strings a wire tray is laid. The whole is inverted and placed in the sun till the strings are dry. It's no won-der evil spirits are appeased temporarily for the odors are delightful.

This was another wonderful experience for the men as well as for myself. Everything is going well. I'm very busy . . . Much love to you, Eddie

39

Dot Plays for a Catholic Wedding

Dear Folks:

I had the surprise of my life last night when our supervisor came in and asked if I would consider going to the Pacific right away since a hospital unit needed an AFD. It took the breath out of my sails but I did some tall talking. She said it would be voluntary but she really wanted me to go. I don't want to go just yet. I couldn't imagine getting everything caught up and getting myself ready to leave on such short notice. I had wanted to go to the Riviera but the Army took over the hotel that the Red Cross had been using. No telling how long it will be before another arrangement is made. Our supervisor will be coming around soon and say I must go immediately. I understand that soon Switzerland will be open and I wanted to go there. I don't want to leave this unit. I hope Red Cross will give me a little time before they move me onward. Everything is interesting here right now. Next week we expect to get our new car. I could make good use of it traveling around.

Later

We've been told that workers in the East Asian and African areas go home at shorter intervals than those in England or on the continent where the weather is considered more healthful. I can't go home from here till October. I filled out a questionnaire stating my preference for the CBI theater rather than the Army of Occupation because I wanted to be with Eddie. Now if I'm sent, I'll lose my chances of getting home for much longer as I can't expect that Red Cross would start me in a new theater and let me go home in October. I'll talk with Miss Harwood and say that I'd like to remain here. Everything is so mixed up at this point. If I hadn't done some tall talking the other night I would have been on my way to the Pacific right now. I can't understand how I got out of it. The trouble with the CBI Theater is it is so large and spread out that it would be difficult to see anyone there unless the person is stationed nearby. Over here it's easy to get around from one place to another. So at this point I don't know my own mind.

Today one of the recreation workers and I went with the patients on a boat trip up the Meuse River to an island where we spent the day. The weather wasn't very sunny but we had lots of fun. The island is being rented by the Army through the Hospital Center and the boat takes patients there every day. Our hospital has the use of it once a week. A doctor and several nurses go along, also an officer from the Special Services Department. The island has several amusements and the place is quite attractive to our patients for we have no space here for outdoor athletics. Belgium musicians—one playing an accordion and the other a guitar—went along with us. Some of the patients and one of our enlisted men jitterbugged with the nurses and us. Then two of the fellows jitterbugged together. It was a regular floor show. We sang all the popular songs we knew and the Belgiums kept up with us. How they knew all the American music I don't know. We passed through two locks which made me homesick reminding me of the Erie Canal. While we waited in one of the locks, I hopped off on a barge and asked a Belgian on the bank to pick me some poppies. I paid him with some chewing gum. At noon a truck from our hospital carried food which was transferred to a small boat and brought to us—the food still hot. We had a delicious dinner with roast beef, mashed potatoes, cauliflower, canned peaches and iced tea. Of course we took along doughnuts and coffee, which we had obtained from a nearby Red Cross Service Club.

The Rawson family is hard to keep track of these days. I'm grateful the three of us are still alive. Yet each of us knows what this war has done in destruction and waste and heartaches to so many . . . Love, Dot

Belgium (11)

My dear Folks:

I've decided not to go to the Pacific at this time but wait and see what happens to our unit first. In the meantime I'll get in some of my leave and see some places.

I haven't heard from Eddie since Dec. 26th. I do hope she doesn't come home too soon or she may have to leave again before I get there. We're now getting patients from other hospitals that are moving out of this area and taking over other hospitals where the units have left for the CBI. Our hospital will undoubtedly move elsewhere, maybe to France, until the unit returns to the States. The newer units are being sent to CBI.

The Riviera is now open to us again. I met a pilot from the air strip outside Liège who has given me an invitation to ride by plane if there is extra room when they take passengers. I may have to go to Paris first to pick up my orders. I wouldn't mind seeing Paris in nice weather. When I was there in January the weather was terrible and also I was extremely nervous from the buzz bombing. I've never fully recovered from that and still feel quite nervous and tired. I could use a rest and change.

I played for a Catholic wedding here this past week—15 minutes before the ceremony—rather easy classical music that I could handle on the reed organ—amazing, isn't it, when I'm only an amateur! I even played for the Mass with a coach behind me to tell me when to play and when not. I spent quite a bit of time picking out the proper music for only certain kinds can be played, also music is limited here so I had quite a struggle. One of the enlisted men sang a solo. The chapel looked lovely decorated with flowers bought in the Liège market. They had borrowed fancy kneeling stools with back rests and had 2 darling Belgian altar boys dressed in white robes with red capes. It was our first Catholic wedding. Another comes very soon and the nurse involved asked me to play for hers. I had a beautiful corsage given me made with red carnations (red for RC, of course)! Following the ceremony, we all went to the Officers' Club for wedding cake and coffee and pictures. The bride was in uniform. They left for a week's honeymoon at a famous spa.

The army has now given me a service ribbon with 4 stars, the fourth for the Battle of the Bulge but, of course, I can't wear it.

I've been over into Germany quite a bit, mostly in the Rhineland from Cologne down to Bond and Aachen both by truck and by plane.

Perhaps you'd like a quick review of my travels up to the present time for I realize it could become confusing. In England we were set up in two hospitals, one at Malvern in the central part and the other near Bristol. We staged at Hoylake near Liverpool for two months and lived in English homes, then came down near Bristol again within two miles of our former hospital for bivouacking before coming to the continent where we arrived on July 24th, 1944, landed at Utah Beach and settled near St. Lo before St. Lo was taken. The first three nights we bivouacked in fields, artillery was sent up all around us and the road was strafed. Later our hospital was set up across the road where we operated until November. Liège, Belgium, was our next and last move. I have made many friends in Liège and have been in many homes. This part of the world is very advanced but the Germans come the nearest to our way of living. Their homes were beautiful and modern but there isn't much left of the cities now. Some are mere shells with a few walls sticking up. People have returned and are living in their basements, attempting to reconstruct. It will take a long time to clear away the debris and procure materials. Even the beautiful oak desk in my office was covered with debris and smashed up a bit.

Later Still

We've received word that we are to take no more patients and that our patients are all to be evacuated to another hospital at the end of this week. We haven't received our orders yet but we'll be leaving Liège before too long after we get through the packing stage. I'll let you know as soon as I get further info.

My secretary, Terry, was hospitalized and sent home. Tests showed a serious condition and the medical group didn't have knowledge of the cause or cure. They felt the nervous strain of the bombing had aggravated it. One of our recreation workers has gone to the Pacific. There are just two of us originals left, Mary, Senior Recreation Worker, and I. This week I did get over to Brussels and down to Ciney with a group of doctors and nurses...Love, Dot

40

June Program Report to ARC Headquarters: Dragon Festival

Excerpt from June 13, 1944 Letter to Dot

My Dearest Dot:

About a month ago I received a letter from you dated May 21st 1944. It went everywhere and finally back to Washington, then was sent on to me here. Your letter of Nov. 5th 1944 came stating you had arrived in Belgium Jan. 12 1944. I received three V mails dated February and then nothing till now. The only APOs I've had in China are 627, 488, and 210 plus a short time at the Rest Camp.

You asked about supplies. We get nothing in the PX except chewing tobacco, cigars, a few cigarettes and hard candy no one wants. Flo and Margaret have taken care of me in sending cosmetics, jewelry and knickknacks. I do need stockings. Mine are shot.

I hope I can stay on till October. Miss Phillips has suggested my being Program Director at the Kunming Town Club since Ned Sparks is leaving for the States, but I don't want to go there. If it had happened earlier I would have loved it; now I'm satisfied that I've had to start from scratch in two isolated airbases and have succeeded.

Excerpt from June 18th Letter Home

Dear Mom and Dad:

I practically turned somersaults and hand springs this morn when your June 5 letter came. Have been so worried that many a night I waked and lay and wondered and prayed. Today the tears have flowed off and on all day. I'm upset over mother's condition and you, Dad, having to bear the heavy burden. Today I talked with the Field Director, told him I was needed at home and wanted to resign. He sent a telegram this afternoon to Dr. Waters for a report on mother's condition. As soon as I receive it I'll send it to Headquarters with my resignation.

This has been a strange day. I received your letter, set the wheels going for my returning home, and received a letter from Headquarters that I am to become Club Director day after tomorrow. How can I do that and program too? I don't know why Miss Thompson was withdrawn from our club and why I was left with so much responsibility. We have two new Chinese girls. Betty Hu has five and a-half years of medicine, is daughter of a Chinese general and is very lovely. Jenny Chen arrived tonight. She is a Chinese-American who lives in Chicago. When our Chinese staff of seven men heard I was to be club director they grinned broadly, raised their thumbs and shouted "Ding hao." I love them and know I'll have their full support. But I hope this won't last for too long for I still have the responsibility of being Program Director.

So I'm back directing the kitchen staff again for each and every detail. It has bothered me many times that the eggs coming from the village market are not more carefully washed of their clinging tiny feathers and excrement and are not more carefully checked for rotten eggs. I demonstrated for the men how this should be done—washing and then breaking each egg separately to eliminate any that were rotten, stressing necessity of pure and healthwise cooking. When I finished, one of the men imitated me slowly, very slowly, and the whole staff began to laugh. It takes 200 eggs for one batch of cookies or cake. What I was demonstrating would be an endless task—or so they thought and made it look so. I gave up. Everything that has come out of the kitchen has been delicious. Maybe that extra excrement, a few feathers, and a few rotten eggs are necessary for the final super taste?

A few of our men, with a hungry longing in their eyes, had mentioned good old American chocolate chip cookies. I said we were low on chocolate but I spread word that if the men would give me the chocolate from their K rations I would see that chocolate chip cookies would be served at the next Sunday afternoon Coffee Hour. I explained the procedure very carefully to our First Cook. He smiled agreeably and I was sure all was well. We all looked forward to this forthcoming special American treat and on Sunday we watched eagerly when a large tray was carried in from the kitchen. Our upturned smiles fell mightily when we saw the contents—white cookies with chocolate frosting. Our highly trained and experienced cook knew that one doesn't put broken pieces of chocolate in a batter so he ignored my lack of knowledge in the field of baking and made frosting with finely crushed egg shells and melted chocolate. Either I'm not too good at explaining or American ways are peculiar and baffle the Chinese . . . Love to you. I'll be home soon, Eddie

June Program Report to Headquarters, Kunming

I was bewildered when word came through from Headquarters that I was to assume directorship of our club. How am I to assume direction of the club and program together? I was grateful for Betty Hu's arrival though she is new to everything and quite naive. Jenny Lind came on the 14th. This last week with two new reports facing me I've had to let down on my program work and in that work I've been so happy and proud of achievement.

SUNDAY AFTERNOON COFFEE HOUR has continued to be attractive and appreciated. Brownies have been served twice. Our First Cook has the real Stateside touch. But of course he was previously a city hotel cook of high repute. He's made peach shortcake and lemon cream puffs that are super.

CANDLELIGHT CLASSICAL MUSIC HOUR from 3:30–4:30 in the darkened Snack Bar continues to give the men joy to say nothing of what it does for my morale.

JUNE BINGO NIGHTS. Sixty-some men participated in each of the two Bingo nights. June 3rd we gave invitations to a Stateside Picnic, also cigarettes. June 20th we tried DRAW BINGO for variety and it worked out successfully. We wrapped fourteen small Indian gifts, ten packs of cigarettes, and one corn-cob pipe in attractive paper and numbered each. When a man

241

made Bingo he drew a number from a GI hat and won the corresponding numbered prize.

STATESIDE PICNIC—The day for the fifteen Bingo winners turned out to be sultry. Our Snack Bar was cool in comparison so we held the picnic inside. Frances decorated the tables with paper over which she arranged flower blossoms forming Chinese characters for happiness, good health, etc. The men enjoyed potato salad, Vienna sausages, dainty meat sandwiches, pickles, cranberry sauce, fruit juice, and apricot pie.

WHIST GAME NIGHT was suggested by three GIs. A clever poster announced it, preparations were made but the night brought forth no players. It was our only complete flop.

TWO PINOCHLE GAME NIGHTS were held in which twenty some competed each time for four really fine Indian prizes. Following the second night we had a REFRESHMENT PARTY in the Snack Bar of jelly roll and cold lemon tea.

PICK IT AND PLAY IT GAME NIGHT poster attracted plenty of good comments. A Chinese bridge was sketched in the center and over it rose a red moon with black shadings (checkers). A horse (a knight in chess) floated through the sky. A red heart bearing the Chinese characters for "I love you" decorated one corner (Hearts). Two Dominoes drifted about below the bridge and a boardwalk (Cribbage Board) appeared beside the water. Four of us had combined our ideas in working on it. Twenty-eight men chose their games and competed with their pals for packages of cigarettes. At 9:30 they were invited into the Snack Bar for cheese sandwiches. As they ate I presented the prizes including the door prize.

CHECKERS TOURNAMENT continued over a two-week period but was finally completed June 9th when Sgt. Quintard won over ten players.

INFORMAL DISCUSSION GROUP ON WORLD AFFAIRS ended with "Post War Problems in the U.S." Our marvelous chairman, Sgt. Danchik has left the Base. Unless he returns there is no one to lead the men effectively. He was outstanding.

Our FISHING TRIP showing a man fishing by sampan and announcing that we had the equipment and would furnish transportation and picnic supper appealed to thirty-three men. But the river suddenly rose and we waited for a better time. Then I had the direction of the club dumped in my lap which has tied me up. I'll have to wait till July to accompany the men in search of bigger and better fish.

SECOND TRIP TO THE BUDDHIST TEMPLE was as wonderful to the new group of men as the last one had been. I wore a white blouse with slacks, felt and looked a little more presentable than in the GI fatigues. I was snapped tickling the "Tickling Tree"—when touched it wiggles all over. A huge white elephant on a very high stone pedestal intrigued the camera men so they hoisted me up and shot "us" from different angles. Elephants are the symbols of heavenly stairs,

DRAGON FESTIVAL—THURSDAY, JUNE 14, 1945. A Sgt. made a spectacular red poster with a large dragon made out of copper covered canvas announcing the yearly Chinese Dragon Festival. I attached to the poster a write-up of the history and the Chinese customs connected with the Festival. Below I announced that a party of men who wished to sign up would leave the club at 10:00 A.M. on June 14th with a lunch prepared by our wonderful First Cook and our kitchen staff. Beside the poster on the bulletin board I tacked six festival souvenirs I had purchased in the village for a ridiculously low price. There were two ducks, one in red silk and the other in green silk, two green frogs, a dog and a coolie in red and green wearing a hat. They were exquisitely made with those tiny stitches and extra touches these Chinese do so beautifully. Four of them had long tassels hanging from them and all had silk threads at the top by which they could be hung. Obviously these were not to be thrown in the water as cruder made ones filled with rice would be thrown.

* * *

History of the Dragon Festival
Posted on the Bulletin Board

Over one thousand years ago in the Song Dynasty, there ruled a cruel, selfish, and lazy Emperor. He surrounded himself with government officials who were as greedy as he and who willingly carried out his orders which brought sufferings and hardships to the common people. There were, however, a few officials already in office when he began his rule who loved the common people. Among them was the famous Shu Yuen. He was promised wealth and luxury by the Emperor but he refused to carry out the Emperor's cruel orders until finally his life was threatened if his persistence continued. Rather than be disloyal to his countrymen he jumped into the river giving his life for his people. Fishermen paddled furiously after him but couldn't save him. Today's races recreate their heroic attempt.

In the decades that followed, a festival was held yearly to honor Shu Yuen. This festival, which became known as the Dragon Festival, became a national holiday and was celebrated on each fifth day of the fifth moon. Small figures of ducks, frogs, chickens, etc. were made of cloth, filled with rice, and thrown into the river to feed the fish thus preserving Shu Yuen's body. For entertainment there were exciting boat races. Narrow crafts decorated with banners and parasols, each holding as many as sixty Chinese, were paddled by peasants who kept time to the rhythm of a drum in the center of each boat. These boats were 20' to 100' in length and on each bow was carved a dragon's head, its body continuing on each side by additional carving or colorful design. Attending boats, decorated with bunting, added even more color to the river scene. Races developed with three or more crafts competing. As the racing crafts gathered momentum they cut through the water at high speed while the crowds, dressed in holiday attire crowded on the river banks, cheered loudly. These dragon boats were often owned by temples. After the festival the temple boats were buried until the next year and then dug up and repainted.

Though events have changed through the years, each year on this Dragon Festival Day the Chinese people pray that the fish will not molest Shu Yuen's body. On the morning of this day they eat rice balls (sometimes chicken or eggs are added) wrapped in special bamboo leaves and then boiled. Duck eggs and a special bitter medicine (yellowing powder) in wine will keep them healthy all year and prevent any skin diseases. Special long slender grass is hung on the walls of the homes to keep the evil spirits away. Everyone wears his best clothes, the women with flowers in their hair and thread bracelets on their arms. At 10:00 the festival begins. Cloth figures of tigers, frogs, ducks, etc., filled with rice are thrown into the water feeding the fish and preserving Shu Yuen's body. Ducks are thrown into the river and everyone catching a duck may keep it. Wash basins are tossed in and men who are successful in diving and pushing up a basin with their heads are awarded prizes. Also prizes are awarded to those catching eels with their mouths. But the boat races are the biggest event of all when the spectators go wild with excitement and joy.

*　　*　　*

And so it came to pass (in Biblical language) that on the Chinese fifth day of the fifth moon (our July 14, 1945) thirty-one men and I along with two kitchen staff carrying our picnic lunch on their shoulder yokes arrived at the river which was already filled with boats and the banks covered with people. About five shells bearing twelve men each were practicing their combined strokes for the ensuing races. We knew that purchase of ducks for the races was too costly for many of these poor Chinese so the men decided to chip in, buy some ducks and contribute to this great occasion. Thus we had the opportunity of "engineering a few races" getting the shells all lined up, giving the starting signal, throwing our first duck in the water and screaming our heads off as the shells came toward us in the river. At the close of each race the yelling seemed to grow even louder as winning crew members dived in for the prize duck which consistently popped up in some other spot.

When we had reached the stage of hoarseness, the festival was finally over and we had become so duck conscious that when the men suggested buying eight more ducks for a DUCK DINNER CELEBRATION the following night I said "Yes" without giving it a second thought—till I fell into bed that night. A second celebration when they had just had a super lunch prepared by our First Cook? Oh well, my duties as Club Director concerned about expenses are close to an end so why should I worry.

I'm sure we created good international relations that day while we were having a hilarious ball. We not only helped to provide extra entertainment for the Chinese (by our purchase of more ducks) but became one with them as a people.

It's strange—there was a dead man floating on the river and no one paid a bit of attention to him.

*   *   *

I received the following note of praise but it did nothing to alleviate the burden placed on me.

AMERICAN NATIONAL RED CROSS
CHINA - BURMA - INDIA COMMAND
INTER OFFICE

June 29, 1945

Edna May Rawson:

Dear Edna:

Recently a splendid commendation of you and your services in club operations was received in this office from Margaret Thompson.

We are sure you would be very pleased with her expression of sincere appreciation with which we heartily concur.

Sincerely,

MP/b

41

China-Burma-India Command—
My Last Report

*   *   *

My June Report to Headquarters became my last Red Cross Program Report although I wasn't fully certain of it at that time. I was utterly amazed at the program and club responsibilities I bore during my last period there. I had never had experience in handling business matters, other than my own simple affairs, but I was proud of the efficiency I developed through necessity. Betty Hu was too immature and inexperienced to be of much help. I bore the load and was grateful to have Jenny Chen by my side helping. Yet I recall delightful moments spent with the kitchen staff eating rice with them almost every day for lunch while we discussed food for the Snack Bar and for special events, trying to get them to wash the eggs more carefully and remove the rotten eggs, etc. etc. They were a joy to be with and I treasured them.

*   *   *

To: Mr. Ralph A. Brandt, Director of Club Operations, APO 465
From: Edna May Rawson, Club and Program Director, APO 210
Subject: Club Report for the Month of June, 1945

I—Problems Facing Me
   A—Salaries
     1—Jenny Chen, U.S. citizen locally paid

Mrs. Chen arrived at our club June 18th. At APO 878 she was receiving $75.00 monthly and assisting Mrs. Los. She was promised that when she would be sent to her new station she would assume the position of Canteen Manager, for which she is exceedingly well qualified, and would, consequently, receive an increase in pay. Instead she was sent to APO 210. She has already proved herself to be a valuable asset to the club and a tremendous help to me. Will you notify me if I may increase her salary for July and how much.

2—Employees Salaries

The CN rate is jumping up fast which means that already our staff are receiving lower pay than a month ago. May I consider, for example, our first cook's pay of 13,000 CN as comparable to $13.00 gold and raise all the salaries according to the CN rate on July 15th? Mr. Taylor thought that this would be wise.

3—Frances Chen

Frances Chen is being paid the full month of June at Miss Thompson's suggestion although for the last two weeks we have been counting on her for advice only. Her baby will be born in a month or two.

B—Staff Problems

1—Squeeze in Kitchen

I am making a complete survey each day of the day's total output and intake according to the following plan

a —Snack Bar Consumption.

(1) Date

(2) Session—afternoon and evening added

(3) Number of food servings—coffee, tea, doughnuts, other foods

b—Cash intake, CN and gold

c—Ingredients used in Kitchen

Each night Jenny Chen is checking the exact number of catties* and pounds of all ingredients used whether they be market W.A.E.C., Q.M., or ARC India gift.

d—Food produced

In many cases this will be exact while in others approximate to within five or six servings

e—Food unaccounted for

The production minus the sales. As an additional check I'm

*A catty = one and a half U.S. pounds

investigating one day of each week on what should be the output per day for food produced. This involves looking through standard recipes put out by Cornell which should correspond approximately to our cook's recipes. I have found three and a half catties of bacon missing and a few minor losses. My staff know now that I'm checking carefully for I told them that I personally am responsible to Red Cross Headquarters for all money spent and supplies used but I have in no way indicated to them that I think there might be a staff squeeze. I trust them and though I know they are getting a squeeze it has been comparatively small. I think I can keep it down to a negligible amount. They are an outstanding staff of Chinese men.

2. Jenny Chen

Jenny Chen has a nine year old son in APO 879, fragile and left alone with friends, her husband being in the U.S. Naturally she wants her boy with her if possible and assurance of his welfare. Mr. Taylor said he saw no reason why the boy couldn't live with her in her private room here in the barracks. His Mess Hall bill would be paid out of her salary. If this is all right with Red Cross we simply have to get permission from our Commanding Officer who likewise would handle the boy's transportation here. Personally I feel Jenny's boy should be here and would in no way disturb or inconvenience any occupants in our barracks.

C—Entertainment Expenditures Listed in Cash Book

From June 19 through 24 I have listed entertainment expenditures according to Snack Bar prices. Theoretically this would be correct but actually there are discrepancies. For example, on one day we sold 427 cups of coffee in the Snack Bar using approximately seven pounds of coffee costing $1.40, approximately 8-1/2 pounds of sugar costing 5950 CN, powdered milk negligible. We expended about $7.35 and received in sales $21.75 at five cents a cup with a difference of $14.00 gain. This gain is compensated for in the Snack Bar where we lose on food but for entertainment I'm not sure if you want actual food production cost or an indication of what we lose in food entertainment through not selling it in the Snack Bar. You realize, undoubtedly, by above remarks that I am listing under entertainment even refreshments for ten to fifteen men—a thing that Miss Thompson did not do.

D—Revolving Fund

I started June 19th with a balance of zero. Is there a revolving fund coming soon so that I can pay salaries, W.A.B.C., and market bills? You know by my statistical reports what I should have in

250

CN. A gold revolving fund is unnecessary as far as I know now.

E—Snack Bar

1—Flour

We have ceased making doughnuts temporarily and are substituting plain sugar cookies. We have had nothing but rice flour recently and rice flour doughnuts are Boo Hao. So many were left over on one night that we cut them in tiny bits, mixed them with lemon sauce and served them as lemon pudding. Can we get doughnut flour from India? It will also cut down on the terrific price that we have to pay A.A.B.C.

2—Strictly Gold in Snack Bar

In responding to Mr. Taylor's request for our opinion as to charging only gold (no CN) in the Snack Bar, I definitely say "Yes." I have asked a cross-section of the GIs. It is OK with them. As for us, it would save us many a headache in computing losses and gains and also in trying to keep CN change on hand.

3—Redecorating of Snack Bar

I have wanted for ages to rebeautify our Snack Bar but could never gain permission. You asked me to assume direction of the club which makes me boss in a few minor things at least. Yesterday the walls were whitewashed and the draperies laundered and pressed beautifully. A dilapidated and unused Ping Pong table has been occupying space in a corner of the room and driving me more insane every day. A Sgt. has made it into a hectagon table to fit around our central post. This is just the beginning. Thursday morning, June 18th, four GIs and we women are starting pell mell on the room and in one week's time it is going to be super deluxe costing Red Cross only one bamboo mat and possibly five or six lamp shades coming from India. Incidentally, the Snack Bar will be closed at no time. I will tell you of the grand transformation in my July report. Meanwhile at last I'm wonderfully happy, for the renovating has begun.

F—Inventory Reports

Please notify to Whom it May Concern that our inventory taken June 19th of food, expendable and nonexpendable property is absolutely perfect regardless of what Miss Thompson may have stated in her closing-out report. A Sgt., Betty, Jenny, and I have fine toothcombed even the rat tracks and posted them in the storeroom and recorded them in our books.

G—Flower Beds in Front of Club

Sgt. Caldwell has earned our keenest appreciation for bringing nature's beauty to the front of our club. He has created three large flower beds outlined by whitewashed stones and has transplanted banana trees and hollyhocks which are growing well. He waters them and cares for them daily.

H—Music Needs

1. No piano has arrived though it was supposed to have been sent from APO 465 some time ago. Will you check on it?

2. Could you send us four or five complete sets of violin strings for club use?

3. I need more GOOD classical records for my Candlelight Music Hour programs. If there are any immediately available at 627 I would appreciate your sending them. If not, I can manage for a few weeks with repeats.

Conclusion

I can conscientiously say that in my time overseas I have always put in more time than required. But these days in June carrying the burden of two jobs have been a nightmare of hours from 9:00 A.M. straight through to 12:00 and 1:00 P.M. with no let-up. I must have relief.

42

Riviera, U.S.A.'s Victory Spree
for the ETO Personnel

My dear Folks:

There is rumor tonight that our unit is going to the Pacific. No one seems to know, however. Our hospital is entirely cleared of patients and equipment and all departments have been closed down. We're now closing up our Red Cross building. A PW and some enlisted men have been helping us in the packing. It's a big job as our building is large and we've accumulated so much stuff. My office looks a mess—really dismantled. I don't know what to do with Red Cross equipment since I don't know what I'll be doing. If I go to the Pacific I'll want lots of these things for they say supplies are scarce there. Two of our girls have been transferred to other hospitals, one of which will be leaving for the States. Terry, my secretary, is on her way home. Mary is in the hospital in Paris. If they send her home, I'll be the only one of the original ones left in the RC unit. It gives me a queer feeling.

One Week Later, July 13

I'm completing my work here and will be going into Paris Headquarters for reassignment not later than Wednesday of next week. Miss Harwood, our supervisor, said today that I probably will be assigned with a unit going to the Pacific by way of the States and that I should have a chance to get home first since I've been over here so long. I had a chance to read two evaluations on me sent in to Washington. They do me too much praise but that's okay with me for the records. Most of the units are sending their personnel to the Riviera while staging in France.

We've cleared out the Red Cross building and the place is like a morgue. Everything echoes. I still have to finish my

253

records and then pack my personal belongings for the Pacific. One of the carpenters is making me a locker which I will appreciate for it's so hard to find things in a duffel bag. Evidently lockers are permitted in the CBI theater. I'll also have my bed roll, suitcase and extras. I gave most of our collected furniture, equipment, and supplies to one of the other Red Cross Hospital units in this area and the rest to a civilian hospital. I am not ready to quit but am anxious to continue till the end of the war with Japan and serve wherever I feel I am most needed. I enjoy working with the battle casualties. These are the boys who need help and encouragement. I've enjoyed hospital work. I always had a leaning toward nursing. No matter what condition I find the men in, my spirits always rally and I can't do enough for them. They have gone through so very much . . . Love to you, Dot

Riviera, France—July 31

Dear Folks:

I closed up Red Cross and went to Paris for reassignment. I asked for leave at the Riviera which was granted. So I stored my belongings at the warehouse, went out to the airfield and managed to get a plane ride down to Marseilles and from there over to Cannes by train.

The whole area of the Riviera has been taken over by the U.S. for a Rest Center. All the beautiful hotels at Cannes and vicinity are now occupied by officers, nurses, and Red Cross while the equally lovely hotels in the Nice area are occupied by the enlisted men. I have a private room and bath in The Provincál, a luxurious hotel. We have a large orchestra that plays during meals as well as at night on the starlite terrace. There has been moonlight every night—most romantic. The officers are billeted about four miles from the women but we all go back and forth milling around, chasing from one hotel to another enjoying the various orchestras. I've picked oleanders and put them in my hair for now we can wear anything we wish. We dance every night and there are always comedians around who keep the places in an uproar. It's one continual round of gadding about—a great mental relaxation but physically exhausting. Yet who cares? I can't imagine the Army making such a wonderful place for us to celebrate and let off steam. I've heard a number called "Symphony"—composed by a Frenchman. discovered by a GI and popularized—that's quite beautiful. It's becoming well known all over the continent and will probably get to the States soon.

There are trips scheduled by bus for sightseeing. The one to Monte Carlo was especially beautiful—the rock formations, palm trees everywhere and tropical vegetation. The Mediterranean is so very blue and the coastline wonderfully rugged jotting in and out. An officer from Texas has taken me to his Hotel California for dinner two nights. The hotel is situated high on a hill overlooking the sea—the hill covered with beautiful palms, a most restful place. It seemed to me the most magnificent hotel of them all.

Every day I've basked in the sun on the beach with suntan oil all over me. I have a lovely suntan, the best I've ever had. I've also enjoyed swimming but one night I swam through a jelly fish and, until I was told, couldn't imagine what had hold of me. I got out to the raft and for quite awhile was afraid to go back in. My legs felt as though nettles had stung them. Seven wonderful days are over and now what?.....Love, Dot

SYMPHONY

Symphony, symphony in blue
That compels me to see you again,
Symphony of that eve in spring
Brings back everything all that is pain.
Harmony, heady with sweet perfume
Comes to me haunting my lovely room.
Symphony, symphony!
All alone in my reverie,
It is you I see my symphony,
Symphony, symphony in blue,
You have brought us together again
Let it be, do not awaken me
Stay away dawn of another day.

C'est fini, c'est fini!
Now it's gone, gone my reverie,
Gone my symphony, my symphony, symphony

Symphonie, symphonie d'un jour
Qui chante toujours dans mon coeur lourd
Symphonie d'un soir de printemps
C'est toi que j'entends, depuis longtemps,
Tes accords ont garde leurs parfums,
Je revois les souvenirs defunts
Symphonie, symphonie!
Je revois los rideaux fanec
Que pour nous aimer, tu as fermes.
Dans la nuit, tout comme autrefois,
Il traine parfois un peu de toi
El l'echo et le son de la voix,
Maintenant, je le retrouve en moi.
C'est fini, c'est fini!
Et j'entends, grande a l'infini
Comme une harmonie
Ma symphonie, ma symphonie!

*　　*　　*

1998 Notes

A jellyfish can be as large as 10" in diameter with an umbrella-shaped smooth belly. From the underside, four thick lobes hang and unite to form a square mouth opening. The lobes also give off four tentacles that can sting. It was these that grabbed or encircled my sister's legs.

*　　*　　*

Paris, France

Dear Folks:
I was scheduled to return to Paris by train but I took the

truck ride out to the air field in Nice and was taken by plane. It's most difficult to get plane rides unless written on your orders but I had dreaded taking the long train ride back here. The pilot was Red Cross minded and put me on the plane at the last minute. If I had gone through channels they would have said 'No.' We traveled close by the Swiss Alps seeing those gorgeous snowcapped mountains of Switzerland. I felt so lucky since I'm one-quarter Swiss. Our Grandmother Warth never had this opportunity.

Now I'm in a private room of a Paris hotel in the center of everything and yet removed enough from the traffic that it's fairly quiet. I'll take it easy for a few days while they clear me through Headquarters, get my shopping done at the PX for necessary clothing and get over to see the paintings that have been returned to the Louvre. Headquarters has assigned me to the 99th General Hospital. By the sound of things I will have an excellent Red Cross staff. At least their qualifications sound good. Personalities are another thing.

Tonight I'm very tired. The plane ride was rough. My ears are still dull and I feel a bit dizzy. So goodnight. I'm off to bed and sleep.

Later

By the way, when we first came down from Belgium to Paris we stopped at Rheims and visited the cathedral. It's the loveliest I've seen. The left side has been damaged by fire and many figures are quite damaged. I was very impressed with the many figures inside and I loved the massive figures and the gargoyles outside. I was laughed at because I wanted it to rain so the gargoyles would spit out water.

Last night I had a date who took me for a carriage ride around the streets of Paris, to the theater, and then to one of the famous nightclubs. The girls in the Parisian floor shows leave nothing to the imagination. Their only costuming is on their heads. Nice scenery and backdrops. It was very expensive and then on top of all that it cost 500 francs ($100.00) to get me home by carriage—2 miles and the only means of transportation at that hour.

Today one of the girls and I went by Metro to the Market of Fleas which reminded me of the Ghetto at Chicago. It extended for blocks. I never saw so much junk in all my life with exorbitant prices. Gladys bought a violin bow. I forgot to tell you I have a gorgeous German accordion which one of the patients gave me. Our chief carpenter made me a lovely wooden box complete with hinges, hasps, and a hand clasp. I'm taking it with me though I'll have to learn to play it. Musical instruments will be invaluable in the Pacific.

The other day I had my first banana since I left the States. Some came through from Spain. I held on to it and looked at it a long time before eating it. How wonderful it looked—and the taste was just as wonderful.

Paris was untouched by war and everything is running along as usual. It seems as though the people on the continent and here in Paris have gone by the stage of accepting the Americans and seem to resent our being here. Paris is lovely and the French seem to be artistic. Buildings are beautiful—not overdone. There's much more life here than in London which is on the conservative side. The Parisians on the streets are generally well dressed wearing tall hairdos or large ornate hats. The shoes are quite different with thick soles of wood in the wedgie style with leather or cloth top and strap heel, quite sporty looking. Blouses are from $40.00 to $80.00 for something very ordinary. And you should see the French women at the beaches here—a tiny bra and a narrow strip at the bottom. The men wear a string.

Tonight we walked through the Tuilleries Gardens in front of the palace—very grand with groves of formal trees, formal floral gardens, tremendous statues and vases, fountains and two arcs with the Arc de Triumph in the distance. The gardens extend for miles.

This present time is a dead season for Paris. Most of the nightclubs are closed during August and there's very little entertainment. I'm glad I was here before in January even though it was cold. We'll be leaving here soon . . . Love, Dot

Camp Philip Morris near LeHavre, August 17

My dear Parents:

I left Paris and joined the 99th General Hospital a few days before they left Camp Carlisle which is a staging area near Rheims. We came on by train to Camp Philip Morris near LeHavre on Aug. 12th. We expected to be sailing home in a couple of days but it didn't happen. Meantime I had a hard lump in the Barthelin gland which kept getting larger and more painful by the day. I was afraid to go to the dispensary for fear I would be hospitalized and miss the ship but finally couldn't stand it any longer. They all agreed that I should enter the hospital so here I am. I have informed every doctor that I can't miss that ship and they've been understanding and wonderful. But I was in such pain that I didn't care what happened. They took me to the operating room almost immediately and removed a cyst. Captain Brown from Des Moines did the job and keeps close tabs on me. I really think if that ship arrived and the group was ready to leave he would send me on a litter. He's been hurrying up the healing by having me taken to Physiotherapy twice a day for hot baths. The drainage has practically stopped and the swelling gone down though I'm still sore and am more comfortable in bed than sitting up.

As I walk around the ward exercising, they laugh at me saying it's clear I really intend to make that ship. After the first day I refused to use a bedpan or let the nurse bathe me, determined to be independent and gain strength. Every day brings a new rumor about our leaving. Girls from our unit are nearby and keep me informed. The doctor wants me to stay in the hospital a while longer but I'm sure I'll be ready to go when the time comes. Heard from Eddie—two letters today. She should be home soon.

Later

We are to leave here Aug. 24th to cross the English Channel and catch the Queen Elizabeth the following day at Southampton, England for home trip. It will take five or six days to come across. I guess it's the real thing this time. All I need to do is get my things in a suitcase and musette bag and I'll be ready. I'm

259

still in the hospital for Sitz baths twice a day but I feel fine. Last night I dressed for the first time and went to the movies with a group of girls. Groups have been here to see me every day. They're a most friendly unit. The incision has practically healed now and there's very little drainage. The doctor says I've recovered beyond expectations—old healthy me! The Sitz baths helped tremendously . . . Love, Dot

Edinburgh, Scotland—August 29th

Here I am in Scotland touring around. We *thought* we were catching the Queen Elizabeth but when we arrived on the English soil we found we weren't on the sailing list so we were sent to a staging area in Southern England to await later shipment. We expect it will be around Sept. 8th on the Queen Mary or the Acquitania. In the meantime we all got leaves and went our various ways. A bunch of us came to Edinburgh and tomorrow some of us plan to go over to Glasgow and Loch Lomond. Friday we'll go back to London for overnight.

I did so much walking today that my legs ache but I must see all I can while I have the chance if it does tire me out. It's all so wonderful. Two of us had our pictures taken in Scot kilts today. Will be home very soon . . . Love, Dot

(a card with a string of pictures was sent from Bailoch, Loch Lomond on September 7th stating "Sailing on the Acquitania tomorrow")

43

Japan Surrenders—
I'm on My Way Home

Suddenly the end began to appear. My resignation, due to Mother's serious illness, was accepted and my orders to leave Chengtu for Kunming came through. At our Base Dispensary I was examined thoroughly, given five shots (a good thing for I would be in India for awhile), and a Certificate of Health.

It was sad leaving the men on the Base, sad leaving my staff of seven precious, loyal men, and sad leaving my three girls, especially my darling Frances. Frances gave me a pair of scrolls beautifully embroidered on purple silk. They were originally cuffs from a Mandarin coat that had been mounted on rice paper. The characters of her name were painted in white on the left and of mine on the right. Betty Hu gave me a large collection of 19th century Chinese coins mounted on heavy rice paper and sewed on by crisscrossed red thread. Jenny Chen gave me a porcelain buffalo with a Chinese astride its back to remind me of all the "surprise spyings" into the window of my one room quarters. I was given two flags by the pilots.

The kitchen staff had been stacking away firecrackers in "secret places." I was totally unaware of this until the time came for my departure from the club. At that moment they were brought out of doors in what seemed enormous quantities—strung on poles in fantastic arrangements and designs and colors. The sound of them, once ignited, was earsplitting and exciting. The evil spirits were surely frightened off and for me a safe trip home was assured.

I flew from Chengtu July 16 to Kunming where I spent five days being entertained royally. I saw even more of the city than I had seen previously, ate at the best restaurants, and attended a very special dance (by invitation only). A.B. was no longer there and I missed his special enlivening presence.

July 21st I flew over the Hump to Calcutta. Again good weather was with us. In my quarters at Calcutta I bathed in a large white tub. What a contrast to China where I had bathed out of a small basin of water, water that had been heated in my teakettle over my charcoal brazier. I brought that invaluable teakettle home as a reminder of less luxurious days. In the Calcutta Red Cross Club I helped as much as I could while envying all the materials they had versus our meager supplies in Yunnanyi and Chengtu, China. They had a grand piano tuned and in excellent condition—the ultimate of luxuries. We never did get a piano at Chengtu, not even an old beaten-up upright.

While in Calcutta I received letters from Chengtu saying how much I was missed, that the Bulletin Board was bare, that there was a lack of "Presence" in the club, and that the kitchen staff weren't happy for they missed me. I appreciated being missed though I felt badly to have left when things were somewhat unsettled.

*   *   *

Excerpt from August 4th Letter to Dot from Calcutta

It seems so long since I left dear old China and came into this Indian purgatory. Have had a terrific cold which seems incongruous with this tremendous heat. My clothes are wet through continually leaving me rather weak and pepless. Twice I've hit India in the monsoon season—that's twice too much. I should be home by the first week in September if all goes well. Red Cross has been marvelous to let me go. I hope we both reach home in time to see Mother. Poor Dad . . . Eddie

*   *   *

I sailed from Calcutta August 5th on the U.S.S. *General M. M. Patrick*. We passed through the Red Sea stopping at Port Said, Egypt, for refueling. We were lucky to be given a long shore leave from 1300 to 2400 on August 11th so we could temporarily put our feet on solid ground and spend a brief time in Cairo. I had been there seven years previously and knew it would bring back wonderful memories. We left in carloads. It was a four-hour drive to Cairo and hotter than Hades. Our road was between the Nile and the Suez Canal with interesting scenes (familiar to me) that kept reoccurring. Men pulling boats along the canal weren't singing to "lighten their burdens" as they should have done. I felt it my duty to stop and teach them to sing "Yo Heave Ho" or the "Erie Canal" in rhythm with their pulls and tugs but we had to press onward. Camels were bringing loads of melons down to the canal to be loaded on the boats. Women were washing clothes by hand in the not very clean looking water while boys a la nude jumped and splashed in carefree joy.

We finally came to a railroad track with the bars down but no train in sight. Time was precious and we didn't want to sit looking at railroad tracks. Two of our men joined the nonchalant, unconcerned Egyptian guards trying to persuade them to raise the bars so we could go through. We sat in our car convulsed with laughter over the hopeless gesturing of hands and bodies as our men, filled with impatience, argued a lost cause. E-ven-tually the train came and the bars were lifted.

We passed through very primitive villages seeing ancient methods of farming still being used in the 20th century. Periodically we were stopped by officers who wanted to see our driver's license. Our driver had a wonderful sense of humor and kept us laughing at his exaggerated statements. One of our men asked: "Did you ever hear of George Washington?" Our driver replied: "No, does he run a shop in Cairo?" We became parched with our tongues hanging out and our faces became smeared with dust and perspiration. It was a relief to arrive in Cairo. We found a place where we could get a drink and wash our dirty faces. There were cockroaches running around which, of course, made us feel comfortably at home.

Our time was very short and each chose his place of interest. I revisited the 153-year-old Mosque al Ashar, a beautiful and uniformly constructed mosque with 366 lamps representing the Mohammedan days of the year, each lamp worth $1,000. Large rugs covered the floor, all the same pattern and color. You could see and feel the richness of the place and yet the beautiful simplicity! The weekly service is held on Friday and before the service an Arab must wash his hands, arms, ears, mouth, nose, head 3 times separately and then go to the latrine (that procedure seems backward to me). The priest reads from the Koran for three hours while all face the east. There is no music. During the prayers, the worshippers all stand and at certain points they kneel and bow low to the ground.

I dashed to the Museum of Egyptian Art. I had been there before to see the astounding King Tut display which brought the newspaper headlines of 1922 to vivid life. King Tut had seven caskets—the extravagant devil! The first, containing his body, was shaped like a mummy and was entirely covered with gold leaf with jewels on the head dress. The second was larger and gave the appearance of gold. King Tut died at the age of 20 and was buried with the wealth of his kingdom . . . bracelets elaborate in design, gorgeous material, gold finger coverings, earrings, chairs, beds, chariots, vases filled with perfume . . . an endless array.

I had no time for the shops in the bazaars and had no desire to purchase further than my purchases of a few years ago. In the distance I glimpsed the Great Sphinx and the tallest pyramid that three of us had climbed accompanied by the two guides required by law. One guide led and the other was at the end of the line. Tony, a photographer from New York City, was in the middle between Sue and me. Those blocks of stone were so high I had to stretch my legs to the utmost while the guide behind me pushed my fanny and Tony in front pulled me up. I have a picture, which Tony gave me, of the three of us at the top. I remember how my muscles ached the next day. As I stood there reminiscing I recalled our romantic ride on camels out into the desert with our hired dragomen, our thirteen course dinner in our dining tent lined with Egyptian hangings (later I bought one of those hangings in the bazaar), romping in the sand in our bare feet, sleeping out under the multitudinous bright stars, and much more. What a marvelous experience that was, never dreaming I'd be back here during a world war.

Our trip back to Port Said was a rush affair with little time before the ship's departure. When we came to the railroad tracks, as before, the bars were down and the two Islam guards were praying. Nothing would budge them till their prayers were finished. We stared at our watches and bit our lips. We were sure our captain wouldn't leave us stranded there but we weren't ready to gamble on it. Finally with the prayers completed and the bars down we spurred our driver into top speed.

On August 14th an announcement was made over the ship's loudspeaker:

JAPAN HAS SURRENDERED
THE WAR IS OVER

I felt no excitement. For me, the war was over when I left China. But for all of our men still there I thanked God.

I could have been carefree on that homeward trip but I continued to be involved in providing programs for the ship's passengers. I was wound up and didn't know how to unwind. In appreciation of my efforts I was handed the following before we docked.

U. S. S. GENERAL M. M. PATRICK (AP-150)

At Sea
2 September, 1945

Miss Edna Mae Rawson,
American Red Cross.

Dear Miss Rawson:

This is to thank you especially for your splendid work with your Choir. You have worked faithfully and you have carried through to the end of this long journey.

This is the outstanding Musical organization in the history of our ship. Your contribution to the Worship Services and the entertainment of our passengers and ship's company is invaluable.

May the Lord Bless you and keep you.

Sincerely,

JOSEPH A. GIST
Chaplain USNR

The Statue of Liberty came into view and tears gathered in my eyes and probably in the eyes of those around me as we crowded to the rail. We docked at the New York Harbor September 3rd amid enormous excitement. I was met by a Red Cross representative who took me to a hotel room that had been reserved for me. My accounts were settled there which saved me a trip to Washington. The next day I was on a train headed home.

The war had lasted six years beginning September 1, 1939 when Germany invaded Poland. It ended in part with the surrender of Germany on May 8, 1945 and completely with the surrender of Japan on August 14, 1945 (although I was told that fighting continued in places where word of surrender had not yet gotten through). Over 45 million people had been killed. By October 4, 1945, hundreds of our men in the CBI Theater had poured into camps around Karachi but Karachi's port could dock only one ship at a time so the moving of men to their homes was exceedingly slow and there was no "Riviera" where they could dance with American or French women to good old jazz, sleep in luxurious quarters, etc. etc.—of course not—this was the CBI Theater! The Hump was closed officially. Remaining troops in China were returned through the port of Shanghai.

Dot and I arrived home in time to be with our mother before she died. In November we each received the following letter from American Red Cross, also a certificate of service, and four medal bars for the four six-month periods of service.

An important period in our lives was over, short in time but tremendously long in events. My sister, deceased January 1987, is not here to express her thoughts. I know that she gave of herself fully in every way she could for the morale of the men. Caring about people was typical of my sister. When she returned to the States she remained with Red Cross serving WW II veterans and their families. I know that she treasured her wartime experiences of service. I gave of what talents I had, and of my time and energy, and most of all my friendship. I learned a great deal from the men I worked with or shared experiences with and I express many thanks to them. I hope that through my efforts I succeeded in raising the morale for at least a goodly number of those men in the "forgotten theater."

AMERICAN RED CROSS
WASHINGTON, D. C.

November 15, 1945

My dear Miss Rawson:

Some time ago the American Red Cross Committee on Awards recommended the issuance of a
certificate to members of our staff who returned
home after satisfactorily serving overseas. This
plan was approved and put into effect after many
unavoidable delays.

We are not unmindful of the sacrifices that
our workers have made in leaving their homes and
families to serve the men in the Armed Forces of our
country. We know of the many hardships and inconveniences which many of you have endured, adjustments
which had to be made, and difficult situations which
had to be met with skill and ingenuity.

You have the satisfaction of having helped
to make the lives of men in the U. S. Forces less
burdensome, and of having made a valuable contribution to the war effort. As a symbol of appreciation
for the loyal and faithful service which you have
rendered, we present to you a certificate of service
and the emblem of the American Red Cross, which we
hope you will wear.

Thank you, and best wishes for the future.

Sincerely yours,

Basil O'Connor

Chairman

Miss Edna M. Rawson